This is a work of fiction. Names, characters, places, and incidents
either are the product of the author's imagination
 or are used fictitiously, and any resemblance to actual person, living
or dead, business establishments, events, or locales, is entirely
coincidental.

For information address:
Rita Monday

Pressing her ear hard against the wall, Whitney tried her best to listen into her stepfather's conversation before Erica came back.

"...nothing to worry...he won't win, I have her watched like a hawk."

'Bastard!' she thought to herself. Whitney knew this had something to do with her and her father. Her mother was a fool to think Eric Thompson was good for her when all he had in his mind was to destroy Whitney's father.

"I'll be tearing that one up by the end of the year and after that,
he won't have a dime to his name. He'll be forced to sell the rest of his shares just to pay off the creditors and I will own my father's company back...she's convinced he means to kill her and doesn't mind the extra protection. She thinks it's for her benefit. Her peace of mind." He chuckled wickedly making Whitney even more upset. "His damn temper has finally given me leverage in this situation. Whitney will give over the stock ownership by her birthday and I won't give a flying fuck where the chit wants to go..." He pounded something hard. "She's threatened me several times about finding her father, but since I took away her credit cards and expense account, she's paralyzed..."

Hearing footsteps approach the parlor, she sat down quickly at the piano and pretended to study a musical piece.

"You are full of shit, Whitney," Erica snapped, bringing the tea tray in to set down on the coffee table by the piano. She gracefully went around to sit in the chair next to the table.

Whitney's heart raced thinking Erica saw her hearing in on Eric's conversation. Keeping her voice steady, she said, "What do you mean?"

"My phone was not ringing, but it doesn't matter." She situated the tray like she wanted and pushed a strand of dark yak brown hair from her face. Erica had spent eight hours just yesterday getting her hair done in zillions. Her original hair length couldn't be much more than past her earlobe, but Erica wanted long illustrious hair similar to Whitney's. Things like this had occurred between Whitney and Erica all their lives.

Whatever Whitney had, Erica wanted.

"Austin will call," Erica said. Her voice was filled with confidence. "He knows I've been back for the past three days and just

because I cut off all communication with him doesn't mean I don't wish him to try to pursue me again."

Whitney got up from the piano a little at eased, knowing she hadn't been caught, and sat across from Erica.

Even though her hair was a lighter brown from Erica's, with her assumed weight no one could mistake her for her stepsister, yet they did have the same height and sandy caramel complexion, and moody pout lips. Whitney's body had a very distinct hourglass figure, yet she also had fuller hips and thicker thighs. She would almost think of Erica as her sister, if the girl weren't so spoiled and devious.

If Erica knew what Whitney had been doing, her father would know soon enough. Erica told him everything.

"Austin is quite smitten with you, Erica, but do you really think you can drag a proposal out of him so soon?"

"Of course. Sugar?"

"Five, please. I like my tea like a like my men, dark and very sweet," Whitney teased.

"Why don't you just go fix you some hot sugar water? " Erica said snorting in disgust at the tease and the request. "It'll do the trick.
Besides, you're only just about to turn twenty-one Whitney, what would you know about men? You've been sheltered all your life. You're still in the category when you prefer little boys. You aren't allowed to meet any guys and we both know you're as green as it comes to even relating to the opposite sex."

"Erica, you are peeved at Austin?" she drooled deliciously amused at Erica's upset.

Erica only huffed, trying not to show her true emotions, but it was difficult. "I have worked too hard to acquire him to give up on him. My father wants him, I want him, and even his own mother approves of the match." She put a napkin over her waist to shield any crumbs or drops of tea falling on her brand new Prada outfit. Even though Erica refused to wear an outfit twice, she still didn't want to mess the outfit she was wearing up, although she changed at least twice a day for no reason at all.

"His mother is as selfish as your father," Whitney said disgracefully. "They believe the institution of marriage is only for a financial gain. This isn't the eighteenth century anymore."

"Of course it would be for a financial gain," Erica disputed obviously. "Marriage is a business relationship; lovers are for the pleasure. A husband cannot be a marriage partner and a lover. It's inconceivable." The disgust in her voice was very evident.

Whitney raised a caramel brow. "What about love?"

"Love may be in a marriage. I will love my husband, I will respect my husband, but I don't think making love to my husband has anything to do with my heart. Yes, he will partake of the marriage bed, but to think I will enjoy his touch and his grunts in my ear would be lying. I know I won't." She leaned in close to Whitney. "It's good we are on this subject, Whitney Mae. I know for a fact, sex was designed for a woman to purposely not enjoy it. I've engaged in it several times and I can tell you now, it's an act for only men to enjoy."

"What about romance novels? The women in there enjoy it," Whitney pointed out.

"Trash! Pure trashed dreamed up by women who have a disgust pleasure in enjoying pain. Just imagine some man taking something about as thick as his wrist and long as his thigh and shoving it into you repeatedly until he hears you scream in agony. Then and only then will this horrible member shoot out bacteria filled liquid to infest in your vagina until you become sick by throwing up everyday, then your stomach blows up like a balloon. You ache all over your body and in less than a year, you have to push out something the size of an Alabama rip watermelon from your ass. That's romantic? That's enjoyable?" She snorted in revulsion.

By this time Whitney's eyes were wide as saucers and Erica derived a great deal of pleasure in terrifying the know-it-all stepsister about sex. All Erica's life she had to watch as Whitney was shielded from the world because her psychotic father threatened to take her if he ever saw her in public. Pamela needed her daughter for the money she received in child support, then after marrying Erica's father, she needed her daughter for the stock that was in Whitney's name.

Whitney had been taught at home since she was ten and flown around the world to be educated during the summer in Paris, France and London, England. She was literate in French, Spanish, German, and Russian. At the age of sixteen she had earned her Bachelor's in Psychology and was part of Mensa's West American . She

was now on her way to getting her second Bachelors in Business with an at-home course and a large donation from Eric to Harvard. It was always to be this way until she reached the age of twenty-one when she would be able to sell her % stock ownership of Thompson Enterprises and Eric intended to have the stock sold to him.

That was the only way Whitney would get her freedom from this house and Eric's clutches.

If Lyle Canton, her father, were to ever get his hands on his daughter, he would get the stock and definitely push Eric out of his father's company.

Eric was holding on by a single thread and he didn't like to lose to his greatest rival, Lyle Canton. Erica was not going to let her father lose either and kept up with Whitney for him pretending to like her stepsister.

"You're lying," Whitney said.

"Why would I lie?" Erica asked as if that were just the most ridiculous thing in the world to say.

"Because you hate my guts. Though your smiles and eyes says differently, you want to make my life miserable." Although Erica's description chilled Whitney to the bone, she knew sex wasn't as painful as Erica depicted. The first time could be a little painful maybe even discomforting, but Whitney had gotten her maidenhead removed when she was sixteen because she had started exercising and the strain had become painful in her groin area.

Standing up, not wanting to be in Erica's presence anymore than was necessary, she excused herself to shut herself up in her room.

Erica giggled wickedly to herself as she finished sipping down her tea. Her murky brown eyes gleamed at the thought of her last adventure just six months ago. Love?! Hah! The last smuck who believed in that malarkey was now a homeless bum probably still crooning for Erica. She had stolen his company right from under him and he was the last to know, then left him at the wedding alter. It served him right for thinking he was in love. The smuck!

Although, in her after thoughts, Dakota Traylor had been quite a nice man to hoodwink. It would be good for his esteem to be knocked down a peg or two. Bet he won't go flitting around treating women like dirt anymore after what she did to him.

Before dinner, Whitney snuck into her mother's bedroom and poured a sleeping agent into her mother's vodka. Usually during the third week of every month, Pamela became "deathly ill" and Eric allowed his wife to sleep in a bedroom alone. This was the beginning of the week and Whitney knew her mother like the back of her hand.

Pamela would feign sickness to come into this room to wallow in her misery. No one knew or bothered to care what she did in this room, except Whitney who only pitied her mother. Getting involved with Eric had been the worst mistake of her life and Whitney knew deep down inside, Pamela still loved Lyle Canton.

After dinner that night, Whitney returned to her room and turned the lights off. Knowing Eric would not installed night vision on the camera's until tomorrow morning, she prepared to make her escape at five minutes to twelve. Whitney knew that was when the security guard's changed shift and Eddie, the night guard, would fall straight to sleep soon as he sat down for his shift.

She put on a black shirt and pants underneath the covers and rested for approximately five minutes counting the passing of time in her head. Sliding out the bed to the right, the opposite direction to the angle of the camera, she crawled behind the couch, which created a blind spot for the cameras. She knew this was now or never, because at dinnertime Eric had informed her, the men would be there in the morning to install the night vision, while she was on the shopping trip with her mother.

Behind the couch, she removed the panel, which covered the entry into the air conditioning duct and crawled through quietly being careful not to make a sound. These past eight months she had practically starved herself without anyone knowing. Coming down from to a lean, physically fit . She still wore her larger clothes and never dressed up for anything. Erica was always disgusted to take her anywhere because she looked so "dowdy." Whitney didn't care about the snide comments Erica made.

Just as she was about to reach her destination through the air ducts, she stopped instantly hearing Eric's voice very close by. He was in his room on the phone, she could tell by the one sided conversation.

"...The boy didn't know what hit him. Who cares what rightfully belongs to him, work it out, Sammy...I don't give a flying leap! Do whatever it takes to keep that company!...What? That is fantastic. Putting the company in her name was a great idea and it can stay that way until she reaches twenty-one then I'll just undo it before her birthday. He'll be devastated to see I've sold the company and go after Lyle thinking he has some rights to it, but neither one of them knows it's really in his daughter's name."

Her ears perked up. He was using her to get his business transactions done. Hiding things in her name and claiming he didn't know anything about them. She was still considered a minor even though she would be turning twenty-one in a couple of months, but until then Eric could do whatever he wanted to within that time period and no one would be the wiser. She hated his control over her life and she swore that as long as she lived no man would have control on her life ever!

Her destination was the downward duct, which came from the air conditioning unit. Whitney had loosened a panel in the basement previously. Inside the duct from the top floor she had drilled a hole then put a clamp into the wall strong enough to hold her. Around the clamp was a clothesline rope she was able to unravel, and then slide down. She used the long sleeves of her shirt to protect her hands on the rope to escape from burns and when she got down to the panels, a slight nudge and the panel swung open. It was only attached to the duct by one screw and she knew she had to hurry and get down before the weight took over allowing the panel to fall. The noise would cause an instant alarm.

When she lowered herself to the ground, she quickly ran behind the furnace to grab her bag and a stool the bag was hiding underneath. In her bag, she grabbed the duct tape on top. Standing on the stool, she used the duct tape to secure the panel back in place, and then used a can of spray paint to cover the duct tape, so it would blend almost naturally with the air duct paneling. This would make it a little difficult to find out how she escaped she hoped and they would believe she was still in the house longer before looking elsewhere. Throwing the duct tape in her bag, she put on her socks and shoes, and then went over to the basement wine cellar.

Good old, Jamison, their butler, had come through for her. Underneath the celebrating champagne rack an envelope was taped containing one vehicle key, a security box key, two major credit cards, an ATM card and a post it note, which said good luck and be careful. She didn't need any other directions, if Jamison had listened to her plan. Using the cellar doors, she crawled out closing it behind her and stealthily climbed to the bushes.

In the darkness she found the opening at the bottom of the dividing property wall with her hands and crawled underneath the fence. Before the watchdog in this neighboring backyard smelled her scent, she took off running heading for the alley, knowing the dog always kept his night vigil on the porch. Before the Doberman let out a bark, she was hopping over the back fence and trucking down the alley like fire was on her butt.

Rounding the corner, she passed five blocks until she reached a large park. In the daytime, it was usually filled with people walking around the track, or mothers enjoying a stroll with a baby carriage. There were a lot of bushes and behind one of the bushes was a ten-speed bike with a bag on the front.

Whitney's heart was racing and her lungs burned as she felt someone was following her. Maybe they found out she was gone and was already on her tracks? Maybe they would be surrounding the park?

Peddling down the street getting farther and farther from her home, her mind reeled at what Eric would do if he found her. She didn't want to be caught ever! She wanted to make it to her father and feel the security and safety of his arms. He was the only one who could protect her from Eric. Lyle would be the only one who could make her feel safe.

*   *   *   *   *

His large hands put the car in drive and he looked at the gas tank worriedly. He would have to lose this car soon because he only had fourteen cents to his name. He had not eaten in three days and his belly felt like a black hole, but that wasn't what drove him to his insane state.

Being bamboozled by a two timing conniving tart tore in his gut like a hot knife and he had every intentions of driving a knife right back into her whenever he got his hands on her.

Looking out his back mirror for anyone else on the dark, empty Eighty Interstate, he hoped he could make it to the next town.

Going across country to find Lyle Canton had been on a whim. As soon as he was privy to find out that Canton Industries had bought his company from Eric Thompson, he had made up his mind to find this Lyle Canton, plead his case and hopefully find a way to get his company back. He was sure every man would understand the meaning of being drawn and quartered by a woman. His heart had been pulled across a hot meat skillet and sautéed like pork steak.

If Dakota Traylor ever got his hands on Erica Thompson, he would make sure he give that lying temptress a good taste of what she led him along on a string for five months for. Every time he had thought he was close and that night would be the night, she would find some devious cunning way to avoid him and what he wanted to do.

Well, he would make sure before she uttered a peep of protest, he would have her. He would see right through her ploy to stop him and his lovemaking and just do it.

He just needed one moment with her and his revenge against her deceitful deeds on him would be complete in his soul.

*   *   *   *   *

Riding none stop for two hours, Whitney found the twenty-four hour pawnshop on the Boulevard. The man gladly paid her thirty bucks for her bike and she caught two different cabs to a lone corner on a residential street filled with apartment complexes. She walked a block to enter into the driveway of Elbert Walker's apartment complex, an email correspondent real estate and RV dealership owner. He had several properties mainly in the north, which he was about to sell to a trustworthy bidder and seventeen different RV and Boat dealerships around the United States. This was the bulk of his fortune and he wanted to devote more time in it, by going international. They had spoken many times about it over the e-mails in the past six months. She had been fortunate to come across him in her secret Internet searches for someone to assist her, who Eric didn't know.

Eric tried very much to keep tabs on her browsing, but he didn't know she had three different email accounts and was using each one of them to assist her in finding someone to aid her who didn't know about Eric and trusted her word. Many times word came back to Eric about her attempts of strange requests and she would have to start with a new plan.

Elbert seemed like a nice enough guy and she was glad to have found him. Unfortunately he lived in Oliver, Maine - millions of miles away from San Diego, California.

Yet, when she told him how desperate she was and asked for his aid, he was eager to give it. The first thing he did was purchase an apartment complex about three months ago, site unseen and hired someone to run it. Jamison's cousin fit in this position perfectly.

He then sent down a very nice recreational vehicle, which was custom built for him, but he allowed her to "borrow it" as she had asked him. This was two months ago. Once it was shipped here, he had Jamison's cousin, Frank, to stock the RV completely and keep it full of gas and liquids at all times in the parking lot of the apartment complex.

Frank was never told about her escape because Elbert knew this information being given out would not help her. If anyone knew of her attempt to leave, they would have to deal directly with Eric and he didn't play fair in people's lives. He made them pay for defying him or made it hard to do anything.

She would owe Elbert her first born if she accomplished the great feat.

Pulling out the envelope again, Whitney retrieved the vehicle key. Holding her breath, she slid the key slowly into the side door lock and smiled in relief as the key turned. Stepping into the warm RV she was first amazed by its size. This was no small camper, she had envisioned. He had gone to great lengths for this vehicle and she was awed and a little frightened to drive it. The white-carpeted floors were soft to her sore feet as she stepped in closing the door behind her.

Remembering Elbert's instructions immediately, she went over to the light brown cabinets in the kitchen area and turned on a switch right below the sink area. There was a third generator that powered up other features of the RV, which had been dormant for a while.

She knew she would find out these certain features as she learned more about this RV, but for now she needed to get on the road. Crawling in the cockpit, she sighed at the sheer comfort the feeling of leaving out of California gave her. Reaching above her head, she pulled down the sun visor to get another envelope, which was addressed to Elbert, but she knew it was for her. Elbert had told Frank to put any mail for him in the vehicle.

My sweet Whitney,

By now you should be amazed at the size of this baby. It's all yours until you're done with it and then you can return it. Call me on my cell phone as soon as you get out of California. Please don't be too scared to drive it. I know it's big, but you can do it. I trust you. There is a cell phone in the bedroom's cabinet along with a laptop and modem uplink. I have set you up with an email address of Roadtofreedom@yahoo.com. I thought it would be quite eloquent to you.

Remember: If you need anything, give me a ring. I am at your beck and call.
Elbert

She smiled endeared. He was a special man and she would make sure her father would take care of him. They would owe him a great deal of gratitude. Too bad she had a backup plan.

With that she went to the cabinet in the gloriously decked bedroom with a king size bed, and mirrors about the room, and took the phone and laptop out the cabinet. Getting back in the cockpit, she drove to the train station and went to package express. Driving wasn't as difficult as she thought it would be.

She put the laptop and the phone in the cross-country package, which was a fifteen-day trip on three different trains back and forth across the country. Afterwards, she drove to Edinburgh a city about three hours away from the California/Nevada state line where she knew the Greyhound buses stopped.

Parking at a truck stop near a restaurant, she locked up the RV and pulled out a piece of paper she had tucked away in the bottom of her shoe.

On it, she had written bus schedules and Brigham City, Utah, which had a Winnebago used dealership.

She had left a note in the RV.

Thank you so much Elbert for doing this for me. My father will be quite grateful for all your help. Thank you again.
RoadtoFreedom@yahoo.com .

Eric would definitely get a kick out of this and Elbert would not be able to lead them to her if Eric did pin him down. She had no doubt Eric would be finding something out. He was just too desperate to get his hands on everything not to be.

Buying a ticket to Brigham City, Utah, before getting on the bus she went next door to the bus stop to a pick up and go cell phone place where she was able to obtain a cell phone.

She dialed a trust lawyer she also had listed in Salt Lake City, Utah and left a message on his voicemail to reach her at the new cell phone number. She knew it would be an off chance that he would return her call, but she did add it would be for a very equitable amount of money, which she would want to keep on the down low.

If he was a good trust lawyer she knew she would get preferred treatment once she announced herself.

It was a three-day ride to Utah and she snuggled down into the Greyhound bus seat and pulled out a magazine.

At the first long stop the bus made, she went to the bathroom in the terminal with her bag she had carried on. Inside the bag was black hair dye product, electric hot curlers, a hair blow dryer, lots of makeup, and beauty products. By the time she was done, she looked like a whole new person adorning tight fitting Lycra pants and a skimpy halter-top to show off her new figure. No one would suspect she was the plump heiress stepdaughter of Eric Thompson.

On her second day, Lawrence Begley, the lawyer, called her back seeming quite interested in what she had to offer. She only told him that she was Erica Thompson, daughter to Eric and stepsister to Whitney Canton, but didn't want her father to know she was helping out her sister. He was familiar with Eric Thompson and how he had ruined many people.

"There are a lot of people out there who would love the chance to get their hands on Eric Thompson for what he cheated them out of," Lawrence commented seriously.

"I happen to be one of them."

He seemed uncomfortable. "Well Ms. Thompson, the old saying does go, he who has the gold, rules."

"What if I told you I don't think he holds all the gold, Mr. Begley, and that I can get to the person who does? Would that put a wrench in Eric's perfect empire he cheated people to get?"

"That would definitely knock a couple of socks off. Would this person be you?"

"You've got less than four hours, Mr. Begley, to get all the information about what Mr. Thompson has exactly and why his step-daughter, Whitney Canton, has higher stakes in his empire than he does."

"Four hours?"

"Yes."

"And what would it be in it for me?"

"Millions." She hung up smiling to herself.

The man beside her had heard her conversation, but was quite disinterested. He was more interested though when he saw the smile on her face. The young girl's face seemed to light up a dark room with a smile like that.

"Traveling alone?" the man inquired.

Whitney nodded looking up into the older man's kind, grey eyes. "Going to college," she lied easily.

"Big step for such a little lady."

"I'm not little if you're trying to find out my age. I'm just short.
I'm seventeen and it's about time I did get out the house."

"Where are you headed?"

"Washington DC," she lied.

"Really? Howard University?" He was guessing on where her exact destination for a young black girl to be going.

"Yeah, that's it," she said.

"My brother went there before he had a car accident. It's a good school."

She shrugged wishing he would stop talking to her. He seemed to be a nice old white man, but right now, she didn't feel like being sociable to anyone right now.

The man must have sensed her "leave-me-be" attitude and decided to go back to reading his LA Times newspaper.

Whitney's eyes grew wide in fear as she saw the headline on the front page. "THOMPSON HEIRESS KIDNAPED!"

The man saw her peaking over his arm to look at the article. "Dreadful, isn't it? She was as young as you."

She looked up into his nice dark gray eyes. "Yes, dreadful." She spoke slowly repeating his proper word. "You would almost think that was me, wouldn't you?" she tested him.

He shook his head. "The chit is too fat and in this photo her hair is a short light brown and yours is black and long."

That had been another feat. Three years ago she had purposely cut her hair off and allowed pictures to be taken. When it had began to grow again braided extensions serve very nicely to cover up her new growth and keeping it in braids until it was back to it's shoulder length was very strenuous when it felt like her hair was tied up all the time. "Well, I do pity the man. He must be terribly worried over his daughter."

He agreed. "I would be too if the kidnappers knew she was worth two million dollars."

"Two million?" Whitney gasped. "That's how much they said the girl was worth?"

"Yes, miss."

"Call me Erica." She was getting very use to her new name.

"Nathaniel Parker," he introduced.

She shook his outstretched hand. "Where are you headed, Mr. Parker?"

"Tampa, Florida."

"Really? That's my final destination...during summer break. You live there?"

"I use to. Long time ago, then I moved to California because I thought it had better opportunities." He frowned, as the subject seemed tense for him. "I left my wife and son and now I want to go back to them, if they'll have me. My wife's gotten ill and I just want to spend a little time with them before...well you can understand."

"Yes and your son will be all alone."

"Well, Jared could always take care of himself, but my parental rights were null and void when he turned eighteen. That boy's twenty-seven now and is doing quite well. I've been told he runs a nice marina and boat store in Tampa. Boat leasing is a big thing for the tourist you know and he's about to sign a good deal with the St. Royal cruise line." Nathaniel sounded quite proud of his son and she hoped her father sounded like that when he spoke of how she masterminded this great getaway.

"That's pretty good. How long have you been gone?" she asked.

He flushed a bit embarrassed. "Twenty years."

She felt a bit sad for him. "It must be tough, but I haven't seen my dad in a long time either. I feel almost like he abandoned me and I should be mad, but I won't be when I see him. I'm going to be happy, because I know he loves me, he just couldn't come to me."

"I hope Jared feels the same."

Whitney gave him that dazzling smile again. "I hope so too."

Pulling out a mirror, Whitney looked at herself. Something she had not done in a while and was almost mistaken even by her self-image thinking she was looking at Erica. Now that Whitney was "skinnier" she could pass for her sister on a far away tip, but one had only to see the difference in eye color: Whitney's being reddish-brown and Erica's was a dull brown.

Her father use to say she had cello eyes, because she had the eye color of the red mahogany wood used for cellos. When she became angry or frustrated, Lyle would just laugh because her eyes would become like little red dots with brown flecks. She could never stay mad at her father for long, when he began his infectious laughing and soon she would forget what she was angry with him for - usually some practical joke he enjoyed playing - and laugh with him.

In addition to the difference in eye color, there was the tremendous difference in chest size and figure. Erica, using the right "Body by Victoria" designed underwear advanced her straight-lined figure with endowed hips and curves and even bust, but Whitney didn't need anything for anyone to see she was quite endowed on her own, especially in the chest. For this trip she had bind her chest to appear a smaller size instead of her usually D.

Mr. Parker had gotten off somewhere in Nevada to catch another bus headed south. He gave her a Tampa address and phone number and told her if she was ever in town to call him up or find his son's business, Parker Marina, and she could probably reach him by there if he and his son were on good terms. She wished the best for him and prayed Godspeed on his journey. He did the same for her.

Mr. Begley did call her in less than four hours and he was even more eager sounding. "What about you getting to the gold?"

"What did you find out?" she demanded to know.

"His step daughter holds everything."

"What?" this was a shock to her. "Everything?!"

He sounded a bit triumphant. "Seems you didn't know all of it, did you Ms. Thompson?"

"Ms. Canton's is a very good friend of mine."

"Then you know she was kidnapped."

"That's a lie. I hope you didn't believe it."

"It's in all the papers and they are going to make national news tonight. The kidnappers asked for two million dollars."

"All of it is a ruse to get to her. She's out of his clutches and she wants to stay that way. Like I said, Mr. Begley, this will make you a lot of money. Are you willing to believe me?"

"Hell yes, but I will not do another thing until I've been given some kind of deposit."

"You give me the account number and I can make sure you have it there by the morning."

He did this, then began letting her know what he knew. "Mr. Thompson use to own several apartment complexes, he lost them all to the IRS shortly after being hired by Traylor Industries, an import and export company that has a large stake in Taiwan and Mexico trade. He practically stole the company from underneath the hands of the controlling party, Dakota Traylor. The young man was just taking over the company given to him by his uncle, who recently died and needed some advice. He trusted Mr. Thompson and somehow signed over the controlling stock of the company to him. He went to court, but by the time the judge was even aware of the thievery, the company was sold to Canton Enterprises. Mr. Thompson, on the same day, also sold several controlling stocks in three Internet companies, and other small businesses. Canton Enterprises owns everything, because Mr. Thompson faced IRS audit. He rid himself of everything to the trust of Whitney Canton to be turned over to her on her twenty-first birthday, but until then Eric Thompson controls the trust."

"Now, if Ms. Canton felt, Mr. Thompson wasn't doing a good job as the trustee of her trust could she get someone else to become the trustee?"

"In front of a judge this could all be arranged." "Would she have a hard time making her real father the trustee?"

Mr Begley answered casually, "Oh no. The judge would probably prefer this."

"How long would this process take and once the process is started would Mr. Thompson be able to get his hands on any monies belonging to Ms. Canton or her trust?" she questioned.

"There could be a freeze upon all accounts enacted immediately if so ordered, but I would need to be in the employ of Ms. Canton."

"You will when that money gets into your account tomorrow morning, Mr. Begley. Be available by noon. I will be at your office." Again she hung up and immediately dialed her father's number in Florida.

"Lyle Canton," a weak voice said.

"Daddy?"

A gasped. "Whit? Is that you?" His voice picked up in mood. "Oh Whitty, where are you?"

"I'm headed to you, Daddy. Are you okay?" she asked very concerned.

"No, baby."

He was intoxicated, she could tell. "Oh Daddy, I need you to sober up. I need your help. Can you be sober tomorrow morning, please?"

"Yes, baby."

"Daddy, this is important," Whitney stressed.

"Am I dreaming? Is this really my baby? He said I would never see you ever again," Lyle said weakly.

"Yes Daddy, but I need you to not drink another drop and go to the place you first fell in love. This is important Daddy."

"Alright baby. First place I fell in love," he repeated.

"Tomorrow by noon."

"Yes, baby."

"I love you, Daddy."

"I love you too, Whitty."

She hung up. Her father was drinking his pains away. Lord, she had to hurry, before he became worse. It was probably already too late.

Reaching in her back pocket she found Mr. Parker's number and called him. A young man picked up. "This is Mr. Parker." His voice was very harsh and edgy.

"I don't believe this is the Mr. Parker I am looking for. Nathaniel Parker."

"Who the hell is this?" the young voice sneered.

Whitney was affronted by his tone of voice and wanted to hang up, but decided to try to excuse him remembering what his father said about his son. "Mr. Parker gave me this number to contact him, can I leave my name with you?"

"Are you one of his sluts?"

She gasped now really insulted. "No sir. I met Mr. Parker a few days ago-"

"Then you must be one of his wanna-be hoes. He's not starting any shit like he's done in California, so you can just forget it. I won't be involved in helping that bastard pimp start another illegal prostitution ring." The phone slammed down hard in her ear.

Whitney wondered if it was wise to even keep this number, but she didn't feel Nathaniel Parker was like what the young man had said he was. The man didn't come on to her like that. Whitney decided she would simply call back later to see if he was in or if that young man didn't answer the phone. He was quite ill tempered if one asked her opinion. She didn't think he had good reason to act that way, despite that his father had been absent from his life, but what he thought of his father was even worse. Maybe it was true; maybe it wasn't, but Nathaniel was making some honest effort to start some kind of relationship with his son, at least the boy could at least try to be cordial and open.

Whitney was grateful her mother didn't try to sway her from her own opinion about her father. She had felt strongly about Lyle since she was a child and she believed if her mother had tried, Whitney would have hated and disgusted her just like she hated and disgusted Eric.

She pushed Jared Parker out of her thoughts and looked out the window to the passing deserted earth. Nevada was passing by, and the drab desert was boring her. She was tired of reading her magazine.

At the next stop, she found a small electronic store and was able to purchase an iMac laptop and a modem cord for her phone. She also purchased more minutes for her phone and another battery. An attendant in the bus station was doing her a favor by recharging her first battery, but she knew having one would not suffice with her trying to keep in constant contact with the lawyer who needed to reach her.

Getting back on the bus, she started charging the battery to the computer immediately so by the time she reached Utah; she would be able to get up on the web.

Time was running out fast and hopefully this Mr. Begley could help her accomplish her goal in ruining Eric Thompson and all that he had done.

He didn't know how he had made it to Nevada and the truck driver even gave him some money to make a long distance phone call. The only person he could think about calling was his buddy, but Dakota knew he was taking a chance because the friend was on the move.

After pondering the call for a while, he took a chance and called the Florida number to his buddy. Dakota had an amazing memory and he remembered details like no other.

Most of the details in his mind lately had been of what he remembered of the tart that stole from him. The one who had convinced him to sign over everything he owned to her pappy and then he remembered the wedding gown she had sent over to the church, but never arrived to put it on.

He had held that dress for about three hours after the crowd in the church had left, until the preacher had come and informed him they had to close down the church. Dakota had still paid the man.

He paid all the debts she had ran up, and then found himself broke. Broke than a bad scratched up . When he couldn't drink any more, or shed another tear for the misery he felt, he started to become mad as hell and had it in his mind to go after the bitch and kill her.

First, he would get his revenge. He would force her to marry him, take his rightful marriage bed with the whore until he tired of her, and then he would slowly choke the life right out of her body.

Yet, with no money and no way to go any farther on his journey, he would need some help, which he knew he would have to pay back and this would make his revenge to her take longer to accomplish.

Time seemed to be on his side. The person, who answered the phone, seemed as if they would deliver the message to his buddy as soon as possible. By tonight, Dakota would be speaking to the long time friend and hopefully by tomorrow afternoon, he would have at least a hundred dollars in his pocket.

When the laptop was ready, Whitney first emailed Elbert to give him the location of the RV. She expressed her thanks in all his help and hoped they met soon when her troubles were over face to face.

Afterwards, she called Mr. Begley and gave him the email address to reach her until she could get to Utah. He sent her information about trust and ownership. He knew a lot about them, but he never had large clients like Ms. Canton, but he still was very helpful in assisting her in deciding on him or not.

She felt he could be trusted and he seemed to be eager to help her, yet leery about what she had to offer him. She wired the money in the account with no problems using online banking.

Whitney had sold many things, stolen from her mother's jewelry box and from around the house, plus had a small website no one knew about and using Paypal.com she was able to receive a profit. Once she had enough money, she had closed down the account and the website selling the business to someone else online, and then opening an account without her stepfather's knowledge.

She funneled the money with Elbert's help into another account for Erica Thompson. She was able to get a debit card and a California driver's license using her own stepsister's information. Eric wouldn't be looking for that and wouldn't even question any activity on Erica's accounts. Erica didn't even pay attention to what happened to her accounts because there was nothing really in her name. Only through Eric, did Erica have anything.

Two hundred thousand dollars in all had been funneled and was now in good use for her. Once she took Eric's name off the trust, she would immediately put her father on as the trustee and then be free. No more running. She would have made her own road to freedom.

"Our next stop will be brief, ladies and gentleman. Although it is a scheduled stop, this town is very small and remote. If you are scheduled to get off, please do so immediately, so we can be on our way."

She looked at her watch and sighed. It was now exactly four days into her trip and she was so exhausted she just wanted to fall into the nearest bed and pass out. No rest for the weary, she told herself.

If she could just get to Mr. Begley and then get down to Florida, she would be fine.

When the bus stopped, it was in front of an old run down hotel.

She checked in as Erica Thompson and then got a room. The identification she had told everyone she was twenty-two years of age, like Erica, so no one asked any questions. She also had her own identification that she had secretly gotten out of her mother's vanity.

Whitney was terrified, but she didn't show it in her face. When the bus pulled away, she made sure she was in her room with the door lock curled up on her bed with the laptop in front of her dialing to get on the Internet.

In the email address that Elbert had set up, there was a note from the attorney to let her know there were hotel arrangements. She used the portable printer to pull off any information she needed, but she didn't print too much stuff because she wanted no paper trail. Mr. Begley thanked her for the quick deposit and would get on the items she had emailed him with.

She then contacted the Heart Agency's Florida office. She was very sure the Heart's Agency was the best on the east coast just from what many police agencies said. Although she had never had the pleasure of meeting Mr. Lethal Heart, the owner, she had a feeling her stepfather would try to employ him when he was sure she wasn't in California anymore.

With her old email address, she wrote a short email.

To Heart Securities and Investigation – Florida
Office Please give this note to Mr. L. Heart
I know you will be contacted soon about the Canton girl. Don't believe everything you see on television and don't let him know he's a liar when you know he is. He knows the truth and she can't be found until things are right again.
W. Canton

It would be no mistake if Lethal was as smart as they said for him to guess Whitney was behind the message. He would do the usual trace on his email to find out who originated the message and she had used her usual Netscape.net address. Since she was on a cell phone that could not be traced to a particular location, she knew she was in the clear, for now, but this Lethal Heart was good. Sometimes so good he scared the police he was usually working for.

Missing person's cases were his specialty and she knew that no matter how hard she tried to cover up her trail, Lethal was good enough to find her.

There was still time. Her Erica Thompson identification was still a big secret. Not even Jamison knew about it, so she still had time.

Going over to the nearest yellow pages, she found a car rental place that delivered cars to the person and ordered small Neon. The dealership was getting ready to close, but she paid for any inconvenience and the car would be delivered by tonight. She told them to deliver it to a no named burger joint down the street and she made credit card arrangements.

After taking a shower using her special bath lotion, she always used and had risked a lot in carrying it with her, she changed into a middle thigh sundress and a sweater in case it became cooler before her ride arrived.

Whitney applied the usual amount of makeup to her face and stared at herself in the mirror, wondering did Erica feel this beautiful when she looked at herself in the mirror. Whitney's face had changed a lot in the past month, but no one would have noticed since they saw her all the time.

She loved her new look and confidently after packing her things up, went down the street towards the run down burger joint to wait. As night fell, she sat in a booth by the window ordering a cup of

broccoli and broth soup with wheat crackers. The waitress and cook paid little attention to her and she kept her eyes off the people who wandered in and out of the restaurant.

The salesman on the phone said it was white Neon and they would pull up right in front of the restaurant. She checked her watch to determine that they should be arriving in the next hour.

She sipped her soup slowly to pass the time staring out the window at the dimmed streets of the almost vacant town.

*   *   *   *   *

Dakota sneered to himself. Since the payphone was all the way down past the hotel, he had to walk all the way back down to the restaurant. He had found fifty cents on his way to the phone and decided to use that to buy a cup of coffee. The days were hot, but the nights grew chilly and he didn't have enough clothing on to be warm. He had put on an extra shirt and another thick plaid shirt he had gotten from the Salvation Army type store, but that still didn't stop him from being cold, nor did it stop him from being hungry.

His belly was screaming for food and the smells coming from the restaurant didn't make it any easier. Entering the restaurant not at all interested in whoever was sitting in the seats eating, he went to the counter and ordered a coffee.

The waitress although older than what his mother would be if she were alive, smiled flirtatiously at him. He didn't want to, but he was cordial to the woman, even smiling when she made some off the wall comment that he barely heard. His belly growled as he handed her the money that he had to dig in his pocket to find.

"Are you sure that's all you wanted?" the waitress asked with a wink in her eye.

Dakota flushed in embarrassment and nodded. She poured his coffee, and then set a handful of cracker packages on the counter. Since they were free, she wouldn't be getting in trouble and he thanked her with a nod and quickly stuffed them in his pocket leaving one out to stuff in his mouth just to quiet his belly.

He was waiting for the bar down the street to open. That was where the Western Union in this town was located. The hotel manager said the place didn't open until after eight at night. It was a strange arrangement for them, but since it was a small town, the

opening and closings of businesses weren't discussed or argued about. It was just lucky the town had a Western Union.

The man that had given him the directions, also added, "That's also the preacher too. He runs the bar and can give you a nice little wedding on the spot."

"I've tried that, and it didn't go well for me, sir. Thanks for the offer though," Dakota had said.

His buddy had landed a nice deal down in Florida and made a deal with Dakota. "If you can get down here within a week, help me get this place up and going in a month, then I'll pay you five thousand."

"Just like that?" Dakota had asked surprised.

"Yes. I just stepped off the bus and I met this guy, who was trying to get this place up and running. I learned a few things out in California, so I offered my help, but you can run a business with your arms tied and this one got great potential man. I think you'd do well down here, but I know you got things to do. One month of your time, Dakota, and you are on your way."

Hell, Dakota would be a fool to refuse him, so they agreed on everything, plus the five hundred needed to get down there as quickly as possible. The money would be more than enough to help him on his way to extracting revenge against the woman he vowed to kill.

Checking his watch, he saw the place lights coming on across the street from the window in the front. His eyes drifted to the young woman sitting in the booth by the window, and he narrowed his eyes.

Yes…no…it couldn't be.

Forgetting his coffee and his own hunger, he stood and slowly started to walk across the room towards the booth. The closer he got the angrier he became. All the while he had been trying to figure out what he would do or say if he ever saw her again and now he was seeing her.

Going to the nearest empty booth, he grabbed the nearest butter knife off the table without being seen and used the sleeve of his shirt to cover up the weapon.

Dakota was stealth in his approach upon her and even stood there for a moment seething in his anger that was boiling like acid through his veins. He wanted to kill her, choke her, shake her and demand why all at once.

She had locked her eyes on an inanimate object outside the window as she daydreamed about her father and feeling safe in his arms. With Begley freezing all of the trust accounts until the matter of the trustee was resolve, there was no way Eric could use any of his money in order to get what he wanted. She had taken his power away. She had dreamed about this day for so long, just knowing she could see her father in less than a week made her giddy all over.

"Erica," a voice sneered above her head.

Whitney was startled by the anger in the voice, and slowly looked around, then up to a very tall dark caramel skinned man. He had to be about six feet two and weighed well over two hundred and fifty pounds, with an athletic. He was so rugged looking with his scruffy beard and dirty face, but his eyes were swollen. There was a musty smell coming from his clothing, but not so unpleasant, if she didn't concentrate on him, or got any closer, she could deal with him.

"How can I help you?" she asked with a frown, wondering if he was some kind of messenger from the hotel or a vagrant, who followed her from the hotel, trying to swindle some change from her.

They were still in Las Vegas and people were willing to do anything in order to get money around here to play the slots.

Yet, just knowing Whitney didn't know whom he was seemed to make him even angrier. "You deceive so many you can't even keep up with who you swindle?" he seethed.

Really looking up into this man's face, she was amazed to see that his face was handsome despite the unkempt appearance. She also became very aware that this man's anger was definitely aimed at her and she didn't know what she had done to him. Never being in the presence of a man's anger (Eric didn't count because he was all bark and no bite), Whitney chose her words carefully. "I don't recall your face."

He clutched her arm in a grip and she felt something sharp press against her ribs. Her eyes widened in shock, and then fear came immediately. "You'll be sorry for what you did to me, bitch," he hissed. "Stand your ass up and walk out of here willingly or I swear I won't give a damn and shove this steel straight through your chest."

Wanting to scream, yet terrified to do so, she slowly rose from the booth hoping someone would think it was suspicious that she left

her personal items there and never came back. Damn, why didn't she check to see if there was a sheriff station around the area. She could be right next to one and the right scream would certainly save her from bleeding to death or get her to the hospital before her lung collapsed.

Once outside, they were dimly lit, and he kept her carefully in front as to shield the weapon he was using in order to control her. He guided her across the street going towards the bar.

"Where are you taking me?" she asked, trying to keep the fear out of her voice.

"We're going to do things right, darling." He used the endearment in disgust. "I'm going to make sure I have consent over you."

She abruptly stopped and gasped as the sharp object pressed

hard against her skin. She knew there had been blood drawn by the pressure. "You're making a big mistake," she said now allowing her fear to come to the surface in her voice. "I can't do this. My name's not Erica Thompson."

"I don't give a flying fig who your name is, bitch. I just know you're the one who took everything away."

"You're wrong." She turned to face him despite the pain in her arm and chest to plead with him. "I'm not who you think I am."

"You shut your fucking mouth or I'll shut it for you," he sneered, flinging her around and pressing her back against the church. "Unless you want to go in there looking like I've beat you within an inch of your life, which I will gain an immense amount of pleasure from doing, you go along with whatever I tell you to. And if you tell anyone you're doing this against your will, I will kill you right there and then, damn the consequences."

Whitney had a feeling this man was seriously deranged and for whatever reason, he thought she was Erica Thompson. He didn't want to listen to reason, because obviously if he knew her sister and it seemed as if he knew Erica quite well, he knew she was a liar.

"You don't think I know you by now, Erica or whatever the fuck you want to call yourself now," he hissed in her ear as they started to walk again going inside the bar. "You didn't think I wouldn't catch you? You probably didn't think I would have the balls to do this, did

you?" His chuckle was wicked and sinister, sending Goosebumps up her arm.

"I'm not Erica. M-My name is Whitney Canton-"

"Lies! Lies! Whatever your name is, you're going in there with me and do as I say," he ordered.

As soon as they walked in, he held her arm even tighter and she swore she couldn't feel her fingers because he was cutting off the circulation. It was as if his grip was to remind her of how much her life was in danger. She started to feel dizzy and when a kindly faced older white man with a preacher's cuff around his neck asked for her identification, she passed him whatever came out of her pocket first.

"Whitney?" the preacher asked to be sure.

She blinked the tears away wishing she had given him Erica's identification, but she wasn't thinking straight. Heart would definitely pick this up. He would definitely find her even faster. "P-Please…" she winced, feeling the steel pressed into her skin.

"Are you alright?" the preacher asked. "Do you need to lie down?"

Was she really staring at a preacher standing behind a bar with the Western Union sign behind him? Or was she dreaming? The loss of blood to her arm was really affecting her sight. "I-I just need a glass of water," she said, hoping the man would see her pleading with her eyes.

The white man put a paper in front of her and ordered her to sign on the lines as he got her a glass of water. She couldn't see her perpetrator because he was still standing behind her. Yet there was no doubt he was there from the grip on her arm, to the sharp metal in her ribs and the sharp nudge he enacted when the preacher had his back to them, when she hesitated to sign.

Slowly, she picked up the pen nearby and carefully signed her own name. She didn't know if she stayed on the line or not, because the tears in her eyes were welling up so badly, she could barely see. While the preacher handed her a glass of water, the man behind her signed the paper and ordered the preacher to hurry the hell up.

As the preacher began his speech about love and marriage, she wanted to pass out. She couldn't do this. She was only seventeen. This wasn't happening. What the hell had Erica done to this guy to piss him off to the point that he couldn't see straight?

"Do you, Whitney Canton, take Dakota Traylor to be your lawful wedded husband?" the preacher said for the second time.

"I-I'm…" she started to protest, but he squeezed her arm so hard, she could barely stand and clutched the bar for support. "Yes," she gritted through her teeth.

"I now pronounce you man and wife, you can kiss the bride, sir," the preacher said.

"I'll do that when I feel good and ready," he said with a growl. Grabbed the paper off the bar and practically dragged her out the bar into the dim streets again.

"This is crazy. You can't do this!" Whitney tried to reason with him.

Grabbing both her arms now and viciously shaking her, he ordered her to shut up, and then started dragging her back across the street to the restaurant. Whitney looked around for a white Neon, but there was nothing in sight. She cursed to herself wishing there was someone out on the streets who she could catch their attention, but this town was so small, no one seemed to come out once evening set in.

He wasn't going inside the restaurant though. He was headed to the hotel. Becoming very paranoid, she dug her heels into the sidewalk until she almost fell down. He was forced to stop to allow her to steady herself, but when he tried to walk again, she dug her heels again.

"No!" she hissed. "I won't let you do this to me. You can't do this!"

"I can do anything I damn well." He shoved the marriage license in her face. "I can do it legally too, you stupid bitch!"

"I'm not going to let you!" Bravely, she stood up to him looking up into his face, and raising her chin to show she could be stubborn.

The back of his hand knocked her back on her butt so fast, she lost her breath as she hit the ground hard. He snatched her by the front of her dress and practically dragged her to the side of the restaurant. She kicked and fought trying to scratch his arms and swipe at his face. Her foot tripped him up, and he ended up landing on top of her knocking the rest of the breath from her body.

He grabbed her arms before she was able to regain her breath again and held them high above her head. "So you don't care where

we have our marriage bed, Erica!" he sneered as he tore the front of her dress.

Whitney tried to twist and turn her body away from him, but it was useless because he was so heavy. "You can't!" she cried. "Please stop-" With his free hand he covered her mouth so her hysterics couldn't be heard by anyone else.

"You'll be mine," he hissed. "I'll make you suffer every second of every minute I choose to keep you alive."

If she wasn't terrified before, she was shaking in fear now. His large hand muffled her whimpers.

"Make another sound or say another word, and I'll make sure you don't live another second," he threatened.

Whitney closed her eyes and prayed. Prayed for a miracle! Prayed for anything or anyone to come and save her.

He tore the rest of her dress as if the fabric were nothing but tissue. She didn't see the knife in his hand, and knew that was just how strong he was. He grabbed the back of her head entwining his fingers in her thick hair and pressed his body against her own. His rough clothing chaffed her sensitive skin.

"I'm going to take what you refused to give me," he said before meshing his thick lips against her own.

The rough kiss terrified her even more and she started immediately thinking about those horrible images her stepsister had implanted in her head long ago about what men did to women during sex. Despite the masculinity of his tongue that tasted her, she shook from her own deep-seated fear of what was to come next from kissing.

Damn the fear he evoked, just knowing the pain to come he wanted her to experience scared her to dissolve in the hysterical darkness her mind seem to fall into.

Dakota felt her go limp under him and her complete unresponsiveness. He raised to look down at her and frown. With her eyes closed and her body not so full of life, she looked very different.

Looking down to the full breast that he couldn't help but touch, and he knew instantly this wasn't Erica Thompson. This wasn't who he thought it was, yet…Why did this woman almost look like her?

Moving his hands along the flat of her stomach, he stopped at the tip of her black silk underwear. Jesus what had he done? Why hadn't he listened to her?

Moving away from her, he gripped his own hair and tried to yank it out in frustration. What the hell had he done?

Taking off his plaid shirt, he laid it over her. Should he stay here until she came too?

No, he should go. She would never identify him. He would be long gone before she came to and he would try to put this awfulness behind him and get a hold of his anger before it got the best of him.

As he went down the back of the alley that led to another street, he broke out in a run. He didn't care that his body screamed in hunger. He needed to get away, before they found him. Before she cried bloody rape.

When he got a block away he cursed his stupidity. He forgot the papers! Damn! Damn! Damn!

*   *   *   *   *

"Ma'am," a voice called over here.

She gasped awake screaming and kicking, but realized she was being attacked anymore.

"Ma'am," the voice called again

Whitney found the voice belong to the waitress that had been in the restaurant. "W-Where is he?" she demanded to know.

"Who ma'am?" the waitress asked confused.

Looking around frantically, she got up holding the shirt close to her. "Him! The man!"

"There was no one here. These two guys came asking for a lady who was waiting for a car," the waitress said. "I saw you walking across the street with that man, and -"

"Yes! That man! He…He…." She huffed frantically. "I don't…"

"I'll give you a minute while you get yourself together, alright ma'am," the waitress said and left her alone.

Whitney was shaking all over as she leaned against the cold wall of the side of the restaurant. Whatever had happened, which she couldn't determine because her body felt sore all over, she knew she just needed to get away from here as fast as possible.

Looking down at herself, she didn't look too bad. There was no blood flowing out from between her legs, and she couldn't really say she had or hadn't been molested because her underwear seemed intact.

Grabbing her purse, she put on the black and white plaid shirt, she remembered him wearing. She could smell him and that made her feel dizzy.

'Just pretend it didn't happen,' Whitney told herself. All she had to do was get to Begley and she could put all this to rest.

Steadying herself, she was able to walk out to the front of the restaurant where the white Neon was parked. The salesman greeted her, and handed her the keys. She signed the necessary documents and he left her after letting her know they had an office in Brigham City, Utah where she could return the car.

The waitress brought out the rest of her items from the restaurant and Whitney paid the lady for the soup, which the waitress had warmed to go. Whitney wanted to question the lady more about the man, but she didn't want to garner suspicion about herself. She needed to get out of this city as soon as possible and was glad when she was sitting behind the driver's seat.

Just as she was about to take off, the knock on her passenger's window suddenly startled her.

The waitress held some papers to the window and Whitney let down the window. "These were with you in the alley. I think you dropped them."

Whitney took the papers and looked at them. Dakota Traylor? Was that his real name? Either way, she would make sure Begley took care of any matters and covered up any paper work.

*   *   *   *   *

Arriving in Brigham City, Utah the next day, she went straight to Lawrence Begley small office on the fifth floor the Brigham Towers, the only other large office complex other than city hall in downtown Brigham City. He was a lean man with natural tanned skin and the deepest green eyes she had laid eyes on. Despite how old he sounded on the phone, she was surprised to see he looked about twenty-five and was darn cute for a white man.

By this time, she had resolved whatever had happened with this Dakota Traylor, she would just tell Mr. Begley she had made a grave mistake and that she needed some type of annulment. Mr. Begley could figure out what to do. He was a lawyer.

After Mr. Begley introduced himself, she said, "Before we go any further in this relationship, Mr. Begley, I should let you know that I am Whitney Canton and I have been a prisoner to Eric Thompson for the past year. He's been holding me hostage practically until my twenty-first birthday when I'm to sign over papers to him for the company. I don't want that to happen. I want my trust to go to my father." She handed him her identification cards and birth certificates, which she had stolen from her mother's vanity.

"This doesn't look like you," he said a bit leery, but then leaned in close to her and stared into her eyes deeply. A small smile started from one side of his face and spread to the other. "Whitney Canton, I'm at your service."

Whitney took a deep breath of relief and wanted to cry. Soon everything would be over with.

Erica had stayed in her room the majority of the time while her father practically ranted and raved about what he was going to do to Whitney once she was found. Everyone thought for sure for almost a week, Whitney had found a place to hide in the house, to piss Eric off, but the girl had managed to get out.

At least that's what Lethal had found out. Whitney had somehow gotten out the state supposedly, because Lethal found traces of her from a cabby on the border of California to Nevada. The Bus Company was really helpful in tracing her until she got off in the middle of the state of Nevada and they found the RV with her prints on it. Lethal was working on the man all the way in Maine to find out more about how Whitney had masterminded this plan to change herself.

Tonight, Lethal was due to come to update her father on the case. Lethal Heart was very business-like, but anyone could tell Erica was smitten with the man. Big as a bear, with hands that could cover Erica's whole face, Lethal lived up to his name. He was huge and brawny, and the government had issued his body as a lethal weapon. He was a former Green Beret and had served the government on several different secret missions. He was trained to fight with his bare hands mastering over three hundred different self-defense methods, and was skilled in over a hundred different types of weapons.

He decided to go private ten years ago because he found out he could make more money working for himself instead of the government. His agency was known all over the world for the various successful cases and accounts.

Missing persons and body guarding were the most profound in his business and Lethal took his business very serious.

Erica finished applying her make and when she heard the sound of a loud F truck pull up in their driveway, she knew Lethal was here. She rushed down the stairs arriving at the front door even before Jamison came to open the door.

The butler gave her a wary look as he opened the door and let Lethal to come in.

Swarthy was the only word she could think of to describe Lethal in his black soft silk shirt, ass-tight jeans, and black timberlands. The California sun didn't faze him the least. He had his

thin back length long dread locks pulled back in a ponytail and a black Stetson on his head. He smelled of Calvin Klein and pure man sending Erica's senses reeling.

She would swear with his granite strong-featured face, coffee brown skin, and an after five shadow on his face, she could definitely mistake him for some type of pirate if it was back in the day.

Immediately ducking through the doorway that filled his six foot five frame, he took off his hat, and nodded in greeting to Erica.

Jamison rolled his eyes heavenwards at Erica's properness.

"Hello, Mr. Heart. It's so nice to see you again." She extended her hand and he shook it.

"Likewise, Ms. Thompson," he said politely.

Jamison took Lethal's hat and went to formally announce him to Eric.

Erica noticed across Lethal's belt, he had three different electronic devices most likely to keep him in touch with his business and clients. The devices looked so small compared to the man who wore them.

She guided him to her father's office, as she made small talk mostly about herself. Lethal looked as if he were highly interested.

"Quit boring the man, Erica!" Eric grumbled. "Go tell your stepmother, our guest is here and to come down as soberly as she can."

Reluctantly, Erica left really wanting to stick by Lethal. To be in his presence was like sunshine on a cloudy day. He made a woman remember she was a woman and those part nuns told you were bad to touch yearned to be caressed.

Lethal Heart dripped sex like a bad facet and she wanted to lick him up and down like a lollipop. His dark looks and reputation only made her want to forget her own fear about being with a man and take a chance on giving herself to him. This felt better than anything in the world to Erica. This felt like love.

Taking the servant steps to the second floor, Erica knew where Pamela had been creeping to when she just wanted to be alone, since Whitney's disappearance.

Pamela had been as close to a mother for Erica as a woman. Before Pamela, Erica had grown up without a mother except the many nannies her father employed. Pamela had treated her no different

than Whitney and nurtured Erica when she needed someone like a mother, but Erica was always jealous that Whitney always garnered the attention from both Pamela and her father. Eric paid attention to Whitney because he wanted to use her. Pamela was always proud of the accomplishments that Whitney achieved despite the way she grew up sheltered.

Pamela looked like an older skinnier Whitney, but unlike her daughter, she always kept her shoulder coppery brown hair down.

Immediately upon coming upon Pamela, Erica could tell the older woman had already finished a finished a bottle of Wild Irish Rose. She reeked of liquor and her eyes were bloodshot from her excessive crying all day, since Whitney's disappearance.

"I thought you were Whitney at first," Pamela said, using a Kleenex to wipe her face.

Erica came around the bed where Pamela was sitting on the edge. A picture of Whitney at four years old with Lyle Canton proudly holding his little girl in his arms was lying next to Pamela on the bed. It was clearly wrinkled from being handled so much.

"Daddy wants you to join us with Mr. Heart at the dinner table," she said.

"Soon," Pamela said, so faintly that Erica had to strain to hear her.

Erica took that answer as an excuse to leave and get back to Lethal. When Erica returned to Lethal and Eric, they had not come to the dining room yet, but from her father's previous attitude, she had a feeling he would send her away again. She made her way to the dining room so she could be there before any one arrived.

It was only a few minutes of waiting before Lethal and Eric entered. They were deep in discussion so she was able to peruse Lethal's tight muscled brawn to her heart's content.

The private investigator sat down beside her and looked into her eyes.

"Erica!" her father snapped, drawing her out of her dream world. "Mr. Heart just asked you something! Quit acting stupid and answer his question."

She blushed profusely and lowered her eyes to her lap.

"Are you alright, Ms. Thompson?" Lethal asked genuinely concerned. "Your pupils are dilated. Do you feel well?"

Erica flushed in embarrassment. "I'm fine," she said breathlessly looking up at him. "W-What did you ask?"

"Had Whitney ever mentioned her father's true whereabouts?" She thought about it, but couldn't come up with anything at the moment with Lethal's proximity affecting her brainwaves. "No, sir."

Lethal gave her a curious frown, before looking at Eric. "His last known residence was in Detroit. He still uses a PO Box there for any taxes or contacts, but I have nothing after that. No ones touched that box in the past two years according to the postmaster."

"It should be easy to check that information, since that's where your main offices are located, aren't they, Mr. Heart?" Erica asked just to make conversation.

The servants had begun to bring the food to the table.

"Where is your stepmother?" Eric demanded.

Erica was well aware that her father was irritated by her presence. "She said she would be coming soon."

"Why don't you do me a favor and fetch her?"

Bristling at his attitude, Erica said, "Why don't you send your servants to fetch her?"

Eric narrowed his eyes to slits, "That's why I had you. Now do as you're told."

Every fiber of her nerve told her to say something, but respect and a whole lot of fear made her keep her mouth closed. She glanced over at Lethal who only stared straight as if he weren't in the room.

Stiffly, she stood up and left the room. By the time she reached the stairs, Erica's eyes were overflowing with tears at the embarrassment her father had made her feel. Out of nowhere someone handed her a tissue. Looking up, she saw Jamison standing there with a stoic look upon his face.

She took the tissue and thanked him with a nod. The butler only walked away. Erica rushed upstairs to get Pamela to hurry up.

Pamela was still sitting on the bed in Whitney's room. It took a moment for her to register that Erica was back in the room.

"I'm sorry did you say something?" Pamela asked.

Erica shook her head. "Eric wants you down at the dinner table immediately."

"Come here, child. My eyes…Please come here, Erica, I have so much to share with you."

Impatiently, Erica came to the bed and sat beside her stepmother really wanting to get back down with Lethal.

Pamela was quiet for a long moment, before she asked, "What do you know about your mother, Erica?"

Erica only shrugged. "Only what Eric told me. He said she died having me."

"She didn't die having you, Erica. She died when she made the choice to give you up."

Frowning in confusion, Erica asked, "What's that suppose to mean, Pammy?" She usually called her stepmother this when she was trying to coax something out of her.

Pamela didn't answer the question. Instead, she spoke of other things. "We should have done what Whitney did. Getting away from Eric was the best for her. You should do the same."

Defensively, Erica said, "He's not her father."

"Evil is evil, child. In the end, it kills whatever it touches. You and I are so much alike, but Whitney was different. She was I before I met Eric. My poor baby. She's out there alone in the world. She's never been out there by herself before." Pamela began to cry.

Erica was lost for words unsure how to comfort Pamela when she was jumping from one sentence to another. "Eric will find Whitney. Don't worry."

Pamela chortled. "Is that why you think I'm sad, Erica?"

"Well, she has been gone for a long time."

Shaking her head, her stepmother said, "I'm crying because I know once she finds her father, she'll know the evil I have done. She'll know that I sacrificed my soul and my first child to a man because I thought I was in love, when in fact Lyle Canton showed me true love, yet I turned my back on him and destroyed him."

Erica thought about Dakota Traylor and how she had deceived him.

"At least I did one thing right for Whitney." Pamela smiled a weird dreamy smile. "I lied to your father about Whitney's birthday."

She pressed her index finger to her lips as if she were keeping the secret and not telling it out loud.

"When is her birthday?"

Pamela giggled. "Yesterday. She turned twenty-one yesterday."

Erica gasped, "How did you fool everyone?"

"I simply had some crack head help me out. He knew this identity specialist who forged fake papers for Whitney when I came back here. Her trust is in the right birth date, but I made the trust lawyer swear to give out the wrong date of birth. I told him in the end that it would protect the trust against misuse. He believed me, and he is seeing the benefits of it now." Pamela shrugged. "We're all pawns in his evil game, Erica. You and I have been used, but Whitney found the , just like she said she would. She found a way out. You should too."

"What about you?"

"I'm doomed, child. I'm doomed to die." Erica

frowned. "But you aren't dead, Pammy."

Pamela looked deep into Erica's eyes. "You have my nose. You ever noticed that? You have my nose and my eyes." She kissed Erica's forehead. "It's too late, Erica. I'm already dying a very slow death."

Standing up, Erica said, "Just wait here. I'll go get Daddy. He'll make you feel better."

Pamela made that strange chortle, but a little bit more softly as

if it took a lot of effort to produce the sound in her chest. "It's too late.

Get out before it's too late for you, too."

Erica started to run for the door, but halted at hearing Pamela call her name.

"Tell Whitney I love her. And Erica?" Her eyes rolled briefly in her head, but returned to their rightful place.

"Yes, Pammy."

"I'm sorry I sold my soul and yours to the devil. I've love you all your life, too my daughter."

Erica was scared, as Pamela turned away and stared at the picture of Whitney and Lyle. Quickly running from the room, Erica found her father and Lethal still in the dining room talking.

"Daddy," she said at the doorway loud enough to make Lethal look at her worriedly, but Eric just continued to talk as if she hadn't spoke.

When she called his name again, Eric put up a firm index

finger as if she were a ten-year-old child pulling at his coat
strings. Angrily at how he had been treating her, she
snapped, "Eric!" "What?!" he sneered heatedly.
        "Pammy's not feeling well. I think she did something drastic."
        Eric looked as if this news was ruining his entire life. "Fine.
If
you can't handle something so simple as to get her down here, I
will have to do it myself. Please excuse my daughter's rudeness,
Mr. Heart." He threw down his napkin and stalked out the room.
        "Do you think it's really serious?" Lethal asked.
        Erica shrugged very confused. Pamela could have just been
feeling more depressed than usual and Erica could have blown it
out of proportion. "I don't know."
        "Is she usually like this?"
        "She's been depressed over a lot of things. Her
depression just seemed really bad just now. It scared me."
        Lethal stood up. "Show me where she is."
        Erica didn't hesitate as she took him up the back stairs
to Whitney's room. When they entered together, Pamela was now
laying down on the pillows with her back to the door. She looked as if
she were just sleeping. Lethal called her name before lightly shaking
her.
        Staying at the doorway, Erica immediately sensed
something was wrong, as Lethal knelt on the bed and rolled Pamela
onto her back.
        Eric appeared at the doorway with three empty
prescription bottles in his hands. He had gone to Pamela's bedroom
before coming here, because he had assumed when he had left the
dining room that was where his wife was without asking Erica of
her whereabouts.
        "She's not breathing. Call nine-one-one!" Lethal ordered
after checking Pamela's vital signs.
        Looking down at the prescription bottles in her father's hands,
Erica knew what to assumed as Lethal began to perform CPR.
Falling to her knees, Erica began to scream at the top of her lungs as
if that would bring her mother back.

        Opening her eyes, she was in the stinking dark alley all over
again. He was there and she began to fight him with all the strength she
had, but the anger and madness was on his side and he overtook her
pressing her arms over her head into the concrete. She was so aware of
his muscular body pressing tightly against her own body and she could
feel his manhood trying to find her softness. Despite her fear this time,
she was very aware of an awakening between her legs, and looking up into
those maddening deep honey-brown eyes of his, she found herself actually
wanting his closeness and more
        "No!" she screamed, sitting up in the massive hotel bed still

trying to fight off the dream.

Looking about frantically she saw she was alone and sighed in relief. Whitney wiped the sleep out her eyes and put her feet to the floor taking deep long breaths. Her dreams about him felt too real. Praying, she never saw him again for the rest of her life she convinced herself that her mind was deluded to think his touch would be pleasurable. He was a street lowlife and she wanted no part of him.

Mr. Begley put her in a Ritz Halston hotel near his offices to give her a chance to wash up and change clothing, which she had not done in two days. Whitney was so glad to have the opportunity to just get somewhere and rest.

Getting out the bed, she went to take a shower to get the smell of 'him' off of her. It was as if he had done something to the chemistry of her body and no matter what she did, she could smell him. She could taste the masculinity remembering how his tongue licked her teeth and entwined around her own tongue like an anaconda. He had drawn the strength and air from her body in just that moment and that was the last thing she remembered.

Pressing her face against the cold bathroom tiled wall, she tried to relish in the discomfort of the contact in order to make herself forget him, but even that was useless.

A knock on the door was a good distraction and she put on the hotel provided bathrobe hoping it was Lawrence with something for her to wear.

To her pleasure it was along with a dark skinned Hispanic male standing about six feet and very lean. He had a black bushy

moustache and his hair was slicked back. Immediately she noted whoever he was, he had money because he was sporting a two thousand-dollar custom-tailored suit, and a Rolex with diamonds on the band and face. Yet, he had to be no more than thirty.

Lawrence made introductions immediately because it was evident of the mistrust in Whitney's eyes. "This is Kenneth Bellini, Whitney. I know you knew very little about your own trust, but I contacted him as soon as you first spoke to me and I made arrangements for him to come here. We've been speaking for the past couple of hours about your predicament and he sees a solution to your problem."

"What problem? The annulment?"

"As your trust lawyer, Ms. Canton, your father set up strong foundations, so not just anyone could dip into the pot. He wanted to protect you because he assumed you would be in his custody at all times. He never thought your mother would divorce him and take you, nor would your stepfather use the trust as his own account in order to take over your families company," Kenneth Bellini said as he entered the room.

Like a gentleman, he offered her a seat and put his briefcase on the table nearby. "Over the years of living with your stepfather, Eric acquired various companies and assets, which were placed in your trust and earned the trust money. In order to keep control of the trust, he had to make a certain amount of money for the trust. These were the provisions and he met them all, but by giving all his own assets to the trust."

"Where is all this going?" Whitney asked.

Kenneth looked a little bit upset as he took out the wedding certificate. "This paper now gives your husband legal responsibility over the trust. Eric Thompson no longer holds any assets and your husband controls everything."

Whitney stood up. "That's impossible if I'm only seventeen! That marriage agreement is null and void! Look at the date on the certificate."

"The date of birth on the certificate is wrong." He pulled out a birth certificate. "Your mother had your date of birth changed in order to protect you from Eric getting his hands on your money. Eric's intentions were to make you sign over all assets the day before your

twenty-first birthday, which everyone assumed it was six weeks from now, but your birthday actually was yesterday."

Grabbing the marriage certificate, she read the date over and over again. It was impossible. She couldn't be legally marriage to some mangy streetwalker that raped her!

Slumping down in the chair, she covered her face trying to suppress the scream that wanted to come out of her mouth.

"I take it this marriage was not to your choosing?" Kenneth asked, coming closer to her and kneeling down to her eye level.

She could see the compassion in his eyes and nodded allowing the tears of despair to run down her cheek. "H-He forced it on me. It was like some bad dream gone terribly wrong and he forced me in the alley and…" She couldn't stop it. As strong as she had tried to be in the past days, Whitney couldn't hold back any more emotions. She let out the sobs and shook in desolation.

Kenneth held her close until she calmed herself apologizing for losing it like that.

"It's fine, Ms. Canton." He handed her a personal embroidered handkerchief.

"Please call me Whitney," she insisted.

He smiled which took away his geek-like appearance to make him cute. "I met your father one day and I thought he was pretty crazy to set up a trust for a child so early in life, but he said you were a smart girl and you would do well by his company and his interest. He didn't trust himself to hold the stocks to his company. He paid the money to set the trust up, knowing I charge a lot of money, and he left. I never saw him again."

"He thought he and my mother would be together forever, but she left him for Eric," Whitney explained.

"I know, but she insisted I give out false information in the interest of the trust. She even convinced you that your birthday was different and no one was the wiser. Yet, your father, who thought he would have the opportunity to choose your husband, made it clear that if you married the trust would immediately turn over to your husband. I must go with the foundation of the trust."

"But I don't want this man to have it."

"There is a solution to the problem, Whitney," Lawrence said handing her the bag of clothes. "Why don't you get dressed and we'll discuss this over something to eat."

She really wanted to discuss it now, but she was also famished. Taking the bag, she went to the bathroom and put on the skirt and blouse. She had given Lawrence's secretary her old sizes and the outfit was too big on her, but there were some safety pins in the drawer of the bathroom and Whitney made use of those to straighten out her clothing. A nice sweater that matched the beige outfit went over her shoulders nicely to cover up the safety pins.

Coming out the bathroom, they were all set to go and took her to the hotel's dining area. She saw how highly regarded the wait staff treated Mr. Bellini and she curiously paid attention to him wondering just how much power did this attorney possess.

After ordering their food, Kenneth immediately got down to business. "Lawrence told me you were on your way to see your father. Considering the man Eric Thompson is, I don't think that's a safe idea."

"I thought we were here to discuss what to do about my marriage,"

"Yes, we are," Lawrence said. "Please give Mr. Bellini, a moment to finish everything so you fully understand what is going on."

"I understand Eric Thompson is a man who will do whatever it takes to get his hands back on the assets he lost, Mr. Bellini," Whitney said impatiently.

"He's also a man that will do away with whomever to get what he believes is rightfully his," Kenneth added.

There was quietness at the table as she digested this information. Leaning forward, she asked, "You think he will hurt my father."

"Yes and now is not a good time to see him. You'll be putting your father's life in jeopardy."

Whitney felt Kenneth Bellini had a point, but what was she to do? Nathaniel had called her back on her voicemail and before falling asleep at the hotel; Whitney spoke with him and asked for his assistance in helping her father, who was also down in Florida.

Nathaniel apologized for his son's rudeness and told her it was just a misunderstanding, but Whitney had been too exhausted to really care.

"What do you suggest I do?" she asked Kenneth.

"I suggest you stay here in Utah a married woman until we track down your husband and get him to sign divorce papers. If he is some bum off the street as you have told Lawrence, Eric should have just as much difficulty. Once we have located this husband, we will convince him it would be to his best advantage to divorce you."

She clicked her tongue in disbelief. "He'll see the money and know it isn't, Mr. Bellini."

Kenneth leaned forward with an arrogant grin on his lips. "Trust me, Whitney. He will bow to your wishes and dissolve the marriage immediately."

Whitney didn't want to know what this lawyer would do, but she realized despite his nice appearance, there was something pretty damn sinister about Kenneth Bellini and she didn't want to know what it was. She just chalked it up that he was a lawyer and lawyers could do things normal people couldn't.

"Fine," she said. "Do what you must, but I must ask Mr. Bellini, why are you doing this at all?"

Sitting back, Kenneth answered, "Although you have hired Mr. Begley to oversee your interest, your trust is still run from my law firm, unless you say differently of course. I've come here to look out for your interest, Whitney."

"And of course your profit," she assumed.

He nodded. "I take my client's interest very seriously because I'm in charge of their future finances. With me, you will never have to worry about your money."

By him saying this, she knew he was serious. She felt confident her 'interest' would be looked over.

"Mr. Begley and I will work closely and he will receive a stipend from the trust to pay for his services whatever you wish him to be in charge of. We will forward the money to him, but I will be always there to make sure your interest and your money are used the way you want them to be used," Kenneth assured her. "Just think of me as a guardian angel, Whitney. I may not be around, but I'm always there."

She smiled liking the assurance her gave her. "So you will find my husband and he'll dissolve the marriage, but what if he's not intimidated by you, Mr. Bellini."

"Then we'll negotiate, if that doesn't work, we will go to the courts," he answered.

"Will I have to be present?"

"Through negotiations, no you won't, but the court proceedings must be attended if it makes it that far, which I highly doubt," he said confidently.

Whitney shivered in disgust. "What if I don't want to see him?"

"I can't control what must be done, Whitney, but hopefully it won't come to that."

Whitney prayed they would find this man, dissolve the marriage and she would never have to set eyes on him ever again.

They spoke well into the night and she found out why Kenneth had so much control. He belonged to the most powerful real estate family in the world. Albeit he was adopted into the family when he was five, he was still considered part of the first generation of Bellini's.

The Ritz Halston Hotel chain was owned and operated by the Halston Corporation with Antonio Bellini Sr., Kenneth's uncle.

He took the celebrity of his name with stride and wore the name with pride although he was adopted. It wasn't just the fact that he was a Bellini, but that he was apart of a very close knit family that loved and cared about him.

Whitney envied that and wished she had siblings or cousins that she could turn to for support, but Whitney knew Erica would never be that close to her.

When she was returned to her room, Kenneth told Lawrence he would meet him down at the limousine, because he wanted a private word with Whitney.

Lawrence didn't hesitate and left them alone in her hotel room together.

"This guy that forced himself on you, Whitney, what exactly did he do?"

Whitney felt that uncomfortable feeling that she always had after her dreams of him. "I really don't want to speak on this right now, Mr. Bellini."

"I must know. In order to negotiate properly, I must know all the details."

It took a moment, but Whitney began to tell him the details of what she remembered doing her best to keep her emotions at bay.

"So you aren't sure if he penetrated you?"

"No, but he was unbuckling his pants, I distinctly remember that, Mr. Bellini."

Kenneth didn't refute this. "Did you feel violated? Was there semen present afterwards when you awoke?"

She shrugged. "I'm not sure. I've never…" She blushed so hard she was positive her cheeks were going to burst. "I've never been with a man…I've never done any of that before."

"Any of that?" he asked, coming closer because her voice had gotten to a whisper.

"The kissing and touching." She forced herself to swallow because it felt as if her throat was closing.

He gave her a long stare in her eyes and she was aware of a soft hazel that entered his green eyes. "Is that why you didn't press charges, Whitney?"

"I don't know. I didn't know what to do and when Lawrence asked me I just told him no, because I wanted to forget the pain."

"The pain of being violated or the emotional pain of being forced?" he asked.

She shook her head. "I can't really say right now."

He pulled out a card. "There's a doctor I want you to see in the next city. She'll run some necessary test and check you out."

"What if I don't want to stay in Utah?" she asked.

"You can't see your father. Not until the heat is down."

"How long should it be?"

"A couple of months. Why don't you let me send you on a nice trip around the world? It would be great!"

She shook her head. This was the first time in her life on her own and she wanted the freedom to do what she wanted without someone over her shoulder. "I liked being on the road, Mr. Bellini. Can't I just travel around until the heat clears up? I mean I'll head in the general direction of Florida, but until you give me the all clear, I won't go anywhere near there. I can hide pretty well."

"That's not very safe, Whitney," he disputed.

"But it's what I want. I'm twenty-one and I think I can do whatever I want," she said stubbornly.

"Like go out and get married?" he questioned, raising a dark brow.

His brutal honesty knocked her confidence down a notch, and Kenneth didn't apologize for his remark, but he consoled her in a comforting hug. "I'm flying back to Chicago for the night. Give me until tomorrow to think about it okay and I'll give you a call tomorrow afternoon."

She nodded solemnly and watched him leave. Yes, she was glad to have Kenneth Bellini in her corner, but she didn't want to feel trapped.

If she stayed in Utah any longer, she would feel like a prisoner. Damn Eric and his deceitful ways.

*   *   *   *   *

Whitney arose early in the morning and made an appointment with the doctor's office on the card, which agreed to see her that morning. While at the doctor's office, as she was waiting for her test results to come back, she received a call from Lawrence.

"Did you speak with Mr. Bellini?" she asked hopefully.

"No, but I did find out something else," he said becoming strangely quiet.

"What?"

"It's your mother, Whitney. She's dead."

Whitney wasn't sure if she heard him right and sat in the nearest chair as if that could clear her mind from the fog that suddenly enveloped her. "What did you say, Lawrence?"

He spoke even slower. "Your mother committed suicide yesterday afternoon."

She covered her mouth to cover the gasp. "Why? Did they know why?"

"No, Whitney." Lawrence sighed aggrieved. "They found her body in the house. She had taken three bottles of pain pills."

Whitney took several deep breaths. "Was it because of me?"

"I'm finding out the details as we speak, but I don't think it was over your disappearance."

Whitney controlled herself well. "You will let me know, won't you?"

"Of course," he assured her. "Mr. Bellini said he would also contact you as soon as he makes his decision. I think he wants to hear your test results first."

Whitney said her goodbye and disconnected the call. Immediately she went to the bathroom for some privacy and grieved to herself.

*   *   *   *   *

Erica looked out the window not really paying attention to Miguel, their gardener. He waved at her and even blew a kiss, but she was so far gone from reality she couldn't respond with her usual fakeness.

The police had come and gone, asking the question she had the answer to, but her mind was not really there because she had questions of her own that now only Eric had answers for.

In the past whenever she had asked her father about her mother was, he became evasive and Erica had always assumed it was grief over losing her, but now as she thought about the past, she knew she had the answers. Erica had seen so many things over the years, but never paid attention to it. Eric had always handled her personal matters and all-important papers were kept in the safe, which Erica was not privileged to know the combination.

Yet it had been one time when she was fourteen and had cut herself. She needed to go to the hospital; Eric had been in Canada and Pamela needed Erica's paperwork to go to the emergency room.

Even though Erica had been screaming her head off, she remembered Pamela saying "your worst day?" in the receiver.

Erica turned away from the window and looked at the portrait of Pamela's picture, which hit the wall safe.

Her father entered the study and stopped short when he saw her there. "You're up early, Erica. Did you have an appointment?" He proceeded over to his desk.

"I never went to sleep," she admitted and came to the front of the desk that he was sitting at.

"Well, don't worry, I'll have this funeral out the way by the end of the week and you'll be back to your normal life, traveling, beauty shops and Rodeo Drive."

Things that were important in the past to her didn't seem so important now. Her entire life all felt pretty stupid in reality when something like this happened to her. "She said some things to me, before…before we found her, Daddy."

He was busy doing his work and didn't bother to look up at her as she spoke to him. "Things like what, Erica?"

"Things like who my mother was."

Eric immediately stopped what he was doing and looked up at Erica. "What did she say?"

"What should she have said, Daddy?"

Narrowing his cruel brown eyes, he threatened, "Don't play games with me, Erica. You got something to say to me?"

"I've got questions that would like to be answered with the truth."

"You don't need to know the truth. You need to just do as I say and accept the fact that I'm your father and that's all you need." He came around the desk and faced her. "Get your ass upstairs and don't you ever question me about anything."

Erica wanted to scream, but she didn't. Turning to the door, she gasped seeing Lethal standing there. This was the second time her father had embarrassed her in front of him.

Lethal only nodded to her as she walked by him, but she didn't stop too upset over how her father had avoided her questions, threatened her and made her feel like she was nothing. Instead of going to her room and pouting, she waited until she heard the study door close and went back down the stairs to the parlor room, which was right beside the study.

Pressing her ear against the wall, she was able to pick up Eric's conversation with Lethal.

"Have you spoken with the trust attorney lately?" Lethal asked.

"No, I use my own attorney who handles all the matters with Mr. Bellini."

Lethal said, "It seems Mr. Bellini has been contacted by a Kenneth Begley in Brigham, Utah as proxy for Whitney Canton."

"She can't hire an attorney," Eric sneered.

"If she has the money and he accepts the service, she can do whatever she damn well pleases," Lethal said. "I spoke with Mr. Bellini this morning. I just happen to have accounts with the Bellinis, so it was no problem finding out what Mr. Begley wanted."

"Which is?" Eric demanded to know.

"To transfer the trustee over to someone else," Lethal answered.

Eric cursed harshly and Erica heard something breaking. "That bitch is trying to take away what I own."

"Not only is she trying to do that, but whatever the matter she wanted to discuss about her trust, made Mr. Bellini jump on a plane and fly to Utah yesterday when Mr. Bellini is known to never go anywhere. He doesn't like to travel, but obviously the matter was dire enough to get him face to face with Whitney."

"What the hell happened?"

"He couldn't tell me. He said it was client-attorney privileges and that the details couldn't be discuss, but I will say this, whatever it was, it didn't sound as if it was in your favor," Lethal said.

Erica could hear Eric working the phone and trying to get his lawyer on the other line.

"One more thing," Lethal said, "The reason we lost all trace of her, was because she was using Erica's identification. I checked Erica's credit card usage and identical cards were ordered three months ago and a copy of her bank statement shows there was a separate account opened in Erica's name four weeks ago."

"Did Erica know this?" Eric asked.

"From what I've seen, Erica probably was too busy spending money and living in her own world, while Whitney must have copied her id and cards."

"So now that you know where to find her, why don't you go get my daughter?" Eric sneered.

"Whitney had this planned for a long while, sir. I've got people going to Utah as we speak, but I have a feeling I'm not going to be able to sweep in there and just take her, Eric."

"And why not?"

"Because just in case you didn't get the memo, Whitney's birthday was three days ago."

Erica heard something being slapped down on the desk.

"I pulled that copy straight from Detroit where she was born. The one you gave me was a fake – a damn good fake, but unless Whitney's coming along peaceably, there's no way I can get her to come back to California. She's not a minor anymore and no longer your responsibility even if she were still a minor. Did you know about this, Eric, and just decided not to tell me?"

"Hell no! Hell! Hell!" Eric did a lot more cursing. "That bitch of a mother did this to me. That fucking whore! She deceived me and then on top of that she goes off and tells Erica the truth about who the girl's mother was when we swore we'd keep it a secret."

"I think you've got some explaining to do, Eric and I want to know the truth this time."

Erica moved away from the wall. She knew she couldn't be in this house anymore. Not with the deceit her father had driven her

mother to do. She had to make things right and if finding Whitney and apologizing would make things right, she would do that.

      "Miss? Are you okay?" Jamison asked, seeing her leave the parlor in a hurry.

      "Yes, Jamison, but…" Erica knew Whitney and the butler were close. "Jamison, Whitney didn't tell you where she would go if she ran away, would she?"

      "No, she didn't," he said stiffly. "But Ms. Erica, I think if you think about it long enough, she's told you."

      Erica didn't know how to take that information. Did Jamison know and just didn't want to say anything, or was he trying to clue her in on what she should already know. "What's my dad's worst day?"

      Jamison smiled knowingly. "The day his father lost the family's business. June eleventh, nineteen seventy-four."

      She thanked him and ran upstairs to pack for Utah. Going in her closet, she found her traveling case and as she was pulling it down, something hard fell by her toe.

      Gasping, she picked up the ceramic figurine Whitney had made for her on her past twenty-second birthday just a month ago. Erica remembered throwing it in the closet because she felt it was worth nothing.

      At the bottom of the figurine of the dolphin that Whitney had created by hand, it said, "Sister: May you always know where I am and may we always find each other."

      Carefully she put the figurine in the traveling case and made plans to drive her car to Brigham City, Utah.

      Whitney didn't know how long she stared at the phone, but it had to be for over five hours before she realized she hadn't eaten all day.

      Using her cell phone to call room service, she ordered a salad and a large container of fresh water and then she checked the messages on her phone. Nathaniel had left a message to assure her that Lyle Canton was safe and would be until she contacted Nathaniel.

      This put her mind at ease and she hoped that she could trust Nathaniel until she got down there. After eating she looked at the time again to see that it was going on nine p.m. She called down to the desk to see if there were any messages, but the desk clerk told her there were none. Whitney asked if a map of the US interstates could be provided for and the desk clerk let her know they would send some thing up for her.

      She would wait as long as she could for Mr. Bellini's okay, but not for long.

           *   *   *   *   *

After speaking with his lawyer for over an hour, Eric ordered the entire staff in the house to leave. Erica stayed in her room the majority of the time, but Jamison delivered her afternoon tea to her room as usual and let her know, her father had dismissed everyone for the rest of the month.

Erica came down to place the traveling bag in the trunk of her Chevrolet Camero. Instead of going back through the front, she took the servant's entrance that led to the kitchen. Just as she was about to round the corner to go into the kitchen she heard Lethal's deep voice on his phone.

"There wasn't much to go on, but he didn't seem as if he really cared that his wife had died. Only that it was all an inconvenience for his life. I saw more emotion when he found out that her birthday was yesterday and from his reaction he had no idea that Pamela had changed the information…yes, I saw the email you forwarded me, Onyx, but I don't know what to make of it. I should have sent your ass out here and stayed in Detroit to work on the Watson case…" He sighed frustrated rubbing the bridge of his nose. "Once you finish up

the paper work in Detroit, head down to Florida to get the real lowdown. Maybe it all means she'll make contact with the office there and I want you to be there when she does…No, but Jay can put you up by the marina if you don't mind the water nearby…" He chuckled. Erica knew Onyx to be Lethal's sister, who was just as deadly as her brother was and was the vice president of Lethal's company. It was the only known woman in Lethal's life.

Lethal continued to speak on the cell phone. "Yeah, that was a complete dead end. The sister knew about as much as the tip of a pencil. She's been flying by the coat tails of her daddy like a good little puppy and letting the ass pull the blindfold over her eyes. It's a pity because she could have been the smartest of the bunch. I don't think she has any answers for me, Onyx. She's about as flighty as a bird and self-centered as she can be. If I hold one more conversation with her my damn migraines' going to pop my fucking eye out."

Erica was aware this was the second time Lethal had insulted her.

Lethal continued to speak. "I'm flying out tomorrow to Bringnam City and find her or any clues of her destination. Once I do that, I can get some more answers. I don't think Eric Canton can tell me the truth to save his life…Forget the damn money, it's personal now."

Knowing sooner or later, Lethal would know she was sneaking up on him, Erica made her appearance at the doorway. Lethal immediately spotted her and ended his phone conversation abruptly.

With narrowed midnight eyes filled with suspicion, he asked, "How long have you been listening?"

"Long enough," she said.

He came up to her until he was inches from her face. "What should I do with you, Erica?"

Coming from any other man, she wouldn't have been intimidated, but this was Lethal Heart, one of the most dangerous men in the world who could kill her with his bare hands and not think twice about.

"W-What do you mean?" she asked nervously.

"I mean do you plan to be your father's little birdy and tell him what you've heard?"

Disgusted and insulted, she said, "I'm not a snitch and I'm certainly no puppy."

"You follow his commands very well."

"I do not!" she disputed angrily.

"Could have fooled me."

Why hadn't she noticed how frustrating he could be? "I am not going to go running to my father. I wasn't even trying to listen to what you have to say. It's none of my business." She did her best to pretend indifference.

Lethal obviously took that excuse and rolled with it because he turned away.

Remembering his comment about speaking with her, she blurted out, "I see your eyeball didn't pop out."

Lethal turned so fast, the wind from his movement made Erica step back a bit, but his reflexes were so fast she found her arm being gripped and her body being yanked against his. With venom in his voice, he sneered, "You'll do well keeping that flighty ass attitude to your self. Take your mother's advice and get the hell out of here, because once your father knows the real deal, your ass is grass, little girl. He'll chew you up and spit you out just like he did your weak ass mother."

Erica snatched away from him and ran up the servant's back steps. How could she have had a crush on someone so cruel? How could he say those awful things? Soon as she reached her room, she locked the door and fell to the floor to cry.

How could things have gone so wrong?

*   *   *   *   *

The plane ticket Dakota wanted to get cost way too much, so he decided he would hitch to Chicago to catch a cheaper flight in order to make it down there by the end of the week. Finding a trucker outside of Salt Lake City, Utah to take him up to Cheyenne, Wyoming was great luck. Instead of going on through Colorado, he took a detour up there in case…just in case the police were looking for him.

Knowing what he did plagued him in every waking hour. Knowing he terrified some innocent woman to death and then had the nerve to marry her didn't make sleeping easy for him. As soon as he reached Chicago, he would try to find his lawyer friend from college and see if he could get this thing annulled to save the young lady the trouble. Until then, he would have sleepless nights trying to get her out of his head, when all he could do was think about those full stubborn lips he had tasted only once, yet it was as if they were made for him.

As guilty as he felt, he craved more. Dakota's thoughts were not filled with what he should have done, but what he had wanted to do. Damn!

Since that time, he hadn't thought much of Erica. Matter of fact a whole day had gone by before he realized he hadn't thought about his road to vengeance. Getting off in Cheyenne, he decided to leave a message on his lawyer friend's voicemail.

"Hey buddy, it's Dakota. Yeah, my ass is out and about and I'm calling in one of my favors. Can you check out a marriage that happened two days ago in Brigham City, Utah between this chick and me? I don't remember her name and I don't know where she lived or came from. I'll give you a buzz in a couple of days or I should be swinging in town by the end of the week to make a detour on a flight to Florida."

Hanging up the phone, he was glad he had done those favors for Kenneth Bellini in college.

* *   *   *   *

Whitney received a call from Kenneth near midnight. She knew if he was in Chicago, it was about three o'clock at night. "Can I go or not?" she demanded.

"I sense you don't really care if I give you my permission or not, Whitney," he said.

"I sense you think I can just sit around and let myself be found by Eric. I think the best decision is for me to be on the move and not outside the country, Mr. Bellini," she said impatiently. "Going abroad is out of the question."

"Yet you'd rather go journeying around this unsafe country all alone?" he asked.

"I can take care of myself."

He paused a moment and sighed. "Whitney you know how I feel about you out there."

"I know, but it's what I want." She borrowed a sentence from him that she remembered he liked to use. "It's in my best interest, Mr. Bellini."

"Don't shit with, Whitney. You're talking to one of the head shitters," he said chuckling. "Look outside your window across the street and then come back to the phone."

She placed the hotel phone receiver down and went to her window just as she was told. Across the street from her was parked a dark colored Winnebago in a parking lot. Going back to the phone, she asked, "Is that Winnebago for me?"

"Of course. I had it delivered there this afternoon. The keys and codes are with the front desk and it's your to drive wherever, but it has it's own tracking device system and there is an Onstar button on the dash if you need anything. Anything!" he stressed. "I want you in Chicago by the end of the week too and then you can go off again if the heat is still on and if I feel it's safe for you to go at this

alone." She giggled. "Thank you, Mr. Bellini. Any word on that husband thing?"

"How fast do you expect me to work, girl?" he asked with a snort.

"Well you are a Bellini."

He laughed. "You've got me there and trust me, I think I knew where to find your husband before I left the state of Utah, but I'm just waiting on my contacts to get back in touch with me."

Whitney frowned wondering how he had managed to work so fast. "What about anything else you have to tell me?"

"Lawrence informed me he told you about your mother."

"Yes," she said solemnly.

"According to the reports, the last person she spoke to was Erica. Pamela told her she felt guilty for what she kept from you. Something about the evil she has done, but I don't have the report in front of me yet. By the time you get here I should have the full report for you to read and keep," he assured her.

"Is there anything else you want to tell me, Mr. Bellini?" she asked.

"One more thing I wanted to inquire. Did you get involved with any of Eric's business? I know he had you sign some things that he wouldn't allow you to read over, but was there ever a time, when he

had people over in his business to the house that you can remember?" he asked rather evasively.

"No one familiar that I can remember. His lawyer came a lot of times and I know even some people from overseas came through as interested business partners or buyers."

"So you don't know about Canton Industries?" he asked.

"Only what Lawrence told me about it. What is this concern with?" she questioned.

"Nothing really. I just thought you would be able to clue me on Eric Thompson's dealings, but I guess I thought wrong." He changed the subject. "Just remember to be careful and keep your phone on at all times."

She promised him, excited about the opportunity of hitting the road again.

Arriving in Brigham City, Utah in the morning, Erica checked into the Ritz Halston hotel. She used her credit card to pay and went upstairs to get a hot shower and some rest. From what she had heard, Lawrence Begley's office shouldn't be that far from the hotel. The desk clerk gave her a very familiar smile as she was on her way out to Begley's office.

"Didn't you just leave this morning?" he asked.

She frowned and shook her head. "No, I'm just getting in from California."

He looked a bit confused. "I'm sorry, I must have mistaken you for one of the guest who checked out about four this morning."

Lawrence Begley looked a little apprehensive when she arrived and took her in his office. "I haven't been so busy before," Lawrence said.

"I would like to know if you've heard from my sister, Mr. Begley. I want to catch up with Whitney Canton and Mr. Heart pinpointed her location to be here," she said firmly.

He shook his head. "No, Ms. Thompson, I wouldn't know where you sister is."

She could tell he was lying because he sounded phony. "I'm not working for my father, if that is what you think. I'm just trying to find Whitney to…apologize and be with her. I think with out my father's presence I can be a very good sister for her. Please help me."

Lawrence looked very disappointed that he couldn't assist her. "Leave me a number and when or if I speak to her again, I'll give her the message."

Erica dug in her purse to write down her number, but then realized that she hadn't brought her phone. She had been so busy trying to sneak out the house that she hadn't bothered to get her phone out her charger in the parlor. Cursing to herself, she ran a frustrated hand through her hair. "I don't have a number."

"Where are you staying while you're in town?"

She gave him her hotel room number. "I'll be there until tomorrow and then I'll be heading to Florida."

"Why Florida?"

Looking at him with distrust, she said, "Don't worry about it. Just tell her when or if you speak to her, I got the message she left for me on my birthday and we can catch up with each other there." Before leaving she grabbed one of his business cards.

Six hours later, someone was hammering at her hotel door as if the place was burning down. She swung open the door and was knocked out the way by Lethal storming in the room as if fire was on his ass.

"You spoiled rotten, little bitch!" He seethed. "Your father calls
me screaming in my fucking ear about how you've been kidnapped

too."

"I took your advice!" she cried. "You told me to get out of there."

"I was talking about killing yourself you little tramp!"

She had enough of his insults and forgetting herself, she slapped him as hard as she could. It didn't seem to do anything to him physically, but it certainly made him shut up. "Quit calling me names, you bully!" she cried, nearing tears of fear. "I'm not a tramp and I'm not stupid. I maybe be spoiled, but I'm not that self-centered."

Quietly as if there was a storm brewing and he had to keep his voice low in order to hear it, he said, "Why are you here in Utah?"

"I'm looking for my sister," she admitted.

"You were listening to us from the parlor?" he asked.

She nodded and said, "I heard what you told him, so I just went on that. How did you know I was here?"

"Mr. Begley thought it strange that Whitney's sister and a private investigator were here to see her."

"I wanted to find Whitney," she said defensively.

"You wanted to get in my way," he growled.

"I'm not working for my father. This is for me to know."

Lethal huffed angrily. "You need to take your ass back to California and let me do my job. I'll let you know when I find her. I'm the best in the business at missing persons and I think I can catch your sister."

"I'm not going back there!" she protested.

He snorted. "Where do you suppose you're going then? Haven't you heard the news? Eric Thompson is broke. All those credit cards he's given away will be dead by the end of the day."

She couldn't believe what she was hearing. "How is he paying you?" she demanded to know.

"He isn't, Erica. I'm working for personal reasons, because his damn check bounced. I just don't like to leave something unfinished until I have all the answers."

Erica knew her credit cards were all she had to make it to Florida. She had two or three traveler's checks, but that was just in case of emergencies and that didn't total up to any more than eight hundred dollars. "What am I suppose to do?" she asked, not really wanting him to answer.

"Like I said, take your ass back to California, find yourself a good job and get your ass on your feet. Your credit is shot to hell from your old man using your numbers and signature and you've got no one else in the world. You think Whitney's going to want to support a sister who use to be her step-father's spy?"

Erica had to admit Lethal was right. When she went to Whitney, her sister would immediately suspect she was just trying to use her like Eric had done. Erica didn't want to be compared to her father, so she knew she would have to make due on her own. Her accounting degree from college had to account for something.

"I want to get to Tampa, Florida," she said to Lethal. "You

think I can make it on the eight hundred dollars in traveler's checks?" He
shrugged a large shoulder. "If spent wisely, maybe."

"You sent your sister down there. I could meet up with her
and she could help me find a job or something. I'm good at crunching
numbers, but I don't have that much experience at it."

Lethal huffed annoyed and scratched something out on the
hotel's notepad. "Here's a guy, who runs his own business down
there. He could probably help you find something out there, but don't
associate yourself with knowing me," he threatened.

For the first time in days, she smiled because for some
reason she knew Lethal was going way above his call for duty to give
her this opportunity. Before she could help herself, she jumped on her
tiptoes and planted her lips firmly on his.

His arms circled waist and she thought he was about to
yank her away, but instead, Lethal's thick arms tightened about her
body and his tongue snaked between her lips to deepen the kiss. She

could feel his body respond immediately to her as her own body
seemed to want more of what he had to offer.

Suddenly, she was wrenched away from the kiss and set
firmly away from him.

"Don't try that shit again, Erica!" he said as firmly as
he possibly could and stormed out the room as harshly as he had
walked in.

Wickedly, Erica touched her lips savoring the deep erotic
flavor of Lethal Heart.

*   *   *   *   *

Whitney felt so free driving down the interstate. The
Winnebago was just what she needed and she couldn't thank
Kenneth Bellini enough in her mind about what he had done.

Two days had passed since she left Brigham City, Utah and
she found herself passing Lincoln, Nebraska. The Winnebago was
specially built with a second gas tank, so she could drive longer
distances without stopping so much.

Along with the keys to the Winnebago was a credit card with
her name on it and one thousand dollars in spending cash, plus a
note for her to go to the Ritz Halston in Demoine, Iowa if she ran out
of cash and needed more to be wired to her.

The nights in Nebraska seemed colder and she changed into a
nice pair of khaki pants with a jacket to match and a short sleeve shirt.
By the time she was on the outskirts of Iowa, she found a Texaco
near a truck stop and filled up both tanks so she wouldn't have to
stop again until she got in Illinois.

Before getting off the exit, she saw a tall man thinly dressed
for a cold night like this, walking on the side of the freeway with
his thumb out. She kept driving because she didn't feel it was safe to
pick up a hitchhiker.

While there, she decided to fill up her refrigerator and cabinets since the gas stop had a small grocery store as well. Whitney figured Mr. Bellini was watching her credit card spending and would know exactly where she was every time she used it.

"Will that be all miss?" the cashier said to her.

"Don't you think that's enough?" she teased as he bagged her items.

The bell to the entrance rung, but she didn't bother to turn around to see who came in as she handed the cashier her credit card and told him she wanted to fill her gas tank up. "I'll be back to sign the receipt and get my card," she said.

After she put her items in the back of the Winnebago, she filled her gas tank. She entered the store again and saw the cashier staring out into the darkness.

Following his eyes, she faintly saw a tall man walking away from the store in a plaid jacket and some dirty pants with bright red baseball cap on.

"Looks like a cold night, don't it, Miss. One of our coldest for this season," the cashier said as he handed her the credit card slip. "Poor man came in here to ask me if some trucks would be pulling in heading for Chicago."

"He was hitching?" she asked, signing the slip.

"Yeah, hitching, but this ain't a night to be out hitching if you know what I mean. Good thing you're doing the smart thing, missy by driving that pretty camper. That poor fellow ain't even dressed for a night like this. He'll freeze to death before the morning."

Whitney had a feeling the guy was trying to give her a hint. "There aren't any trucks about this part that can take him part of the way."

"Nope, all them fellows heading south and west. Ain't no truck due east for two days and that fellow didn't look like he wanted to wait around for that long." The cashier looked to the window again after he took her credit card receipt. "Nope, ain't a night to go out hitching. The cold here will certainly kill you."

She didn't say anything else to him, except goodnight. He was a nice enough cashier, but she was not going to pick up someone she didn't think she should be associated with. Whitney could just imagine Mr. Bellini's anger if she told him she picked up some strange man.

She had made that mistake before about strangers and she certainly wasn't going to make that mistake again.

Before leaving the station, she neatly put up all her food and cooking items she had bought and made sure the water tank on the Winnebago was filled before she found the freeway again. A mile onto the freeway, she could see the red-capped man in the distance and by the time she was a few feet from him she changed her mind and decided she should give him a ride. It would probably be nice company for her on her way to Chicago and she could get there faster with a little company as well if he was nice enough.

Stopping ahead of him on the side of the road about ten feet she honked her horn and put on her hazards, while unlocking the doors.

Reaching underneath her seat, she checked for the knife she had strapped down there in case of emergencies, but put her hands back on the steering column and waited for the hitchhiker to open up the Winnebago's passenger door.

The light came on indicating that the door had opened and she smiled her friendliest smile as she heard his smooth deep voice of relief, "Thanks for stopping miss."

He tipped his hat up to reveal himself and her eyes opened wide in fear as she looked into the face of the man she had married just a few days ago in Brigham City, Utah.

Whitney wasn't sure how long she had stared at him thinking it was a dream, before shaking herself back to reality and digging under the seat frantically for the knife. He must have assumed her intentions because he lunged over the passenger seat.

She screamed as he grabbed her wrist and twisted it until she bent to his will. "Let me go!" she demanded as he held her wrist pressed against the driver's window, while his free hand made its way down under her seat to grab the knife.

"So you can kill me?" he asked, moving away from her and sitting in the passenger seat.

"You deserve it, rapist!" she sneered.

"Rapist?" he asked incredulously. "I never raped you, woman."

She didn't care what the doctors had told her. He had overpowered her and initiated the deed and that was just as bad as doing it. He would never understand how terrified she had been in those moments when she thought she would be violated in the worst way and the pain.

She couldn't imagine the pain she could have suffered and he had made her face her greatest fear. A fear she couldn't run from no matter what.

"Or are you the type who thinks that if that's what I was going to do, it's just as bad as the doing?" he questioned, reading her thoughts.

"You were going to rape me. You forced yourself on me in the act of doing something I didn't want!"

"I thought you were someone else!" he said, raising his voice angrily. "I thought you were the bitch that ruined me."

The invective made her ears burn. "Get out," she ordered. "Get out of my sight and get out of my life."

Dakota looked at her as if she was crazy. "I'm not going anywhere, lady!" he said adamantly.

That was the last straw. Whitney leaped at him, meaning to scratch his eyes out, but he grabbed her arms, twisted them behind her back and pressed her chest against him, while forcing her legs to straddle his waist. He was too close!

He only needed one hand to keep her in place as he pushed her now messed up hair out of her face. They were both breathing hard from the struggle, but he didn't look upset over her intentions to hurt him.

"I hate you!" she seethed and spat in his face.

He wiped the spittle away, but Dakota still didn't get upset. "You have every right to be. You have every right to hate me for the rest of your life."

The madness that she remembered being in his honey colored eyes before was not there any more. They were looking at her in wonder as if he couldn't believe she was there now.

Whitney forced herself to calm down. Losing her temper was getting her nowhere with him and she needed to get away from him. She didn't like the way her body was reacting to his proximity. "Let me go," she ordered calmly.

"Not until I know you won't fight me anymore."

"I won't promise that," she argued.

"Alright, you won't hurt me for now until I say what I have to say to you."

"Fine," she conceded.

Dakota released her arms and she was aware he still had the knife in his hands. When she started to get off of him, he gently held her down. "Wait," he insisted.

She warily paused impatiently lingering where she was sitting to hear what he had to say.

"I've never gotten that angry before in my life, and it drove me into some kind of madness that I couldn't see straight. I thought you were that bitch. I thought you were the woman who took everything from me and stomped my in the heart. I wanted to hurt her and take what she wouldn't give to me," he said, explaining his actions. "I know what I did was wrong, and I must have scared the shit out of you."

His swearing again made her uncomfortable and she shifted her weight a little.

He must have assumed she was trying to get up, because he moved his hands to her waist firmly as if to hold her down. "I apologize," he said.

"Is that suppose to make me feel better?" she snapped.

Dakota looked shocked by her callousness. "No, but I've wanted to say that to you. I've been thinking about you for the longest." His tone had gotten deep and smooth, making the goose bumps on her back increased.

Forcing herself to stay focus on her anger, she said, "Now you've apologized, so get out!"

"I want to make things right," he said.

Whitney didn't care what he wanted to do, all she wanted was for him to get out, but she knew he had no intentions of being left on the side of the road by the way he was dressed. Whitney recalled the cashier's words about the night. It was going to be one of the coldest nights. Perusing him, she saw that even though his clothes were old and worn, he smelled like pinecones, grass, and sweat. The odor wasn't bad.

The more she observed him she saw he was well groomed despite the scruffy appearance. His hair was braided back in cornrows and his hands had been well maintained. His teeth were pearly white and straight.

It was as if he was putting on a scruffy appearance in order to hide something about himself. Even the way he spoke despite the southern drawl when he became angry and the curse words seemed somewhat educated.

If she really thought about it, Whitney needed to get his acquiesce to sign the divorce papers without fighting her about it. "Are you asking me what I want?" she asked warily.

"Is that what you want me to do?"

"Of course! My lawyer's looking for you. You won't contest the divorce?"

Dakota shrugged to say that was no problem. "I had no intentions of it. I was going to get a lawyer friend of mine to do the same."

She tried to get back up, but he held her down firmly. "What else is there to talk about?" she snapped upset that he wouldn't let her go and she was tired of trying to fight him, only to end up losing in the end. Plus, he still had the knife in his hand and she didn't want this to become a situation where he had to use it.

"I still haven't made it better," he pointed out with a very deep expression on his face.

She narrowed her eyes suspiciously. "What do you mean?"

"I mean you're still scared. I feel the fear in your body," he said.

Audaciously, Whitney said, "You do not!"

Leaning forward to her, he said, "Trust me, I'm a man who knows a woman's body very well and I can feel your fear. Why do you have this fear over what you want?" he asked.

"I don't!" she lied.

Dakota smirked knowingly. "Who did that to you? Who made you scared of men?"

Whitney couldn't believe he could read her mind like that. "You don't know anything!" she said spitefully. "If you know women so well, why didn't you see the woman that hurt you was lying?"

His eyes narrowed and she could see that was a touchy subject with him. "She managed to escape my detection, but I've made sure not to make that mistake again."

"How?"

"I won't love with my heart anymore." He changed the subject back. "Nice try, woman. You're trying to get away from your problem." His brawny long arms circled her waist and pulled her closer to him.

"You can't make me feel better," she protested, pushing away from him.

"I think I can." One of his strong hands snaked to the back of her head to hold her securely.

The panic returned and the shaking increased. "Please," Whitney pleaded, trying her best not to sound as if she was crying.

He stopped pulling her so close, but he didn't release her. "The only way to get over a fear is to face it, woman," Dakota tried to explain.

Whitney didn't want to face anything, let alone that! "Let me go," she pleaded.

"I will if you'll do two things for me," he said.

Cautiously, she asked, "What?"

"A kiss and a ride to your lawyers office," he said.

The second she could do; the first she didn't want to do. "I don't know you!" she cried.

"Last I checked, I was your husband," he pointed out.

Narrowing her eyes, she said with a great deal of anger, "Last time I checked, I was forced!"

That smirk of humor returned to his face again as he said, "True, but that does mean I have rights."

"You have the right to let me go or I'll scream!" She knew this was stupid to say. They were in the middle of nowhere. If she did scream, no one would hear her.

"I've made concessions with you, why can't you make concessions with me?" He was trying to reason with her and his rational worked.

Whitney asked, "How do I know you'll keep your word?"

"I'm a man who only has his word that is worth anything," Dakota said proudly.

She was given a moment to think about, before she sighed in resignation. "Fine, one kiss!" she said, stressing her words.

He relaxed his hold just a little bit more, but before he could prepare himself anymore, she leaned in quickly and brushed her lips against his and then tried to get up, but his grasp tightened on her again.

"What?!" she asked exasperated.

He snorted in disgust. "What the hell was that?"

"A kiss. You never specified what kind of kiss," she said smartly with a triumphant smile.

"I don't know what rock you've been under for the past decade, woman, but that was not a kiss. That was a tickle. Now since I asked for the kiss, we should go by my rules of kissing."

"And what are your rules?" she asked suspiciously, knowing it would be something she didn't like.

"Long and hard," he said with a genuine eager smile.

Whitney was not going to point out just how damn sexy he looked when he smiled and his eyes seem to dance in expectation. "How long is long?" she asked to be difficult.

He rolled his eyes in exasperation. "You've got to be kidding, woman."

"Fine!" she snapped in a pout. "Let's get this over with." She leaned forward, closed her eyes and puckered her lips tight.

When he made no move to return her actions, she opened her eyes. "What is the problem?"

"I was starting to wonder that about you. Who taught you how to kiss?" Dakota wrinkled his nose.

Insulted, she said, "No one needs to be taught how to kiss."

"That's where you are wrong, woman." "Quit calling me that."

"I would if I knew your name."

She looked at him long and hard as if he had told her something she just couldn't believe. "You don't remember my name?"

Bashfully, he admitted, "I was so angry, I didn't pay attention."

"Whitney," she said quietly.

His familiar smirk of humor returned again as he looked at her in awe. "Whitney," he whispered, leaning forward. The bass in his voice, made the hairs on her arm stand on end.

She was struck by the tenderness in his voice. As he whispered her name again in his deep mellifluous voice, she answered self-consciously with a soft, "Yes."

Dakota took advantage of her parted lips and connected his own to them.

She felt her whole body come alive as his mouth pressed against hers and his tongue slipped to play with her own. He tasted like dark sweet honey and her mouth buzzed for more as she responded to the kiss wrapping her arms around his neck. She moaned as he broke the kiss to deliver light kisses all over her face and neck.

Before planting his lips and suckling on her earlobe and neck, he breathlessly said her name again sending her senses aflame with lust.

Her body was not shaking in fear anymore. Passion was making her nerves quiver in expectation of so much more.

Dakota returned those beautiful lips back to her and she

pressed against them on her own wantonly taking what he readily offered.

"This is your Onstar operator. Our computers have informed us you've been parked on the side of the freeway for over ten minutes. Do you require assistance?" a high-pitched voice sounded from the dash.

Startled, she broke the kiss. "N-No!" Damn Bellini and his silly security system, Whitney said to herself.

"Please push the require security code on the dash keyboard to assure us that you are fine," the Onstar operator instructed.

Whitney practically fell out of his lap trying to reach over the dash in order to put in the code, knowing she didn't want Kenneth Bellini to find out about this, but also knowing the lawyer would.

Huffing to herself, she seated herself properly in the driver's chair and turned the ignition. The Winnebego screeched because it had been running the entire time.

She looked over at him to see him smiling with that same damn smirk on his face as if he had cured cancer. Biting her tongue to keep from saying anything, she put the vehicle in drive as he secured the passenger door tightly. The overhead light went out as well as the open door light on her dashboard.

"Mind if I get a little shut eye while you drive?" Dakota asked.

Whitney didn't care what he did as long as he didn't speak to her. Not believing she had acted like a wanton slut, she told herself she would keep her distance from Dakota Traylor. She would get him to Chicago and get him out of her life as soon as possible.

As tired as Dakota was, sleep didn't come to him right away, yet he pretended to be a sleep to give him self a chance to look at her through slightly closed eyes.

Her bone structure reminded him of Erica's, but other than that, she was different. He couldn't believe the mess he had made out of her life and would love to make it up to her, if she wanted him to.

Dakota had never hurt a woman before in his life. He had been a lover of women and before meeting Erica he had been a great person to know. Many people thought of him as kind and hard working. He would help a friend out in a minute, but after Erica, he found himself becoming a sarcastic, surly, and selfish.

Going down to Florida would give him a chance to collect himself, get on his feet and get back to his old self.

Although, Whitney had brought him closer to himself in the few minutes he had gotten to know her, than any sole searching he had been doing these past few months.

When sleep finally over took him, Dakota was a bit disappointed because he had enjoyed staring at her even though he could only make out a little of her face from the side views he had.

His mind took him to the last night with Erica. How beautiful she had been in a blue chiffon dress. Her dark brown hair swept up with ringlet of curls everywhere.

"When Erica?" he asked after a very passionate kiss, which she quickly broke off.

"Soon," she promised. "All our dreams will come true very soon, Dakota."

He allowed this answer to suffice for now and led her over to a table where they were having dinner in her hotel room. There was a black box on the table where she sat at and she opened the box quickly. Her eyes danced in excitement at the beautiful diamond necklace.

"It's beautiful!" she gasped. "You shouldn't have."

Dakota helped her put it on. "In two days, you're going to be my wife." Kissing her shoulder, he noted only a little how her body seemed to grow cold as his own passion heated up, but his love for

her was blind and he didn't care that she acted like this. "You'll be Mrs. Traylor soon and I'll make love to you."

"Please, Dakota. Don't talk about that now. Let's eat," she pleaded as if the subject was too taboo to speak about.

He noted the frustration in her eyes and …the fear. The same eyes as…

Awakening with a start, he groaned as the sunlight hit his face hard, making his eyes burn. Checking his watch, he noticed he slept half the night and almost the whole morning. It was going on ten to noon EST and he was hungry as hell.

Her eyes were glued to the road and she had soft jazz playing. The air conditioner was turned on, but all the vents were pointing away from him. Dakota wondered if she had moved them away, or had they been like that all along.

He knew she was aware he had awoken, but she didn't speak to him. Matter of fact, by her body language, she was stiffening up the more awake he became.

"You mind if I give myself some relief?" he asked.

She frowned annoyed he was addressing her as if he should check with her appointment secretary before speaking with her.

"Anyone ever call you a stuck up bitch?" he asked honestly.

"That's enough!" Whitney snapped. "I am trying to be a civil to you as possible considering what you've done to me, but if you keep up your foul mouthed behavior, I swear I'm going to scream."

"I guess that's a no, huh?"

She huffed as if he were jumping on her last nerve.

"Does that mean I can't take a piss in your toilet?" Dakota asked

"Do you have to be so vulgar?" she asked perturbed.

"I'm not vulgar."

"Then you should talk to me like a gentleman would a lady."

He was quiet for a moment, staring at her up and down. "How old are you?"

"I'm twenty-one," she said proudly.

"Jesus, you're borderline jail bait, just legal enough to take a good drink of vodka."

Whitney frowned again as if she had never heard the terminology. When he started to explain what he meant, she cut him

off sharply, and said, "I know what that means, sir, but I'm mature enough to make decisions on my own and I'll have you to know, I'm college educated with almost two bachelors."

"Like going off on your own into the middle of the United States?" he asked.

"You remind me of my lawyer," she said surly. "I needed the freedom. I've been locked down for most of my life. I wanted to get away and this is like a vacation to me."

"I take it my company was not part of your plan?" Dakota asked jokingly, but she didn't find his humor very amusing.

She concentrated on the road again and he began to become perturbed by her rudeness. He rolled down the window and then began to unbuckle his pants.

She served the Winnebago sharply. "What are you doing?!" she screeched.

"I'm going to piss out the window, since you don't want to stop and you won't give me permission-"

"Go!" Whitney cried. "It's the door to the right before the bedroom. Go!"

Grabbing his bag, Dakota hopped up and found the bathroom, chuckling to himself. After relieving his bladder, he decided to wash himself up, trim the extra growth and change shirts and socks. As he stepped out the bathroom, he could tell she was watching for him through her rear view mirror. He still had his shirt opened and tucked it in before closing it giving her a good view of his chest, making sure it stayed taunt in order to give her a good show.

Sitting back in the passenger seat, he asked, "Where are we?" "We should be hitting Des Moines in about thirty minutes," she said as a yawn escaped her lips.

"You look pretty tired, you want me to drive any?" he offered.

She shook her head and he knew this was out the question. "I'm fine," Whitney lied.

Shrugging a shoulder to let her know he had tried, Dakota asked, "Think we can pull up somewhere and grab something to eat?"

"I have something in the back, why would I stop?" she asked.

"Because I'm hungry," he said. "I'm so tired of beef jerky."

"It doesn't sound like you've eaten anything. Your stomach's been growling since you've been asleep. I thought you had a bear

under your shirt," she said and smiled to herself as if she had accomplished a great dig.

"So how about it?" he asked, ignoring her comment too hungry to care right then.

"How about what?"

"How about you finding a drive through and letting me get a burger down my throat?"

"Why don't you just go in the back and toss something together?" she suggested impatiently.

Dakota got back up and went to her kitchen area.

                    *   *   *   *   *

Whitney really hated having a conversation with him and would do about anything to shut him up. He was rude and vulgar.

He probably was a selfish ass too especially since he knew she was driving through the night and had been snacking on only peanuts and coke by her side. A real gentleman would offer to…

"Here you go," he said, handing her a wrapped warmed burrito.

Whitney looked up at him suspiciously.

"Weren't you hungry?" he asked.

"A little," she said warily, wondering were there any sleeping agents he could have snuck from the back and into her food.

"Would you like something to drink too?" he asked as she took the burrito.

She shook her head and he went back to the kitchen area. Watching him duck around because the ceiling was too low, Whitney wondered was he some kind of mind reader, but she remembered his words from last know, "I know women."

When he returned to the passenger seat again, he had four warmed burritos in his lap and proceeded to pop them down like they were gumdrops. She wondered if he even chewed them.

While she was in the middle of her burrito, he was finishing off the fourth. On top of that he had the audacity to start sucking his fingers, which in turn made her watch his lips. She started thinking about last night and didn't feel like eating anymore.

"Are you going to finish that?" he asked, eyeing her burrito voraciously.

Whitney shook her head and handed it to him. He proceeded to chomp it down in one bit, opened a coke and guzzled that down. "Aren't you afraid of germs?" she asked.

Dakota looked over at her as if she had asked him the meaning of life. "If I was licking your tonsils last night, you think I'm really worried about catching something now?" he asked sarcastically.

She flushed forcing the memories from last night out of her mind.

"Is that a blush?" he asked.

Trying to play it off, she sipped on her coke, but she never answered him too worried on embarrassing herself again. She was very glad when he dropped the subject, by saying, "That was the best damn lunch I had in days, Whitney," he said, politely covering his mouth and belching.

Whitney pursed her lips together trying not to say a word, but increased her speed as if that would get them to Chicago faster.

"What part do you come from?" he inquired.

"What part?" she asked confused.

"What side of the country?"

"Aren't you supposed to ask these questions before the vows?"

It took a moment, but he started laughing. Her humor had been a ploy to get of the subject because she didn't want him to really know much about her.

Yet the trick didn't work as Dakota asked again, "Where?"

"I was born in Detroit, but my mother moved to California after divorcing my father to live with my stepfather," she said, becoming very solemn at the thought of her mother.

"Are they still married?"

"No, she's dead. She killed herself."

Dakota quieted down for a moment, but the pleasure of his mouth being closed was short lived for her, when he said, "I grew up in communes in Florida. My old man thumbed his nose at our family's money and took up like he was broke. After he died my mother felt like exploring the aura of her soul and left me to grow up with my old man's brother. My uncle demanded that I intern with several companies after earning my degree before I could work for him and take over his company. I was raised to know the business and cool with it until I let my heart get involved." He looked at the road. "You ever fell in love, Whitney?"

"No and I don't intend to." She thought about how love had destroyed her mother. "I think the idea of sacrificing oneself in order to make someone else happy is stupid."

"Love isn't sacrificial," he protested.

"You have nerve to talk? Didn't you just say you lost it all because of love?"

He was quiet again, but it wasn't long before he brought up a new subject. "Is this your first time out on your own?"

"Yes," she said proudly. It was a safe subject for her.

"Where were you headed?" he asked

She shrugged trying to be evasive again. "Just out and about, but now we're going to Chicago."

"How did you know I wanted to go to Chicago?" he asked

suspiciously.

"My lawyer is in Chicago," she said.

"Did you want me to do some driving?" he asked.

"No, after we pass Des Moines, I'm going to find a hotel
to take a shower and nap, then we'll be on our way again."

"I could save us a lot time, if you'd let me drive," he said. "To be
perfectly honest, I don't trust you, I don't like you, and
I
am not letting you touch any personal property of mine."

He smirked and she had a feeling he was thinking about last
night, but he didn't say a word as if he was letting her fester. Try
as she might, she couldn't stop thinking about last night and when he
decided not to speak to her for a while, she wished he would to get
her mind off of what she was thinking about.

When he asked her about herself, Whitney was eager to
speak because talking about her past education made her not think
about those warm soft lips only five feet away from her.

"So you're a genius?" he asked.

"Yes, I am considered one," she said proudly. "I think I have
always been one all my life."

"Is that why you are so sheltered? Your nose was always in
books?"

"What makes you think I was sheltered?"

He shrugged a broad shoulder. "You said you were and by
the way you act, Whitney. You have so much knowledge about the
world, but your people interactions suck. I never thought I would have
a wife who would be so anti-social."

Protesting, she said sourly, "I'm not anti-social, Dakota.
I'm just not a people and there's nothing wrong with that."

He tilted his head and looked at her funny before
stating, "I beg to differ. How do you suppose to get along with a
man you really want to marry?"

"That's where you're confused, sir. I have no intentions of
getting married. Marriage is something people use nowadays in order
to justify having sex in the eyes of God, but as you can see more and
more people aren't really caring what God thinks."

"So you're a religious person?"

"I'm religious to know that having a sexual relationship with
anyone should only be between a married couple and since I don't plan
to be married, I don't plan on having sex."

He snorted in disbelief. "You're beautiful! You're trying to
convince me that you're going to be celibate all your life because you
don't have any intentions of marrying? What if you get horny?"

"I doubt that," she said, sucking her teeth.

"What if you want children?" he challenged.

"I doubt that. I plan to run my own business and be very
successful. I don't want anyone getting in the way especially children
and especially a husband."

"Success isn't the only satisfaction in life you know," he said.

"You sound like Billy Dee Williams in Mahogany. Are you going to shake me and shout success is nothing without someone to share it with?"

Dakota chuckled. "No, but I was headed in that direction."

"Save your breath, because I don't need anyone. I don't want anyone. Love doesn't do anything, but destroy people and a moment of pleasure with a man can only lead to a lifetime of pain and suffering."

"I think you view love and sex in the same field, when it's not. Sex is not love."

"I'm aware of that."

"But you group it together," he accused her.

"Maybe because the outcome of experiencing both is the same," she snapped.

"That's not true, Whitney. Pain and suffering doesn't come with good sex," he said proudly.

"That's an oxymoron. There's no such thing as good sex."

"That's because you haven't experienced it."

"You don't know what I've experienced, Mr. Traylor," she protested. "I'm not going to deny I'm a virgin, but my views on sex are exact. Men and women have different opinions on the subject. Of course you would think it's good, because you get all the enjoyment."

Dakota cackled. "And you think women don't?"

"Of course not," Whitney said as if it were obvious.

"Like I said, you haven't experienced it."

"I don't need to experience anything to know that it's bad. I just know."

"No, you don't anything of what you're talking about," he refuted. "You can't say something taste bad, until you've tasted it."

"Eating and sex has nothing to do with each other."

Dakota only smiled wickedly. "I beg to differ," he said. "It just goes to show how really naïve you are."

"I'll have you to know, I took sexual humanities in college and they never discussed eating during sex."

He laughed so hard and she was peeved that she couldn't see the humor in their subject. Whitney decided to not try to argue him down about this, because even though she was intelligent, she wouldn't dare say she was an expert in the field they were discussing.

Trying to sound professional about the subject, she asked, "So you are an expert in this field, Mr. Traylor?"

"Call me Dakota and yes, I would say I was an expert in the field. I was a real Casanova if you must know. Before taking over my uncle's business, I bounced around from club to club all over Florida and there was no woman I couldn't have within the first five minutes of walking in the door."

"I don't want to hear about your disgusting sexual exploitations of women."

"I never exploited a woman in my life. They wanted it." She snorted in disbelief. "I doubt that."

"They came to me. They wanted me."

"So you gave them what they wanted?"

"No doubt." He smirked more to himself. "They loved what I could do to them."

Whitney huffed revolted "I don't want to know."

"Are you jealous, wife?"

"Our marriage is a farce," she said. "And no, I'm not jealous of your whoring."

Leaning over to her, he asked, "Aren't you the least bit curious?"

"Curious of what?"

"Well, we're married, we could try it out and no one would be the wiser. It'll be a secret between you and I."

Crinkling her nose, she said, "Didn't I tell you I didn't want any part of you touching any property of mine? I also meant my body as well, Mr. Traylor."

"Dakota," he corrected stiffly again, giving her a look as if he really wanted to make her eat her words, but he didn't say anything else about the subject anymore.

She took the detour around Des Moines instead of going straight through the city. Her plan was to stay away from large cities because that's where Eric would think she would stick around.

"I take it you don't like big cities either," he noted.

"I just feel we'll do better with the traffic during this time of day by taking this route. It's thirty minutes off schedule, but you aren't in too much of a hurry, are you?"

Dakota smirked again. "Not with you, Whitney."

*   *   *   *   *

From what Erica could find out, her father's assets were diminished. All of her credit cards had been cancelled and all money in her bank account that was joined with Eric's was cleaned out. She had gotten in touch with Austin at the country club. He was glad to spread the gossip on everything and as she spoke with him, she had to wonder what did she see in him other than a nice piggy bank.

Desolate, with nothing to her name, she filled her gas tank up in Louisiana and continued on her journey. Her vehicle was a newer model and she was sure she could get more miles out of it. So her

transportation was no problem, but once she reached Florida, she would see after getting a job, could she make arrangements with the bank to pay off the car on her own. It was in her father's name, but she didn't want to lose what little she owned.

Caressing the dolphin she kept on her dashboard, she hoped she could find her sister. Once she was settled with a job, she would start looking for Whitney.

Erica wondered if Whitney would forgive her? They were sisters. If Erica got to Florida, worked hard to change herself, Whitney would see that Erica wasn't like Eric and they would be a family. Erica prayed the same fate would not befall her like it had done to Pamela.

A Red Roof Inn was a cheap nice out the way spot to get cleaned up. She offered to get a room with a double bed, but he said he would feel more comfortable sleeping in the Winnebago if she didn't mind, but he did take up her offer to use the shower.

She went first taking a long hot shower and then laying down in bed. So exhausted, by the time he went in to take his, she was unconscious. Awaking five hours later, she had been bothered by the dream she had been having, which involved Dakota lying naked over her.

She dialed Kenneth's cell phone number only calling him to let him know she was fine.

"I doubt that," he said sarcastically. "Are you going to tell me the real reason you stopped on the side of the road for ten minutes last night?"

Whitney decided to be as honest as she possibly could without divulging the secret that she was presently traveling with her husband. "I picked up a hitchhiker."

"You what?!" he demanded angrily. "Have you lost your mind? Do you realize the danger you could have put yourself in."

"It was all perfectly safe," she tried to reason. "I didn't see anything wrong with picking him up and he was on the way to Chicago anyway."

"Him! You picked up some strange man?" he asked incredulously.

"Yes, and I'm fine."

"NO, YOU ARE NOT!" Kenneth bellowed in the phone. "I'm sending you a ticket down to Des Moines airport-"

"No!" she protested. "I won't do it. I can be in Chicago by tomorrow afternoon."

"You have no business being alone on the road all by yourself."

Whitney refuted this. "I can take care of myself. You can't do this to me!" she cried. "I hate to beg, Mr. Bellini, but please let me do this."

Kenneth was quiet on the line and she pressed her ear hard against the receiver to hear what, if anything, he was mumbling to himself.

"Being out on my own is really important to me," she said calmly, trying to implore to him. "For the first time in my life, I feel so free. I don't want to sit still and I don't want to wait until Eric catches up with me. I want to have this opportunity to see a little bit of the things I've been reading about and seeing in books and on the Internet. I promise I'll be in Chicago by tomorrow night. I promise."

"You know disobeying a Bellini's wishes is like violating a Federal offense," he said.

His tone was serious, but she knew he was only teasing with her. "You won't regret this, Mr. Bellini."

"I better not," he growled.

"Have you heard anything about him?" she asked evasively.

He knew whom she was speaking about. "My source is closing in on him. He made some calls to a close old friend of the family in Florida, but other than that, we don't have anything for sure although the contact did let us know your husband would be joining them in Florida by the end of the week for a job opportunity."

Biting her lip, she decided against telling Kenneth that she knew exactly where her husband was. Kenneth would have blown his lid and probably kept her on lock down until Eric was really out of the picture. "Well, hopefully by the time I get there tomorrow, you'll have the divorce papers ready for me to sign and then you can just leave it up to him to complete them."

"I can do that," he assured her.

She confirmed where she would be staying once she arrived in Chicago and then let Kenneth go. She decided to call Nathaniel Parker in Florida to find out about her father.

Nathaniel assured her, Lyle was doing well and that sobering him up would be easy. She told Nathaniel she was going to Western Union him some money to compensate for his troubles and also to buy her father a ticket to Chicago. She felt the sooner she turned over the businesses to her father, the better it would be for her father's recovery.

There was a restaurant in the hotel's lobby and she sat down to enjoy a salad, plus she had the waitress give her two cheeseburgers to go and then she went to the Winnebago. It was late evening, and the sun was on the horizon of setting.

Iowa was warm and she wore a nice sundress that showed a lot of leg. Wooden heels with a top cover to match the dress along with a hair ribbon to draw her hair back were the only accessories she wore. In the beige jacket she wore, the inside pockets contained her

wallet and keys. She didn't trust herself to keep a purse. Using
the side door, she entered the dim Winnebago and
looked at the bed. He was laid out on the bed in just jeans, asleep.
Creeping up on him, she looked over the well-defined muscular body
and bit her lip. His face was buried in the pillow so coming within
arm length and getting a better view made her bold.
          The nerves in her fingers vibrated as if calling out to his
skin. Sitting down carefully on the bed, she reached out and touched his
shoulder. The muscle twitched, but she really couldn't tell if she had
done that because her hand was shaking so badly. Her breath
became shallow as her palm made contact with his upper spine and
she watched in fascination, as the contact with his skin seemed to
make her own hand come alive.
          Whitney started to wonder what did he do to those women
to make them want it so bad. Was he all talk? Men were known to
brag, but his eyes had been so honest. Could he make her feel
good? Could he make her want what he had to offer?
          Suddenly her wrist was grabbed and she was yanked flat on
her back under him. The moment had been so quick; the yelp was
short lived as she was smothered by his weight.
          "What the hell do you think you're doing?!" Dakota said,
looking around the room as if The Calvary had come in to take him
away.
          When she caught her breath, she said, "I was waking you up."
          "That was no wake up, woman."
          Writhing under him uselessly, she ordered, "Get off of me!"
          Dakota didn't move himself, but he shifted his weight so she
could breath. "Do you really want me to move, Whitney?"
          The deep familiar voice from last night returned and Whitney
shivered at the illicit streak that shimmered down her body. Biting
her lip, she forced herself to nod not trusting her voice to give him
the order.
          Leaning close to her, he gently kissed her cheek. She closed
her eyes and stiffened as his lips caressed her neck suckling in the

familiar spot from before, and then moving up to play havoc with
her ear.
          In a whispery voice, he said, "Your body says something
completely different, Whitney." The inflection he put on the middle of
her name, made her body tremble.

                    *   *   *   *   *

          He could smell her heat and knew she wanted him, but Dakota
wanted to hear her say it. The stubbornness was there in her face, but
her body was primed and ready for anything he could offer. It would be
so easy to break her down, kiss away any resistant, and make love
until the morning, but he wouldn't.
          She had a fear some idiot had put in her head and he wanted
her to really want it - he wanted her to want him to the point she

begged for his mouth and his body. Damn his own need, which he had never gotten rid of after Erica, but he could wait. He could wait for Whitney. He would wait for her!

Releasing her arms, he lifted even more, giving her the out. "There's nothing to stop us, Whitney. We're married, remember?"

She bolted from the bed and stood at the doorway looking as angry as she possibly could pretend to be. "Don't ever do that to me again!"

"I wasn't the one trying to give a person a back massage while they were sleeping," he said.

Whitney blushed ten shades of red and turned away.

He smiled to himself grabbing a shirt and putting it on before going up to the front to sit beside her in the passenger seat. On his way, he picked up the bag of still hot burgers off the floor by the bed that she dropped. "We're these for me?" he asked.

She didn't say anything and he chuckled, knowing she was probably too choked up on her own passion to say much.

After he had munched down the burgers, he noted she seemed thoughtful about something, but he didn't try to pressure her although he wanted to know what she was thinking.

"What could you do that other men couldn't that made women so attracted to you?" she asked, trying to sound as evasive as possible.

He shrugged a nonchalant shoulder. "You wouldn't be interested in the details," he said, being just as evasive.

The pout of disappointment was clearly on her face, but she waited a couple of miles before she said anything else. By this time she was pulling off the freeway and drove to the parking lot of a store with a Western Union. When she came out, she was about to start up the engine, but hesitated and turned on the light inside of the cabin, because it had started to get dark outside.

Turning to him, she asked, "What if I wanted details?"

"You wouldn't be interested in details. Plus every woman is different. What I've done with one, doesn't mean it will work with others."

"And what would I be interested in?"

Dakota looked intensively at her long and hard liking the way his attention made her nervous and she tried hard not to show it. Deciding to leave her hanging on, he clicked his tongue and shook his head. "I don't tell, I show."

Whitney huffed in frustration and he knew she was dying to know, but she turned to start the engine up again, yet she didn't put the vehicle in drive. Again she hesitated and looked over at him narrowing her eyes circumspectly. "What if I wanted you to show me, but I didn't want you to…" She flushed and bit her lip.

"Go all the way?" He finished, with a curiously lifted one-eye brow look.

She nodded and tried to breathe deeply. She was perspiring as her nervousness about the subject grew. "Would you?"

Dakota wanted to give in to her request now, but didn't. His will power was strong and he was going to make sure that she enjoyed every minute of it. When they got to Chicago, he wanted to tear her off of him and be able to walk away. "I could, but what pleasure would I get from it?"

Gritting her teeth, she looked forward and thought about it. "There is a way I could…please you without you going all the way, isn't there?"

He wanted to hear her say it. "What way?" he asked.

Blushing while making eye contact shyly, she barely whispered, "My mouth."

Smirking with pleasure, he said, "There is, but what makes you think you can do it well enough to please me if you can barely say it?"

"You could teach me, because I've never done it before."

He broke their eye contact looking forward as if deeply pondering the thought, but in truth trying to hide the triumphant look on his face. "I think I can be appeased, Whitney."

There was a moment of silence between them, and then she asked, "Do I go first?"

*   *   *   *   *

Dakota chuckled at her innocence. "Do you go first? Is this where you want it, Whitney?"

"Would a bed be better?" she asked a bit flustered.

He laughed even more and she became angry. He seemed to be making fun of her.

"Fine," she sulked. "If you're going to make fun of me, Dakota, we can just forget it."

Shaking his head and clicking his tongue again, he said, "We won't," he said casually, gently placing his finger underneath her chin and making her look into in eyes. The space between them seemed to disappear as his mouth claimed hers in a sweet gentle kiss.

Staring deep into his eyes, she could see he was going to enjoy what he was about to do, but she was so nervous she couldn't breath straight. Had this been the right decision? Should she allow him to do this to her? What about the pain? How was he going to make her forget the pain?

Her cell phone rung startling both of them and she used that opportunity to back away and answer her phone.

"It's Nathaniel," the voice said on the other end.

"Hold on," she said and looked at Dakota. "This will only take a minute." Getting out the RV, she put the phone back to her ear. "Is everything okay?" she asked.

"It's fine, I just wanted to tell you I received the money and I'm going to get your father a ticket to Chicago by tomorrow. I'll call your lawyer to confirm the flight."

"Thanks Nathaniel."

"Don't you think you sent a little bit too much money, girl? What did you do? Win the lotto?" he asked incredulously.

She laughed. "Like I said, you keep all that's left over for what you need to do, Nathaniel. You don't know how much help this has been for me."

"Well, I do have some investments in mind and I got a partner whose joining me soon, so I think we can really do some things," he said excitedly. "I'm going to make sure I pay you back."

"You already have, Nathaniel."

"I should thank you for giving me this opportunity to show my son, I can do some things the right way."

"Just keep me informed and if you need anything, please don't hesitate to call me."

They hung up and she leaned against the RV to catch her breath and clear her mind. Whitney knew what she had waiting for her inside could change her life forever. Going around the RV to the side door, she stepped inside to throw him off a little bit, but she was thrown off when she saw he was standing in the kitchen area leaning against the counter and waiting for her. She noted he had to crouch down some because the ceiling was too low, but he didn't seem as if he was put out by the interruption.

"That was about my father," she explained. "He's-"

He placed a finger over her lips to stop her from talking. "We aren't about to change the subject, Whitney. I want you to close your eyes and turn around."

Frowning confused, she wanted to protest, but followed his direction. Her ears peaked as she tried to listen to what he was doing.

Gasping, she felt him move up behind her and place his hands on her shoulders. Her heartbeat was double timing and she felt dizzy all over.

"If you breath any faster, Whitney, you'll hyperventilate," he whispered in her ear. "Concentrate on your breathing and take deep slow breaths."

She listened to his relaxing voice and did as he said. His hands began a gentle massage from her neck to her shoulders, and then moved down to her back. He repeated this several times until she was very relaxed and she felt his hands moved toward the front of her shoulders for a brief moment, while his own body pressed against her backside. Whitney forced herself to keep her breathing steadily,

while he continued his massage. She noticed he would occasionally use one hand at a time, but she didn't wonder what happened to the other hand because she was so consumed with her thoughts and how her body was feeling.

The RV seemed to grow very warm, but then she realized it

wasn't the RV, it was just herself and then she realized his hands were touching her bare skin. Somehow he had removed her dress, which was lying at her ankles and all she wore was the matching strapless bra and panties. She was amazed at how he had accomplished this feat without her knowing, but she didn't get upset.

It seemed natural as his hands came around her waist, to gently turn her around in his arms. His shirt had been removed and his chest was like candy to her eyes as his muscles defined him so powerfully well. He smelled so natural and the warm contact their skin made was electrifying to her senses. She wanted to touch him all over, but at the same time relish in this innocent contact.

He looked very focus as he stroked her back gently and smiled down at her. It wasn't even a smirk as if he had accomplished something. She didn't feel like she has lost something in giving him this opportunity to hold her like this, which she thought she would feel if she had allowed him to get this far.

"Relaxed?" he asked, his voice thick with arousal.

She nodded. "I thought…I didn't know what to expect."

He chuckled. "I'm not done yet," he said as he kissed her with passion.

Whitney's body was easily swayed to what he wanted to do. His kisses were long and luxuriating, his hands were tender and teasing. His massage moved from her back, to her breast and she tensed a little as the sensation was new to her, but he was gentle about his ministrations easing her down until she bent to his will. His lips left hers to moved down to taste her neck, shoulder, and then replace his hands on her breast.

Her back arched as his hot mouth aroused her body even more. She wanted to move him away, but make him do more all at the same time. It felt good and frightening and she held on tight to his shoulders, biting her lips praying she wouldn't scream. Her legs had begun to go weak, but he compensated by holding her. When she couldn't stand anymore as his delicious tongue attacked the other

peak, he cradled her body lowering her to the carpet, but not letting go of his sweet war to her skin.

What his mouth couldn't touch, his hands were there to excite her. Before she could get use to the tantalizing sensations that he extracted from her body, he was kissing down to her stomach tickling her belly button with the tip of his tongue. Whitney was able to look down and realized her underwear had magically disappeared, but at the same time watched as this man placed his mouth full on her womanhood.

Her eyes widened in shock, because she could have never imagined a man's mouth there, but also that seconds after Dakota did this, her entire pelvis had a mind of it's own and radiated a wave of pleasure all the way to her brain.

She felt she was going to die in one moment and become reborn in the next repeatedly. Now knew why the French called it the little death, because as she felt her orgasm grip her heart in an invisible vise, while sending hot bolts of energy through every vein.

Yet, this didn't stop him and just as she came down from a high, he was sending her back up again. The look of serenity on his face, showed he was very much enjoying what he was doing to her.

Whitney became a mindless writhing embodiment of pleasure and joy. When she could only whimper her gratification, he held her close resting her head on his chest. His heartbeat lulled her into a deep sleep.

Sitting up in the bed abruptly, she looked around in a panic desperately. Dakota was not there with her, but she was still naked. Wrapping the covers around her, she got out of bed and went to the front to see him sitting in the driver's seat, whistling to a tune on the radio and driving.

When he was aware of her just standing there, he looked her up and down with that sarcastic smirk and then turned his eyes back on the road.

"Nice outfit. Your clothes were lying at the end of the bed," he said. "I didn't think you were the type that left things lying around on the floor. Although it isn't such a bad place to lay."

Blushing from his remark clearly meant to remind her of what just occurred. "I didn't give you permission to drive," she said.

He shrugged. "I couldn't sleep, but I didn't want to bother you and thought I could accomplish something for the both of us, by driving. Do you mind?"

No she didn't, but she wanted to sulk about it, so she didn't answer. Instead, she went back to the bedroom, turned on a light and dressed. Looking back up at him, she saw he was watching her in the rear view mirror intensely and she blushed again. Going into the bathroom, she threw cold water on her face and did her best to compose herself. She was not going to let him get the upper hand in this situation.

Coming out, she fixed them something to eat, before joining him by sitting on the passenger side. He thanked her for the food and noted her dress.

"I think I like the blanket better," he said.

"Why don't you wear it then?"

He chuckled as she fought the blush again.

Whitney decided to change the subject before her cheeks broke out in flames. "What do you plan to do after Chicago?"

"I'm meeting a friend in Florida for a job. I want to get on my feet so I can do some things in California."

"Get revenge?" she asked.

He didn't answer, but the glare he shot her told her enough. "What are your plans after Chicago?" he questioned.

"Live, be free. Do all the things I couldn't do before all this."

"So you are running away from someone?"

She only shot him a glare, which clearly told him she didn't want to talk about it. He didn't press it. They had their own secrets and they were both very aware any emotional involvement would get in the way of their plans. She stared at the road until she dozed off to sleep again.

Whatever he had done to her drained all the energy from her body, but she felt so wonderful. Whitney would cut off her tongue before she admitted this to him and wondered when was her chance to do the same to him?

* * * * *

Dakota pulled in the rest stop at five in the morning. Not because he was tired, but because he couldn't fight the need anymore. Listening to her sleep had been torturous because she had made those whimpering noises as if she were reliving what he had done to her, plus he had gotten in Illinois and was only three hours away from Chicago.

Looking at her face, he wondered what she was running from. She was too young to be any real trouble with the law, but whatever it was drove her to go across country in order to get away from it.

Lightly, Dakota caressed her cheek awakening her. Her eyes fluttered, as she smiled not realizing she wasn't dreaming anymore. He took her hand and motioned her to be quiet. Her eyes were filled with curiosity as he led her back to the bed area. Whitney hesitated at the doorway, but with a passionate kiss, her fears were pushed away and she allowed him to lead her into the room with many more kisses.

He guided her hands to his chest and prompted her to remove his shirt. Dakota didn't stop kissing her and marveled at how she found it difficult to concentrate on unbuttoning his shirt and kissing him. She wanted to please him and this made him so attentive to her needs.

"How do you feel?" he asked softly.

She nodded with a little fear in her eyes. "I'm good."

"I didn't hurt you, last time?"

Shaking her head, she blushed again. "No. You didn't."

"But you're still scared?" he asked.

"A little. I want you to show me how to please you."

Those words were all he needed and groaned as they kissed again. Did she know how good she tasted and that he could smell her arousal? He wondered was she as wet as she was before. It had taken all of his will power not to make love to her and when she was lying there in his arms after those beautiful orgasms shuddering from her experience, she hadn't notice his own shudders as his body cried for release.

Now, he was going to have that release, but didn't know if he could hold off long enough for her to enjoy doing this to him and he did want her to enjoy it. He wanted to watch her take him in those pouty lips of hers, tightened her mouth around him and feel that soft tongue lick him to heaven.

He moved her hands down to the front of his pants and she opened them up. Her fingers were shaking, but she didn't stop as she hurriedly unzipped his pants and pushed them down.

Stepping away, he removed his clothing to give himself time to calm himself down. Dakota was very aware of her eyes watching every inch he revealed and his arousal grew knowing she liked what she saw.

"Come here," he ordered as he sat on the edge of the bed.

Whitney moved in front of him hesitant and anxious. He tugged on her hands until she obeyed his wishes to move down to her knees. She started to move her hands towards his waist, but he pulled them up to his lips, kissing each fingertip, then suckling them in his mouth. She watched in fascination as he carefully applied his own oral massage from the peaks of her palm all the way to the crook of her neck, suckling deep at the skin leaving a very dark mark before moving up to capture her lips again.

He moved his hand up to her mouth and she immediately caught on suckling every finger with relish and moving up his arm over his broad shoulders and to his thick neck, where she placed a similar love bite before meeting his lips again.

His look of approval encouraged her to move over his other shoulder down his arms and do the opposite hand. This time, she used her teeth gently nibbling as she went. Whitney moved back up his neck where she found a tender spot near his collar bone and sent his eyes rolling to the back of his head.

He had to grip the bedpost to keep his composure at her newfound discovery of his passion spot.

"Wait, Whitney," he said breathlessly. "Please have mercy, woman."

She moved away to await further instructions.

Dakota quickly composed himself and took her hands gently placing them around his thick stiffening shaft. Her eyes were wide as saucers as she stared down at her hands as if they belonged to someone else.

"Are all men this long?" she asked curiously.

He flushed and kissed her tenderly. "I can't really say, Whitney."

"Do you hurt them when you use it?"

He frowned at first not getting her meaning. Releasing her hands allowing her to massage him to full titillation, he gently cupped her face. "I wish I knew who told you these lies, Whitney."

She gave him a look as if she didn't want to talk about it, so he didn't press her. Changing the subject, she asked, "When can I kiss it?"

"Remember how you kiss my finger?" he asked softly. When she nodded, he said, "Just take it slow and remember, it's most sensitive at the tip." Leaning back, he gave her the room she needed and watched as she hesitantly started to use her mouth to give him pleasure. Giving her instructions took his mind off losing his control and he was able to guide her into giving satisfaction with her lips. When he knew he couldn't hold out any longer, he groaned her name in warning.

"It's…wait…hold on, Whitney."

She didn't stop despite his warning and never missed a stroke as he released his liquor deep into her throat. Even he was surprised at how deeply she was able to take him.

When he was able to collect himself, he looked down at her. She was still gently stroking him, marveling at his manhood.

"Why is it still hard?" she asked curiously. "Didn't I satisfy you?"

He chuckled and kissed her brow. "Yes, you did Whitney, but sometimes men can continue."

"For how long?"

He was too relaxed to go into sex education , so he kissed her to take her mind off everything. That did the trick and once he pulled away, she was mindless again. He knew he could have his way with her, if he chose to, but decided against doing so because he wanted to hear her say she wanted it.

"Can we do it again?" she asked.

This was what Dakota had been waiting for. Pulling away from her, he shrugged, "We could, but I don't think that would be a good idea." Finding his clothes, he began to put them on to her disappointment.

"Why not? We are married."

"That's the point, Whitney. Married people do other things that what we did, but you don't want to do them."

She was quiet for a moment, before she said, "Why should it matter, Dakota, when we find pleasure like this."

Sitting next to her on the bed, he said, "You will never find complete satisfaction, until you truly experience love making with a man, Whitney."

"But I was satisfied," she protested. "I had orgasms."

Smiling wickedly and licking his lips, he said, "There are other pleasures and more satisfaction to achieve than what I did to you."

Curiosity was killing her, he could tell, but she would not say what she wanted to say. Biting her lip, she narrowed her eyes at him warily. "I am not going to be another notch in your bedpost, Dakota." She stood up and left out the room angrily.

He followed her. "I didn't ask you to be any notch," he said disgustedly. "You asked me for it."

Sitting in the driver's seat, she started up the engine and

proceeded to take off. Dakota had to hold onto something quickly as she turned sharply. He sat down next to her. "You wanted me to show you."

She had the nerve to be offended that he was using her words against her. "You are deliberately trying to seduce me, Dakota, into compromising myself for you. You're trying to make it seem as if all this is my idea."

"I admit, I want to make love to you, Whitney. You're my wife, why wouldn't I want to sleep with you? You're damn beautiful and you come so hard you shake like an earthquake."

Whitney blushed so hard, her cheeks looked as if they were going to burn off.

Dakota hadn't meant to admit so much, but it was hard not to let her know the truth if that was what she wanted to hear. Calming himself down, he said, "I'm not going to give you what you want, Whitney, until I can get something else out of this deal. Tit for tat."

"But I gave you what you wanted and I'll do it again." "I want more."

She grinded her teeth in frustration and Dakota had to bite his lip to keep from smiling. He could feel her thinking about everything. "I won't, Dakota. I can't." There was an immense amount of anxiety and disappointment in her voice. "I just can't get over something like that right away and…I need more time."

"But we don't have time, Whitney," he pointed out. "In three hours we'll be in Chicago."

Keeping her eyes on the road, she didn't say anything. Dakota didn't press the subject, but he could almost hear the wheels in her head turning. She was a stubborn chit, but he was sure she would give in.

Two hours later, he wasn't as hopeful. She hadn't spoken at all and he could see she was still bothered by the subject.

They arrived in Chicago and she finally spoke to him, only asking where he was staying at while he would be in the city.

He told her a hotel by the airport he knew about and she drove in that direction.

"When does your flight leave?" she asked.

"Tomorrow afternoon," he said, trying not to show his own upset. For the life of him, he couldn't understand how she could let this opportunity go when she wanted it so bad. He could tell that just by looking at her she wanted it.

She hesitated a moment before saying, "And you won't forget to go to my lawyers this afternoon to sign the papers?"

"I have some business in town. I want to speak to my lawyer first before anything, and then I'll proceed to your lawyer if that's alright with you."

Whitney pursed her lips together never taking her eyes off the road. His bad mood was coming to the surface and there was no telling what he might say.

She found his hotel and stopped in front of the office door. Dakota didn't even try doing anymore convincing. He was not going to beg her. He could tell she wanted to say something, and all he probably had to do was just say anything, but he wouldn't give in. He wanted the control she relinquished to him. He needed that in order to be satisfied with this whole situation.

Grabbing his bag, he was about to close the door, but she called his name. Bracing himself, he looked over his shoulder at her, hoping she would say what he wanted to hear.

"I didn't tell my lawyer you were with me. I didn't want him to know," she admitted.

"Why?"

"He's a little over protective of me and I didn't want him to worry."

Looking away, trying to hide his disappointment about what she was saying, Dakota gritted out, "Fine, Whitney."

She didn't say anything else, so he slammed the door and stormed into the office. There were windows everywhere, but he didn't have to look back to know she was still there watching him as he registered for a room.

Coming out the office, the RV was gone and he cursed in frustration, but a little bit relieved, because he knew he would have begged her if she had still been out there. Going to his room, he took a long shower. When he left came out the bathroom, he thought he saw movement outside of his door and looked out the curtains. There was no Winnebago parked outside his room. Closing the curtain holding the towel around his waist, he leaned against the door cursing under his breath.

Going to the phone, he called up Kenneth Bellini, but only received his voicemail. "Hey, Ken, this is Dakota from college. I'm in town and I wanted to let you know I was still looking for some help on a legal matter." Dakota said his hotel and phone number briefly. "Give me a call fast. I've got to swing around to another lawyer this afternoon and I wanted some advice."

Damn Whitney for her stubbornness. Damn her for making him want her so bad.

Suddenly, there was knocking at his door. Forgetting all he wore was a towel he opened the door and looked down at his wife.

Whitney drove around the block twice trying to get on the freeway that would take her to the hotel room that was waiting for her. In her mind, she had convinced herself that she was not going to even think about what he could do to her that would be so satisfying, but all she could really think about was how pleasurable it had been having him and to those things he had done with his mouth. Yet, she wasn't willing to make the sacrifice.

Somehow she ended back in the parking lot of the hotel in front of the office. He had registered under his own name and it wasn't difficult to find out what room he was in.

She stood at the door for a moment just staring there, but then walked away. Whitney almost made it back to the Winnebago, before her body defied her and she was turning back around and knocking on his door.

Dakota stared down at her as if she were a dream. He just stood there in the doorway looking sexy as hell dressed in only a towel.

"I was in the neighborhood," she said, trying levity to hide her nervousness.

Taking her hand, he gently pulled her into the room closed the door and let her lean up against the nearest wall while he stood in front of her just looking deep in her eyes. He didn't speak and this made her even more nervous.

"I told myself not to come back," she admitted. "But then I said, what the hell, we're married."

He smirked a little before dipping in for a glorious kiss that sent her toes curling. It didn't take long for her to lose herself in his million kisses, nor did her clothes stay on her body for long. She didn't know how they made it over to the bed, but as he gently placed her back on the spread, she looked up into his face.

"You won't hurt me?" she asked terrified.

"I won't," he promised, kissing her in so many varieties; she couldn't keep up with him. His hands and mouth pushed her fears away as she fell blissfully into a world of desire and she was crying for him to quench the passionate thirst he arose deep in her womanhood.

"Now, Dakota," she begged. "Now, please."

He didn't give up on his teasing and she was driven senseless, as he adored every inch of her body without mercy. Only when she screamed his name and begged for him, did he finally cradle her in his arms, give her a long sweet kiss, and tenderly sheathed himself deep within her. She didn't have time to think of the pain as his mouth suckled her neck and breast, and soon she was taken to a new height of craving. He had been right.

Her body shook so hard, she thought she would explode as he drove deeper and deeper inside of her. She could actually feel her muscles working with him as they danced together in an arduous tango until the climatic end, reveling in the wonderful explosion they created.

*   *   *   *   *

She wasn't sure how long she laid there, but she knew if she didn't get away from Dakota, Kenneth Bellini would come and get her out of the bed himself. The last thing she wanted was Kenneth to know that she was with her husband.

Yet every time she had made an effort to get out of bed, Dakota found ways to keep her in. He seemed inexhaustible and gained renewed strength after every episode.

"Is this normal?" she asked after his forth time.

He chuckled more to himself. "No, but you're speaking to a man that had a lot of pent up frustrations. We won't even discuss how long it's been."

She sighed thoughtfully and asked, "What time is it?" He looked over at the digital clock on the bed. "Noon."

Lifting her head from his chest with a frown, she said, "I should go."

"No," he said, wrapping his arms around her waist protectively. "I think we should talk about some things."

"There's nothing to talk about, Dakota. I have to see my lawyer."

He frowned this time. "I don't think we should do it?" Sitting up, she looked at him incredulously. "Don't do what? Get a divorce? We should have never gotten married in the first place."

"I know, but now that we are, don't you think we should try to see if we can make the best of it."

Whitney was positive he had no idea about the money, but she couldn't do this. He would get in her way. Eric would find a way to use him.

He continued. "Whitney, I know I don't have much, but all I'm asking you is to wait. I know you'd be proud of me."

"Wait?!" she asked upset. "Wait for what, Dakota? Wait for you to get rid of that revenge in your heart for a woman who scorned you? Or wait for you to finally get enough money to get to California to leave me like a bad habit?"

"That's not what I meant? That's not what I said!" He started to get angry, but forced himself to calm down. "I'm just saying that my flight leaves tomorrow. We can lay here for a while and think about it."

Getting out of bed, she cried, "You promised! I kept my end of the bargain and brought you to Chicago. Are you going to break your promise, Dakota?!"

This was a challenge and she wouldn't take anything other than what was promised. He stared at her long and hard, then gruffly said, "No Whitney, I won't break the promise I made to you."

Hurriedly she put on her clothes before she was inclined to climb back in bed with him. He wanted to protest, but she saw the dilemma he was in and once she was dressed, he still didn't speak. She looked back at the bed as she opened the door.

Their eyes met and she knew his passion for her had not dispersed. Her own yearnings grew knowing he still wanted her, and she forced herself to break eye contact and walk out.

Once she was outside she broke into a run. This was for the best, she convinced herself. They each had too much in their past in order to plan for a future together.

Driving swiftly to the hotel, an attendant at the desk passed her several messages. All of them were from Kenneth Bellini. She was shown to her room and quick hot shower. Getting out the bathroom wrapped in a thick white terry Christian Dior rob, she stopped startled at who was sitting in the front room of her hotel.

"Why in the hell did it take so long for you to get here, if you've
been in Chicago since early this morning?" Kenneth asked calmly as if he had been sitting there for years.

She wasn't surprised how he got in the room. He was a Bellini and his cousin owned this luxurious hotel along with thousands of others around the world. "I was busy."

"Busy my ass."

"I don't want to talk about it," she said tiredly and went into her
room.

He didn't follow, but she knew that wouldn't shut him up. "So you were out by the airports busy?"

"You could say that," she said evasively. "Did you come looking for me?"

"If you'd miss your appointment I would have."

She didn't have any doubt about that. Changing the subject she asked, "Did you bring the divorce papers?" Coming out the room, he was just letting a waiter out the room. Looking in the corner, she smiled at the light fruit bowl and toast. She was famished after her morning exertion.

"Of course," he said with a pompous snort.

She sat down at the table as he handed her the papers to read over. "Did you get into any contact with him?"

"Actually I had and you'd never believe it," he said. "He's in town staying in one of the hotels by the airport. Could you imagine my shock knowing you were also out there too."

Forcing her face to maintain its nonchalant disposition, she said, "Do you think he knew I was there?"

"I was going to ask the same of you."

Whitney took several bites of juicy watermelon pretending to be very immersed in her eating just to give her time to slow her roll and get on the same page as Kenneth. He paid too much attention to detail, which was probably why he was such a good lawyer. "Well, it's true what they say, Mr. Bellini, it is a small world."

Kenneth stared hard at her for a moment, and then relaxed himself chuckling. "You're a pretty smart girl, Whitney. You know that?"

She only shrugged and pretended to be deeply involved in reading the divorce papers. "So once I sign these and he signs these I'll be divorced, right?"

"Unofficially yes, until I file the paperwork with the state of course." He handed her a pen.

She started to sign it, but then hesitated. "Mr. Bellini, do you think I'm being deceitful by not letting him know how much I'm worth?"

Kenneth raised a hazel brow. "Did he suspect you were rich?"

"No but-"

"Did he ask?" he questioned, cutting her off.

"No," she responded.

"Then what deceit would there be?" he asked.

She thought for a minute before saying, "I'd like to give him a little something."

"What's a little something?" Kenneth wanted to know full of suspicion.

"Five hundred thousand."

He gasped as if the breath had been knocked out of him. "That's the first time I've heard anybody getting a reward for a forced marriage."

"You think it's too much? You're often touted as being frugal."

"I may be frugal, but I am highly intelligent if I may say so myself. I really don't feel that half a million dollars is something you just give away for no reason at all, Whitney." He sat down across from her. "Let's agree to a smaller sum that won't seem cheap, yet won't look so rewarding."

"A hundred?"

"How about fifty?" he suggested.

Frowning in thought she felt Kenneth knew what was best and nodded in agreement. "Do we need to fill out anymore papers?"

Kenneth shook his head. "Oh no, we're fine. This will be a gift which I'll present to him in your honor after he signs the papers."

Whitney signed the divorce papers looking down at Dakota's name longingly wondering that if she had stayed in that hotel room what would they have been doing now?

Kenneth took the papers and enclosed them inside his briefcase. "Why don't you stay here and rest. Tomorrow come in about eleven and we'll discuss what to do about your newly acquired

assets and stocks, plus which ones are to be transferred over to your father, so by the time he arrives at one, we'll be all set to do the paperwork."

She smiled enthusiastically at the though of seeing her father.

"I can't wait to see him.

"Good day, Ms. Whitney."

"Good day, Mr. Bellini." She watched him leave, but not hungry anymore, she went over to the phone and called the hotel Dakota was staying in.

He answered his line half-asleep.

"It's Whitney," she said quietly.

There was no answer on the other end, but she could hear his breathing and knew he was there waiting.

She spoke softly, "I didn't want us to depart on a bad note, Mr. Traylor."

"Then you should have stayed, Mrs. Traylor," he said quietly.

"If I had stayed I would have never wanted to leave," she admitted.

"I wouldn't have minded."

Closing her eyes, she convinced herself this was all in the past. Changing the subject, she said, "I never told you where the lawyer's office was. That was my excuse for coming to your hotel room."

"Really? I thought it was so I could put another notch in my bedpost," he said sarcastically.

Whitney decided not to let his acidity rub her raw. He was angry because he had expected her to stay, when he really wasn't thinking clearly. "Do you have something to write with?"

"Just hurry up and tell me, Whitney. I think I can remember some greedy divorce lawyer's address."

"His offices are at the Bellini Towers in Downtown. Take Michigan-"

He cut her off. "I know how to get there. What's his name?" "Kenneth Bellini. His offices are on the-"

"Third floor." He finished her sentence. "Your lawyer is Kenneth Bellini?"

"You know him?"

"Let's just say he knew me before I started swimming with sharks." There was a pregnant silence on the line. Neither knew how to end this conversation.

Checking the time, she saw it was going on one-thirty. "Did you meet with your lawyer friend yet?"

"I was on my way."

"Won't you be late to my lawyers office? We agreed by two," she insisted.

"Damn, Whitney. I think I can keep track of the fucking time. Quit your bitch nagging." He knew his foul mouth annoyed her. He cursed under his breath angrily more at himself for allowing this situation to affect him so much. "Dammit woman, I wouldn't have cared about revenge. I would have given everything up to be with you."

"I'm not like you, Dakota. I have my past chasing me. I have to put it to rest before I can go on."

"Then do what you must Whitney and don't worry, I'll keep my fucking promise." His line clicked.

This was best, Whitney told herself. He would just get in the way.

Dakota wanted to tear the room up, but he knew that wouldn't accomplish anything. Jumping out of bed, he called a cab while he dressed quickly.

As exhausted as he was, he forced himself to find the strength to get through this without losing his temper, but it would be hard to keep the sarcasm and evilness out of his character.

The stubborn chit! He kept telling himself. All she needed was one excuse to call him some kind of Welch. He wouldn't give her that opportunity.

He arrived at the Bellini Towers five minutes after two and the receptionist showed him to a conference room.

Armando Bellini entered the room looking very glad to see Dakota. He was about Dakota's height, which was rare for a true bloodied Bellini. Most true bloodied Bellini's stood over six feet two. Armando was one of the shorter ones, but there was no doubt about his bloodline with his deep hazel eyes of green and pitch black thick hair that was soft to touch. Armando was clean cut. Wore a suit that could feed an entire homeless shelter for a week and carried himself elegantly in style at all times. His expensive watch, thick diamond pinkie ring and a gold thick chain around his neck clearly told anyone the man rolled in money as if he shitted mountains of it on a daily basis.

Unlike his other cousins, Armando was also one of the lighter true bloodied, Bellini's with their Hispanic – Black American ancestors intertwined making a very handsome young man of thirty.

"You son of a bitch," he swore, taking his glasses off and giving Dakota a hug like a long lost brother. "When Kennie told me you'd be here I thought I'd shit bricks." He took out his wallet and pulled out a hundred dollar bill."

"What's that for?" Dakota asked when Armando handed him the bill.

"The bet you won. Remember the last time we hung out together; you were swearing you could bed that cold bitch. Next thing I know, she's your fiancée."

Dakota went a little cold as he thought about the night that he first met Erica. That had been so long ago, but thinking about it made it feel like just yesterday. "Yeah, well, not anymore."

"Now you're married."

"It wasn't to her," he quickly admitted.

"Oh, I was well aware of who you married," Armando saying knowingly. "Whitney Canton is no joke, Dakota. You got the crème of crop."

Dakota frowned, wondering what Armando meant by that. "How do you know her?"

"Only that she's been in every major city newspaper as missing for the past week."

"So she was running away."

"She was in her right mind, after what she did to-" Armando stopped as Kenneth cleared his throat at the doorway of the conference room. Abashed, Armando said, "Hey once you get done here, why don't we hit the bar to catch up."

Dakota only shrugged.

When Armando was gone, Kenneth came over to Dakota allowing the table to be the only barrier between the two of them. "You look like shit," Kenneth remarked.

"Well, life's been hard for me these past years," he explained gruffly.

"I don't think it was life, Dakota. I think it was the women you chose to be with." He looked him from head to toe in distaste. "You reap what you sow."

Dakota remembered hearing Whitney say how over protective "her lawyer" was. Kenneth had beef with him before over a woman and now he was probably relieving that beef with Whitney. Before Erica they had been pretty close and Dakota knew the majority of the Bellini family through Kenneth, but after Dakota became involved with Erica, his relationship with Kenneth disintegrated. Facing his old friend, Dakota had a lot of questions for Kenneth, but had a feeling he wouldn't get the answers he wanted. "My past has nothing to do with why I'm here," he said.

Kenneth placed the paperwork in front of Dakota. "Sign it and be out."

Dakota didn't even care about what it read. He just saw Whitney's signature and signed beside it. Hoarsely, he asked, "When do I get a copy?"

"Leave an address with the receptionist on your way out, and you'll get one when I get everything official," Kenneth answered, reaching inside his jacket pocket and pulling out a white crisp envelope with Dakota's name on it.

"Can I ask how you became her lawyer?"

"Her father appointed me over her trust. Actually I extended a few services for him and then he felt I was the only one he could trust. You remember that word, Dakota, don't you?"

"Like I said, I'm not here to discuss the past."

"You should. You're still there."

Dakota wasn't getting Kenneth's animosity. "If you have something to say to me, then say it, Kenneth."

"It's nothing I want to say, Dakota," Kenneth seethed through clenched teeth. "It's more what I want to do."

Noting the lawyers clenched fist, Dakota took slow deep breaths and said, "Is this over that girl?"

"Fuck that! When has a Bellini ever let a woman get in the way of life or friendship? It's over what you did to the old man."

Dakota gritted his teeth remembering. "That was a long time ago, man. I was wrong. I'll admit, but I was blinded by love. I thought-"

"Don't give me that shit!" Kenneth sneered, tossing the envelope on the table in front of Dakota.

Opening up the envelope as Kenneth collected the divorce paperwork, Dakota frowned very bothered at the amount of the check. "What's this for?"

"Let's just say, your soon to be ex-wife, holds no grudges for what you did although I thought differently and you better be glad I owed you or I would have loved to have convinced her to go to the police. Whitney felt you should have that."

Handing it back to Kenneth, he said, "I don't want anything from her."

Holding his hands up as if Dakota was pointing a deadly weapon at him, Kenneth said, "I'm just the messenger, Dakota. She insisted. You can use it for tissue to wipe your ass for all I care, but I will warn you, keep away from Whitney if you know what's good for you."

Challenging him, Dakota said, "And if I don't?"

Kenneth came up so suddenly Dakota didn't have a chance to duck, as Kenneth's fist connected with his jaw sending him to the floor.

Gripping his chin, Dakota looked up pretty much in shock at Kenneth's lose of control. "You've been around your cousins too long, Kenneth. Whatever happened to your cool composure?"

"Whatever happened to your fucking sense of loyalty?! You want to really know what will happen if you don't?!"

Dakota looked up waiting for the answer.

"You'll be betraying the same man you fucked over before! Lyle Canton."

Slowly rising with a look of disbelief, Dakota rubbed his jaw. "What does he have to do with Whitney?"

"You stupid shit! He's Whitney's father!"

Gripping the table not believing this, Dakota cursed under his breath. "How? Did she know?"

"Hell no. She was kept in the dark about the whole damn thing. Like I said, I'm doing your ass a big favor. Consider this a repayment for a debt owed." Kenneth gathered his things, shook his sore hand, and started out the room. "Get your ass out of town and never step foot in her life again, Dakota." He turned to leave out.

Dakota watched him leave still not believing what was just revealed to him. Turning his back to the door, he stared out the window at the Chicago streets deep in thought.

There was a knock on the door and Armando entered the room. "You okay, Dakota?"

"Yeah, I'll be okay."

"Were you headed out tonight?"

Dakota shook his head, with a far away expression in his eyes. "Not until tomorrow."

"Good. Let's head out to the bar. We'll catch up on some things, okay?"

Dakota really needed that drink and followed Armando out. Instead of taking a company provided limousine, Armando took his own vehicle to a nice quiet bar and grill. He ordered a light lunch and offered Dakota something, but was refused.

"You take a punch well," Armando said with a teasing chuckle.

"You're still a nosey son of a bitch, aren't you?" Dakota grumbled.

"And you're still breaking hearts."

Dakota didn't remark on that. Maybe because he felt it was the other way around since she hadn't taken what happen between them as seriously as he had.

"Trust me when I say, Dakota, it was for the best. She had some serious problems following her and they wouldn't have been merciful on you."

"What's that suppose to mean?" Dakota demanded to know after downing a shot of whiskey. "What the hell was she running from?"

"You didn't know?" Armando asked surprised. "Man, it was in the papers all over the nation."

"I wasn't paying attention to the damn newspapers, Armando. What the hell was she running from?"

"Her stepfather. Maybe you remember him, Eric Thompson."

This was another blow to his equilibrium. He cursed violently pounding the table in anger. Armando ordered him another shot.

"You really should eat something, Dakota," Armando insisted.

Before the waitress even set the drink down, Dakota snatched it out her hand and demanded another one. "Why was Eric following her?"

"He was keeping her hostage in his home until she turned twenty-one, but that smart chit escaped before then and had been on the lame until she made a mistake and bumped into you."

"Why was he keeping her hostage?"

"Even you knew Eric couldn't be touched, but the reason he couldn't was because he was worth nothing. He put all his assets in Whitney's trust to hide until she reached twenty-one and was going to use the price of freedom in order to make her sign over everything to him. When she escaped it was said she was only twenty, but her mother pulled a fast one over on Eric by telling him the wrong birthday. Whitney turned twenty-one the day you married."

"Whitney had everything Eric owned?"

Armando nodded.

"And Kenneth conveniently forgot to tell me?" Dakota surmised narrowing his eyes suspiciously. "I would have owned everything Eric owned."

"I thought you didn't marry Whitney for her money."

Dakota flushed feeling the past greed and revenge over come him. Maybe Whitney was right in saying he needed to get it out his system. "So she now owns everything all by herself."

"She does, but she plans to turn the ownership of her father's company back to her father and the other companies will be divided and liquidated. I've been summoned to a meeting tomorrow to assist in that since I am a real estate/business lawyer."

With a snide, Dakota said, "Keeping it all in the family, huh?"

"Of course, when haven't we?"

"What about my uncle's company? Do you know anything about that?"

Armando frowned very bothered. "Didn't you know what happened?"

"No."

"Eric dismantled the company and sold it off piece by piece. The only company that he really kept together was Lyle Cantor's Florida distributorship and his own, but even that's going to be sold off. Whitney wants Eric to pay for what he did to her father. Be grateful she doesn't know you had a part in it."

"I didn't know it was her father, Armando."

"And if you knew back then what you did to the old man devastated that girl and had her imprisoned for most of her life, would you have tried to make it right?"

Dakota lowered his head in disgust and defeat because the answer to that question would be a negative because at that time in his life, he was thinking solely about the business and money. He took the hundred dollars out that Armando had given him earlier. "I didn't win that bet. I never bedded Erica. She led me around by the nose until she dropped me at the lowest point of my life."

Armando took out a cigar and lit it. "I don't suppose you want to go on a long vacation with me tomorrow."

"You're taking a vacation? Other than Dalton and Alejandro, you're the third hardest working man in the world."

"Mom's forcing me."

Nothing else needed to be said about that. Mom was the matriarch of the Bellini family and when she spoke all listened. She was the oldest female Bellini and wise beyond her years.

Continuing after a long toke on the Cuban, Armando said, "She said I work too hard and she wanted me to do this for Alejandro, but I think it's just a way to force me on a vacation when I've got a mountain of paperwork at the office."

"Yet you still plan to go? Couldn't you get Alejandro to reschedule something?"

"He's been rescheduling this launching for the past year, but he'll lose money if he reschedules it anymore. I jokingly volunteered for the project when he told me about it initially. I didn't think he'd actually put it all together and I certainly didn't think he'd get my father and Momma to make me go." Armando's mood was pretty messed up.

"You could still refuse. I mean you're a grown man last I checked, Armando," Dakota stated.

"Dalton said I had to."

That was the end of the subject. Dalton was CEO of Bellini Enterprises and he was one of the most feared men in the Bellini family. He was also more or less in charge of the family as well and all of his first generation cousins that all vowed to stay single.

Other than smoking a Cuban, there was nothing else Dakota could think of that Armando loved more than his work. The vacation would be like torture for the young man, more than anything.

"I got a gig in Florida I want to hook up with a friend. I'll give you a call though if I change my mind by tomorrow."

*   *   *   *   *

Of course Armando felt the night was still young and found more bars to visit. Without eating, the alcohol took over his mind and by morning he was so hung over he could barely get out of bed. When he did try, he ended up emptying all his stomach contents in the trashcan by the bed. Picking up the piece of paper by the bed, he read it repeatedly and looked at the phone. It was Whitney's hotel number Armando had given him last night.

Dakota wasn't sure what he had said to Armando in order for the lawyer to give him the number, but it must have been enough to get the information.

Checking the time, he saw he had three hours before his flight, but he wasn't going to call her. Lying back in bed closing his eyes, so he didn't have to watch the room spinning, he told himself calling her would be allowing her to know she was his weakness. Forcing himself to get up to dress and pack, he called a cab to go downtown back to the Bellini Towers arriving near one in the afternoon.

He didn't want to leave Chicago with a bad relationship with Kenneth and he wanted to say thanks to Armando before boarding his flight.

The receptionist was rather stiff as she told him Kenneth was in a meeting and Armando was getting ready to go into a meeting.

"Could you just let Armando know I'm here for a quick minute?"

She called Armando's office and in a few moments, she hung up the phone. "Mr. Bellini said to come on back, but if you could please take the second hall way and go around to his office."

He thought the request was rather weird since the first hallway could reach Armando's office faster, but he started to take the second hallway. Being too hung over, he saw the receptionist lost sight of him and he was too tired and ducked down the first corridor.

Hearing voices coming from the conference, he glanced inside to see Dalton Bellini sitting casually at the head of the table and right next to him was Whitney. He stopped at the doorway just as Lyle Canton who sat across from Whitney, said, "Exactly how much does this make her worth after this deal?"

"It's just an estimation," Dalton said coolly, "But once everything is completed your daughter will be able to lay in about ten million dollars, which of course will be properly invested." His deep hazel green cold eyes looked up at the doorway and narrowed slightly.

Everyone else in the room eyes followed Dalton's piercing stare. Dakota wasn't looking at Dalton anymore. His eyes locked with Whitney's.

Kenneth came up beside Whitney protectively.

"I just came to tell Armando good bye," Dakota said quietly. He met Kenneth's glare. "I also wanted to tell you thanks for the favor."

"I can see you don't adhere to warnings very well," Kenneth sneered.

Armando came up beside Dakota. "Why don't we step outside, Dakota?" he suggested.

Dakota was still peeved at Kenneth for that cheap shot yesterday. "You plan on making your point again like yesterday, Kennie?"

Coming around the table, Kenneth asked, "Do I need to?"

Not backing down, damning whoever was in the room, Dakota sneered, "Ain't nothing stopping you but air and opportunity, bastard." That was a low verbal blow and anyone who knew Kenneth's background knew it was hitting way below the belt.

Kenneth lost the little control he had and lunged for Dakota getting in a good shot to the face, but that didn't stop Dakota from landing two punches to the jaw and stomach knocking Kenneth to the floor by Dalton's feet.

The Bellini stood to his full six foot seven height and unbutton the jacket of his Christian Dior three piece hand made suit. "I don't think this is the time or the place to hash out our personal problems. Don't you agree, Dakota?"

Although Dakota never had a conversation with this Bellini, he was well aware of not only the physical power Dalton beheld, but also the financial and family power he welded.

Just being aware of his presence was enough to calm Dakota down. "I was done saying my piece any way."

He started out the room until he heard the old man call him. "Dakota Traylor?" Lyle asked.

Dakota turned around to face the older man. He could see a lot of Whitney in him. With only a nod, he braced himself for the anger to follow as Lyle stepped up to him.

"You got nerve to show your face around me," Lyle seethed.

Whitney came up to her father. "Daddy, it's fine. Let's get this meeting over with," she insisted, trying to pull her father away from Dakota.

He snatched away from his daughter and clocked Dakota in the jaw. Although it was painful considering his jaw had been bruised yesterday, Dakota didn't strike back. He only stood there.

Whitney gasped. "You know him, Daddy?" She looked at Dakota for confirmation.

"I would never forget the man turned traitorous and helped Eric take my company away from me," Lyle said.

She gasped again and stared at Dakota. "Is this true?"

Dakota took a moment, before he nodded and braced himself for the slap she delivered on the other side of his face. He knew eating would be useless for the next day or so.

"Get out!" she screamed. "Don't ever come around us again!"

He wanted to explain to her what really happened. How he'd been used. How he'd lost everything in the end, but his lips wouldn't move. All he could do was stand there and watch, as she seemed to lose all feelings for him.

Angrily, he said, "Yeah, I've already got what I wanted from you, but you didn't have to pay for it." He took the check out of his pocket, ripped it in half and flicked it in her face before he stormed out the office.

Arriving in Tampa, Florida, Erica decided not to spend her last

twenty bucks on some cheap hotel room. If she could make some
money today, she could possibly afford a nicer hotel room.
Since leaving Utah, she had made great timing by sleeping in
her newly updated BMW.

Since her father's credit cards had become defunct, she was
forced to eat what she could at rest stops using the traveler's check
money. By the time she arrived in Tampa with directions to Jared
Parker's Marina, there were eighteen dollars and seventy-three cents
in her pocket.

The receptionist told her immediately that there were no office
positions available at this time.

Not having anywhere else to turn, she said, "Why don't you
let me speak to your boss and maybe we can arrange something?"

The receptionist looked very doubtful. "Your funeral lady," she
snipped and picked up the receiver to announce that someone was here
about a job.

Erica was wearing her best Donna Karen pants suits with
low heels. She didn't want to shock the man with her clothing or
intimidate his office staff, which she determined was only one.

Walking into the office, she paused seeing the large man sitting
behind the desk and if Lethal was sexy this man was ten times sexier. His
light gray eyes caught her attention first and then his thick dark pink
lips followed. He had this sort of cruel look like LL Cool J with
attitude, but he was much taller and much wider.

Leaning back in his chair, Jared stared at her with his eyes
partially narrowed, his brow furred, and his lips tucked tight. His dark,
honey brown skin highlighted the color of his eyes.

"Are you going to stand there all day and gawk as if I'm the
eighth wonder of the world?" he asked in a monotonous voice.

With confidence, she walked up to the desk and
outstretched her hand. "My name's Erica Thompson, I've come to
apply for a position with your company."

He raised a curious brow as if it took a lot of effcrt to
actually
show some feeling in his face and looked at her outstretched hand
in disgust. "You've come off the street?"

"No sir, I was recommended to try you as an employer."

"Really?" He didn't seem impressed. "Well, I've only got two
positions open and none of them would fit you."

Erica knew she really needed a job and whatever the job
entailed, she could do it. Plus, she didn't know how to go out and get
any other kind of job, so if she walked out that door and refused this
job, she would have nothing else to go on because she knew Lethal
wouldn't help her anymore. "I assure you, Mr. Parker, I can do
whatever you have open."

He looked from her head to feet with doubt in his eyes. "I don't
think so."

"Aren't you at least going to let me fill out an
application?" "And waste paper?" he snorted.

She handed him a piece of paper with her resume. "What about my resume-"

"Never mind. That's just more junk on my desk." He sat up and picked up his phone. "I don't think you can work for this company, miss. Have a good day." Jared started to dial a number and didn't look twice at her again.

Erica had been dismissed before even given the chance. She really had nowhere to go and no money to buy anything with. Realizing she was desperate, she waited for him to get off the phone patiently.

"Why are you still here?" he asked only a little perturbed. "If you can't give me a job I would be qualified for, then I'm willing to accept a lower position. I do need a job, Mr. Parker."

"You've never done a day of hard work in your life, miss. I wouldn't hire you," he said with a great deal of revulsion. "Looks like the only time you ever broke a sweat is when you misplaced the credit card your Daddy got you when you were in line to pay for purchases."

She forced herself to let the smart remark slide. "Why don't you give me a chance?"

"You're not dressed for work," he pointed out.

"That's just an excuse."

He stared at her long and hard, before he stood up and walked up to her. "You're willing to take any job offered?"

As desperate as she was, she nodded eagerly.

The cruel look in his face seemed to glow. "Fine with me," he said indifferently and led her out to a boat dock. "We've got to get

ready for a large contract with the St. Royal line which is owned partly by Bellini Enterprises. These are the last of the boats that need to be cleaned up."

"That's it?" That didn't sound hard. "I've never cleaned before, but I think I can manage that."

He looked only slightly disgruntled, but she continued to get that feeling that she was wasting his time. Jared Parker was certainly a very surly individual and she couldn't understand how he could be associated with Lethal unless they shopped at the same stores for large men. She wondered was all that brawn underneath that tight shirt all muscle?

"Take a bucket, fill it with water, there's cleaning solution and a scrubber. Phillip is around the yard if you have any questions." "That's it? So I'm hired?"

"Take it as probation, Ms. Thompson."

She was surprised he had remembered her name. "So how much do you pay?"

"Eight dollars an hour."

Frowning she asked, "I'll only get eight dollars?"

"An hour," he reiterated. "It's going to take you a couple of days to get it done, trust me. Some have taken weeks, but as you can see those people aren't here now."

"How many boats?"

"Two are left to be completed. Are you going to stand here all day and waste my time or are you actually going to work?"

"So I get eight dollars an hour to clean off some boat?"

He nodded impatiently.

"Fine," she said, outstretching her hand to congratulate on a deal.

Jared looked down at her hand again in disgust and walked around her. "Go through the double doors and I'll see you at the end of the day."

She watched him go back inside his office, before she went inside of the thick green double doors. There was a huge yacht inside lifted out of the water. A very skinny white man was checking off some paper work and looked at her with wariness.

"Can I help you?" he asked.

"I'm here to clean the boats," she announced proudly.

"Is this some type of joke?"

"No sir, Mr. Parker told me to come in here and clean the boats. Is this one of the boats?"

"Yes, ma'am, but I don't think-"

Erica didn't want to hear neither his protest nor the same thing she had just heard from Jared. By the end of the day, she would have sixty-four dollars in her pocket that that could get her a nice hotel room for one night plus a vegetarian meal at the restaurant down the street. "Don't think, just tell me what to do, and stay out my way."

Phillip showed her the cleaning supplies and then instructed her about where she needed to clean. The crud on the bottom of the boat needed to come off.

She had carefully rolled up her silk blouse sleeves and dunked her hand in the hot soapy water. The smell of the cleaning agent burned her eyes and the hot water felt like it was taking the skin off her hand, but she didn't complain.

She promised herself she wouldn't complain. She would show Whitney and Jared Parker that she could work hard for a living and make something of herself without Eric Thompson's money. Gritting her teeth, she started in a circular motion to clean the grin up, but an hour into her job; she had only done about a twelve inches length of work. Her back ached, her arms felt like they were going to fall off, and she had ruined a great suit.

Phillip came in to check on her. Her eyes were red from crying, but he thought it had been from the cleaning solution. "Why don't you wear the goggles?"

"I-I'm fine. What time is it?" she asked.

"Only nine-thirty. In about an hour you can take a fifteen-minute break. The bathrooms are around the other side of this boat house."

She had to pee bad and when she was able to take a break, she went to where the bathrooms were, but she had to cover her mouth at the stench of the bathrooms. It looked as if no one had

cleaned them in years and someone obviously had bad aim. Urine
and feces covered the ground, there was no toilet tissue and the bowl
was so backed up maggots had begun to evolve inside on top of the
water and tissue.

Stepping out the bathroom, she gritted her teeth and went
back to the boathouse praying she could hold out. Around lunch,
Phillip gave her a bottle of water and asked if she wanted
something from the burger joint across the street.

Being a vegetarian, she shook her head. The water was gone
in two seconds though and Phillip told her where she could get a
refill inside of the office.

When Erica came in the front, the receptionist smirked in
amusement. Holding her head up with confidence, Erica strolled
over to the water machine and filled her bottle up again.

Phillip brought in a large bag of food. The smell reminded
her that she hadn't eaten all that day. Jared came out of his office
and said something to Phillip quietly. Phillip chuckled handing two
sandwiches to "the boss" and a thick cup of fries.

Jared looked over at the water machine and raised two
brows of curiosity. "Are you on lunch, Ms. Thompson?"

"Yes sir," she said nodding.

The receptionist laughed under her breath.

Erica was starting to hate the wench.

"Will you be eating for lunch, Ms. Thompson?" Jared asked. "She's a
vegetarian, Parker," Phillip said quickly. "She doesn't
eat meat."

"I think I know what a vegetarian is, Phil, thank you," Jared
growled.

Phillip quickly left the office.

"So you don't eat fries either, Ms. Thompson?"
Jared questioned.

She shook her head. "I stay away from junk food. My body
is my temple. I don't allow impurities to invade it. Fries are high
in cholesterol and very bad for your health."

"I bet that water sure taste good then."

The receptionist couldn't help herself as a laugh burst from her
mouth. Jared and Erica looked at her disapprovingly. The older woman made
herself scarce too.

Being alone with him again made her slightly uncomfortable,
so she decided to leave too. "I'd better get back to work, Mr. Parker.
I wouldn't want you to think I wasn't a hard worker."

"Let me see your hands," he ordered.

Walking up to him, she felt like a small child coming under

scrutiny from a parent that she desperately wanted to please. Raising her hand palms up, she watched as he saw the red blotches that were on their way to become blisters.

"How's it going?" he asked.

"It's rather hot in there," she stated. "The bathrooms are horrible too."

"That's it?"

Obviously he wanted her to complain about the work he had given her, but she wasn't going to let him know she hated it with every fiber of her being. She was going to suck this up, collect her money and get some stability here. With the cost of living so low in Florida, sixty-four bucks would come in handy for a girl starting out with nothing.

"Our janitor quit too," he said.

Snatching her hands out of his grasp, she said, "My break time is over with, Mr. Parker. Are you done chit chatting or were you going to tell me something related to the job you have assigned me?"

His eyes narrowed at her polite dismissal of his company.

When he shook his head, she grabbed her water and walked out the office feeling slightly triumphant. He was nothing but a cold non-emotional bully.

Maybe that's what he had in common with Lethal. They both belonged to the American Bullying Organization. She chuckled to herself at this levity. He was a card-carrying member of the ABO.

This thought lifted her spirits for a while, but the pains continued as she scrapped, scrubbed, and cleaned every piece of dirt off the bottom of that boat. By five o'clock, she knew her body couldn't take anymore, and was so happy with herself that she had actually finished it all.

Phillip seemed very impressed by her accomplishment, but looked worriedly at her hands, which were bleeding. Matter of fact, during her last hour she had cried every time she had to put her hands in the soapy water because they stung so bad.

He found some cream in the fist aid box and made her put it on, then for the largest blisters, he placed strips of tape after he helped her stop the bleeding. Jared entered just as Phillip was finishing with her hands.

Phillip didn't stay around long. He told everyone goodnight and left quickly.

She watched as Jared looked around the yacht before coming up to her with a satisfied nod. "Good job."

Smiling, she said, "So my probationary period is over with?"

"No. There's another one tomorrow. Or will you be reporting tomorrow?" he asked skeptically.

"Yes, Mr. Parker," she said with disappointment, yet she had to tell herself this was the real working world and most probationary periods lasted sixty to ninety days. "I'll take my money and leave."

"Money? What money?"

"The eight dollars an hour you owe me."

He raised one brow again in that annoying curious way. "All payroll goes in at the end of this week. You'll get your check in about three weeks."

Her mouth fell open as if he had slapped her in the face. "Three weeks? I have to wait three weeks! I can't wait that long! I don't have any money! I don't have a place to stay! I don't have anything to eat!" She wailed hysterically.

Jared stood there waiting patiently for her theatrics to end. When she realized he was not reacting to her crying, she forced herself to calm down, although an occasional choked up sob escaped.

"I'm s -sorry. I should have remembered that wouldn't be something that would concern you. I was just disillusioned about-" She stopped herself from saying, "Life."

Going to the sink, she used a rough brown piece of paper towel to blow her nose and her eyes.

"I don't take women crying very well, Ms. Thompson." Waving the episode away like it was nothing but a fly, she said, looking over her shoulder, "I'll be fine. I've gotten this far, I think
I can live for three more weeks…like this." She went to the double doors to leave. "Good night, Mr. Parker." Getting to her car, she cried in the steering column for at least an hour before she forced herself to drive to some parking lot, where she covered herself with a thick wool coat and fell asleep promptly.

Awaking in the middle of the night, her muscles were hurting in places she didn't know muscles could hurt. Getting out the car, she

found a payphone and called the eight hundred number on Lethal's card.

His voice mail came on after seven rings and she cried raggedly in the phone, "I thought you would be at this number," she sobbed. "I hate it here. I hate being here and he's got me hurting, Lethal. Please be here tomorrow. Please." Hanging up, she slumped on the ground and wept.

The knocking on the window startled her and she looked up to

see a police officer standing by her car. He ordered her to move and

she drove to a gas station where the attendant allowed her to use the

bathroom to wash up. Every muscle in her body screamed for a hot
bath and a deep massage, but she knew that if she wanted some
money this was what she had to do.

She threw away the three-piece suit and blouse because it
was ruined from the chemicals and strenuous work she had done in it.
Going through her bag of clothes, she found some jeans and a pink,
silk, short-sleeve blouse. Although the clothes were barely worn, she
knew she hadn't put them on in about a year or so, plus she had
bought them about two years ago on a trip in Europe. She wasn't
going to remind herself that she was going to mess up over three
hundred dollars in clothing today because she knew she would start
crying again.

Washing herself up in the sink with cold water and harsh soap,
she dressed quickly so she could get to work as early as possible.

Getting to the marina, she realized Phillip had not gotten there
yet, but she didn't bother to go inside of the office to let anyone know
she had arrived. She parked in the very back where the other employees
couldn't see her car.

She had her reasons for detesting the office staff; Erica
couldn't stand the receptionist and she couldn't face Jared so early
in the morning.

The other boat had been hoisted up and it was ten times
worse than the first. Biting her tongue to voice her inner protest,
she cleared her thoughts of everything and got to work.

Pretending she was refreshed helped a lot to forget the
pain and humming a song. Phillip arrived two hours later and was
overwhelmed at her determination and hard work. He offered her
coffee, but she refused.

When he left for a moment, but immediately returned, he
seemed agitated. "The boss wants to see you, ma'am," he said
gravely as if she were in big trouble.

Cleaning off her hands with a towel, she did her best to brush
her hair back in place, but her fixing only made things worse, along with
the dirt and grime in patches all over her face and neck. Her hands were
red and swollen from work and blisters and she was glad her inner pain
didn't come to the surface unless she moved too fast.

Walking as best she could in her usual stuck up way, she walked past the receptionist desk without giving the woman even a "good morning." Opening the door to Jared's office, she was surprised to see him in front of his desk looking bothered.

Before she said anything he demanded to know, "How long have you been here?"

"About two or three hours, Mr. Parker," she answered a bit flustered by his interrogation, pulling her hands behind her back so the tape around her blisters couldn't be notice.

"Don't you know how to let someone know when you've arrived for work?"

She couldn't understand his anger and wasn't use to dealing with a man with attitude other than her father, but even then she was quiet to Eric's ramblings. Yet this was her boss and she was suppose to answer, but she didn't know how. "I-I didn't know—"

He cut her off abruptly. "You know the way to this office, don't you?"

"Yes, sir." Why did he constantly make her feel so bad?

"Then every morning you need to walk your tail in here and let someone know you've come to work."

The receptionist came in the room carrying a large Styrofoam platter of food. She gave a humorous glance in Erica's direction, with an almost glad look of relief that Jared's upset was not directed at her.

Erica really couldn't stand that woman. "Fine, now that you've seen I'm here, what else can I do for you?"

Moving around the desk, Jared sat down with the platter in front of him. Erica couldn't help but stare at the food.

"You can fill out an application. I figured since you're on your second day, I might as well waste a little paper on you."

The receptionist stood in front of Erica to hand her a form and pen. Erica took the items quickly and the receptionist gasped at Erica's hands. Since the receptionist blocked Jared's view of Erica, he couldn't tell what had shocked the receptionist. Erica put her hands behind her back and glared at the receptionist with a lethal dare to say anything.

"What's the problem, Ms. Lee?" Jared demanded with a mouth full of food.

"N-No problem, sir, I thought…" She faced her boss. "I'm going to take my break, Mr. Parker." Hurriedly she left out the room looking nauseous.

Jared gave Erica a suspicious glare, while Erica tried to look as wide eye innocent as possible. "Would you care for something to eat?" he offered. "Mrs. Lee is going to get her food, if you give her the money she'd be glad to pick you up something."

She came to the desk to see he was eating a hungry man setting of grits, eggs, and bacon. None of which she ate and if she did eat it, she wouldn't deign herself to eat in front of him. Plus, she thought he had been aware that she had no money after her hysterics from yesterday. "No thank you," she said despite the fact that her stomach was doing cartwheels over the smell of the food.

"You're still a vegetarian?"

"All my life I've been a vegetarian, Mr. Parker. Plus, I don't eat
eggs because they are high in cholesterol and grits are disgusting." "You
are black, aren't you?" he asked with a straight look on
his face.

Insulted, she said, "Yes."

"Where are you from, Ms. Thompson?"

"California."

He shrugged after chewing a large size portion he jammed in
his mouth. "That explains everything, then."

She didn't dare comment on where he came from considering
his manners. This was her boss and she had to keep reminding
herself that. "I'll fill this out by lunch time," Erica said and started
to
leave out the room.

"Wait, Ms. Thompson," he said.

Huffing, she turned making sure she kept her hands behind
her. "What?!"

She felt her heartbeat become louder and louder as he
approached her with deliberately slow stalking strides adjusting his
pants and tucking his shirt in. She noted the lean waist and wondered
was the bulge in the front just the way his pants fit or was it him?

"Stay here for just a moment," he ordered. "I want to check
up on Mrs. Lee." When he left the room her eyes went directly over to
the plate of food still hot and waiting for someone to taste it.

Walking over to the desk, she stared at the food. Her hand
had a mind of it's own as she picked up a piece a bacon and held it in
front on quivering lips. Eating it would be a crime against her own
morals, not including it would be stealing, but she was so hungry…so
very hungry.

Forcing herself to put the bacon back down, she put her
fingers up to her lips and sucked the grease off of them
desperately moaning her hunger pains.

The door to his office opened and she didn't turn around
to see if it was him, but she knew it was just by the way that the
wind moved around his large form.

"Aren't you done?" he asked disapprovingly, referring to the
application.

"I was going to fill it out during lunch," she said.

"Fill it out now." Jared pointed to the seat near his desk.

Sitting down, she tried to keep her hands as close to her as
possible as she filled out the paper work. He sat back behind his
desk and started eating again paying no attention to her.

She filled out the form quickly wanting to get away from the
delicious smell of the food and just as she stood to put it on his desk,
he tossed the half eaten platter in the garbage. It was a total waste of

food and she couldn't help thinking about all those hungry
children around the world.

        Erica didn't wait for him to approve or disapprove of the
application before she walked out and went back to work. Phillip
brought her some water for her break, but she didn't drink it
until lunchtime. That was when the receptionist came in there
carrying a bag of food making Erica become suspicious.
        "Greta Lee," the older receptionist said. "I never introduced
myself to you. You can call me Greta."
        Erica didn't say anything.
        "Look you may think I'm some kind of snob, but I acted
that way to you, because on your first day you were acting that
way to me," Greta explained. "When I saw your hands and realized
how desperately you needed this job, I just couldn't be upset with
you another second."
        "I don't want your pity. I'm doing this because I need the
money and I'm down here all by myself and I have no one else to
turn to." She reached in the bucket of cleaning solution to
retrieve her brush, wincing at the stinging sensation of the water.
        "Dear Lord, child, why don't you use the gloves?" Greta asked.
        Erica looked confused. "What gloves?"
        Greta went under the sink and pulled a box of disposable
waterproof gloves out that Erica had never seen before.
        "Thank you," she said, wanting to cry after all the pain she had
been enduring because she didn't think to ask for them. How stupid could
she have been?
        Going back over to the bag of food, Greta said, "I brought you
something to eat. I saw how hungry you were this morning." She set
down a burger and fries on the counter by the sink.
        Walking over to the burger, she didn't care that it was a cow.
All she cared about was that it was food. Picking it up to take the
biggest bite possible, the large green doors opened and Jared entered
looking curiously at her with a frown. Erica mouth closed instantly as
she met his eyes.
        "I thought you were a vegetarian?"
        She fought the groan knowing she would have to deny this
craving of hunger, just so she wouldn't look like a liar. "I am,
Mr. Parker."
        "Then why are you about to gobble up a thick juicy beef
hamburger?" he questioned.

        "I thought Greta made it a vegetarian burger since I said
yesterday I was one." This was a bold face lie and it took all her
will power to keep a straight face so he couldn't see she was lying.

"And of course you weren't about to eat those fries because they are high in cholesterol, right?" he asked, saying her words from this morning.

Putting the burger down trying to look as nonchalant as possible, she said, "I'll just get some more water." Immediately she left to go to the office to get some water. While doing so, she looked around since no one was in there.

Going into his office, she saw there was a private bathroom in there. Taking this private opportunity, she hurriedly used the bathroom and rushed out.

Returning to the boat dock hoping they were gone with their food, she immediately grabbed the gloves and put them on.

"How do you do it?" his voice said behind her. Startled she turned around to face him. "Do what?" "Don't complain. Usually by now, you women are screaming and crying like babies." He said this as if it were a fact.

"I scream and cry," she admitted. "But I wouldn't do it in front of you…I mean I did, but I learn fast, especially when you've made it so evidently clear that you could care less."

His stone gray eyes were piercing and intimidating. Along with his height, she didn't feel comfortable around him. "I don't care because I find that attachment leads to other things. I'm not a people person, Ms. Thompson."

"I gathered that from my yesterday's hysterics." Grabbing the brush she went back over to the end of the boat and began to scrub.

"You'll be done by the end of the day again, won't you?"

"With any luck," she said hopefully.

"You do work hard, Ms. Thompson. I must give you that credit."

She cynicism quickly came to the surface. "If that was a compliment, Mr. Parker, I think I better check to see if pigs are flying outside or did hell just freeze over?"

"I'm not that cold and I do reward hard work, Ms. Thompson. I'll just have to find you another job around here, won't I?"

Looking over at him to determine his mood she saw this was useless because he looked as impassive as he always did. Going back to work, she knew it would be futile to have a conversation with him when he could be unsympathetic to her. Although she didn't want pity, if she was going to talk about her problems, she at least wanted someone humane.

Moving behind her with his arms folded over his chest, he asked, "You don't like me, do you?"

"Whether I like you or not, you're my employer for now." She faced him looking up into his bitter granite eyes. As remarkable as they made him look, all she could feel was a cold façade. "The only thing I should like is for you to sign my check and make sure it's right."

"So you're all about money?"

She shrugged indifferently. "A girl's got to live, Mr. Parker.

Can't pay the rent liking people, can we?" Scrubbing again, she gave him her back as a sign that she didn't want to speak anymore. Working wasn't so hard when she was alone. These interruptions made her self-conscious and slowed her pace.

"I took the liberty of disposing of that unhealthy food for you,"
he said.

It took every ounce of effort to force out, "Thank you." She didn't turn to acknowledge him. Erica continued to work hoping he would get the hell away from her.

Jared stood there for a moment longer before he walked out the double green doors. She leaned against the boat, giving her back a rest breathing slowly. She wanted this day to be over.

*　*　　*　　*　　*

Phillip came to her at the end of the day and gave her a fresh bottle of water. "You do good work, Erica," he complimented her.

"I don't try very hard," she said apathetically, slumping on a crate by the sink.

He poured her water out and cleaned off her equipment. "I sure would love to see something you really work hard at." He sat beside her and smiled proudly handing her a plum. "You make the men around here look bad, girl."

She smiled genuinely taking the plum and hungrily eating. It had been the first smile in some months that was real. "Thank you

Phillip." She leaned her head on his shoulder feeling very content. "I've learned a lot these past two days. About life and about myself."

"Well, I hope hard lessons like this don't have to come every day for you to learn."

Chuckling, she said licking her sore fingers from the juice of the plum. "I think I like the easy lessons."

They laughed together, but stopped abruptly hearing a throat clearing at the doorway.

Jared stood there with a disapproving look in his eyes and his arms folded over that wide chest of his. "When you two are through, could you come to my office, Ms. Thompson?"

"When we are through," she said tiredly, wondering what kind of trouble was she in now.

He waited a second, but when she didn't make a move to follow him, he left them alone again.

"You should be a little nicer to him," Phillip said. "He's acting rather strange lately."

"I should be nice to him?" she questioned incredulously. "The man deserves no niceness, Phillip."

"That's because no ones been nice to him. No one as pretty as you."

Forcing herself to stand, she trudged to the door. "I doubt that, Phillip. With a face like that, I doubt it." Going to the office, she saw Greta was getting ready to leave for the day.

"He said to go right in and have a seat," Greta instructed her.

Erica thanked her and wished her a good night. No one was in the office, but the door to his bathroom was closed. She went over to a mirror in the far corner of the room behind his desk and gasped as she saw how dirty she looked. Dirty was not the word she would use either and horrible almost came close. If there was a perm in her hair, it wasn't showing itself today. There were dried seaweed particles, sand, crud and everything else practically layering her hair and smelling the strands was just like taking a full whiff of the cleaning solution.

Her face had not only splotches of dirt, but there was the crud in her hair scattered over her brow, in her ear, and all down her neck. She was filthy and the worse thing about it was that her hair smelled better than the rest of her body.

The door to the bathroom opened and she turned abruptly as if she had been caught naked. He came across the room to his desk and pulled out a time card and a folder. "You can take this home and complete the employment forms. From now on I would like you to clock your entrance and exit to work. That includes breaks and lunches too. The time clock is behind Greta's desk."

She looked grateful for this. "I take it that means I'm hired?"

"For now." He turned away to sit down.

Greta came in with two Styrofoam boxes and placed them in front of him. "I'm gone for the day, sir."

He nodded her away. When they were alone again, he opened up the first box and Erica gasped at the delicious spinach Lasagna. The moaning in her stomach was so loud she moved away from the desk hoping the distance between them muffled out the noise.

"You didn't put down an address on your employment application," he noted with a mouth full of food.

She felt so dizzy from being famished, but forced herself to answer, "I-I don't have an ad-address."

"You don't have a place to stay? Is that what you're saying?" he asked with another mouthful of food.

Swallowing because she was salivating too much, she only nodded.

"Where have you been living?"

"M-My car," she barely whispered.

"You know there's a motel two blocks from here. You could stay there?" he suggested.

Shaking her head as if she were dying, she said, "I don't have m-money."

"Nothing?"

"Nothing," she confirmed.

Wiping his mouth, he took a long swig of water, then belched and patted his stomach. "There's a homeless shelter right around the corner, if you're just interested in a hot bath and somewhere to sleep until you can make some money."

Backing up to the door, she clutched the papers he had given her. "T-Thank you." Turning to leave, he called her name again. Her

shoulders slumped knowing she had to spend more seconds in this room with him as hungry as she was.

Slowly turning around, she saw he had filled his mouth again with more food. "I was serious about getting you to do something different tomorrow."

She only nodded not, trusting herself to speak.

"Hey, I'm going to pick my father up at the airport in a few hours and I don't think I could eat all this right now. Would you like the other one?" He held out the box to her

It would be a cruel joke if he decided to renege on that offer just as she was taking it. She nodded in response to the offer and slowly walked over to him to get the box of food.

Once she took it, he said, "Good night, Ms. Thompson."

Hurriedly she walked out and went to her car. When she was inside her vehicle she opened the box and took a deep breath of the food. Before she knew it, she was using her fingers despite the hot cheese, and stuffing the food in her mouth. She felt overwhelmed and joyful and dizzy all at the same time. She couldn't chew fast enough and almost choked herself as she ate, but she continued.

The abrupt knocking on her window startled her and looking up, she couldn't have been more embarrassed with cheese and spinach all over her face as Jared looked down at her. Being unladylike, she used the back of her right arm to wipe the food away and quickly chewed the food out her mouth; while she rolled the window down to see what he wanted.

"I was thinking if worse comes to worse, I have a couch above my office you can crash on," he suggested.

"I couldn't, Mr. Parker. I can handle myself, but thanks."

He shrugged as if it didn't make a difference whether she did or didn't. "To be so broke, where'd you get the car?"

"My father if you must know, but it's mine. I drove it from California." She gripped the steering wheel proudly. "It's practically brand new."

"You ever thought about selling it and getting the money to get a place?" he asked.

The thought sounded appealing, but with her father's accounts in limbo, she wouldn't be surprised if there was a repossession order out on the car.

"Then I wouldn't have anything to drive, would I?"

"There are cheaper cars, Ms. Thompson." He gave her a wink and walked away as if he had actually contributed something to society.

She really hated Jared Parker.

The woman at the homeless place looked at Erica as if she had lost her mind. Erica should have parked around the block because the lady took one look at her and said she needed psychiatric help, not a place to stay for the night.

Going back out to her car, she found a more secluded spot and parked for the night. Finding a payphone only a block away from where she was parked, she called Lethal at the same time she had called him last night.

This time Lethal answered, "You sound much better than last night," he said.

"Where are you?" she asked, hearing loud music in the background as if he were at a club.

"Home. I took a detour home to get some time for myself if you must know."

"Are you taking a bath?" she asked, hearing water running.

"No, that's just the waterfall in my living room. You are feeling better than yesterday, aren't you?"

"I guess. I still hate my job and I'm still miserable, but I think I've come to a humble realization." It felt good to have a comfortable conversation with someone who knew her from California.

"What's that?" he asked interested.

"The world doesn't evolve around me."

He hooted highly amused. "You didn't get that philosophy from Jared Parker, did you?"

Snorting, she said, "Definitely not. Were you aware the man could be so cold?"

"Of course. Cruel as well, Erica, so watch your self. He derives a lot of pleasure on punishment."

"And you sent me to him for help?"

"I had a feeling you would be an asset to him. Are you?"

"My body feels like a boulder fell on it, Lethal, and I'm so hungry I could just die. I'm broke and I have to wait for two weeks just to get some money. I'm all alone down here and I hate Jared Parker."

He paused a second before he responded to her complaints. "But you're free from your father, right?"

"About now, I'm not considering my freedom." Sighing, she said, "Although I do find it liberating, Lethal."

"Is that how liberating sounds?" he teased.

Laughing, she said, "Since I'm not an expert on it, I don't know."

"How can I help you Erica, without giving you the wrong impression or ruining my selfishly greedy reputation?"

She knew he was referring to the major crush she had on him. He didn't want to lead her own and she couldn't help becoming enamored even more about Lethal Heart. "The car I'm driving. I want to know if it's mine to do with. I want to sell it if I can so I can at least find me a place to stay and get some food in my stomach on a daily basis."

"It's practically new, isn't it?" he questioned.

"Pretty much." She gave him the vehicle identification number and the plate.

"I'll get back in touch with you when I find that information out. Is that all?"

Erica didn't want his pity and she didn't want to seem like she was helpless. Having a job gave her confidence that things would start to look up soon. "For now. I don't want to ruin that reputation of yours."

"Are you living in the car?"

"Basically. Speaking of living, where's my father?"

"Trying to stop what little he has left from being taken away. Without you there, you can't assist him in getting things, so with his credit shot, his bank account busted, and his step daughter with everything, he can't find a pot to piss in."

"Are you still trying to find Whitney?" she asked.

"I'm looking, but she's doing well in Chicago preparing to go to Florida to stay with her father, but of course you knew that which is why you're down there, right?"

"I was hoping. Do you think she'll talk to me?" "I don't know, Erica."

Someone in the back called Lethal's name with a giggle, then Erica heard, "Aren't you going to join us in the Jacuzzi?"

"Us?" Erica asked.

He chuckled seductively. "I'm a man who just can't be pleased by one woman, Erica."

Since she didn't want to go into that subject with him, she said, "Then I'll let you handle your business."

He didn't wait for her to say goodbye as the laughter behind him increased and it sounded as if he were right by the water. Hanging up, she shivered in the cold and felt really alone. Her thoughts wandered to Whitney and she wondered what was she doing.

* * * * *

Staring out the window, Whitney's thoughts were not on the Bellini's private jet, which was flying them to Florida. They were traveling with Armando who was going to start on some vacation yacht project for his cousin by meeting with someone down in Florida and then traveling over to the Carolinas, while she and her father were going to start a new life together.

"You're doing it again," Lyle said.

Looking at her father, she smiled guiltily. "I know I said I would
stop, Daddy, but it's hard."

"Even after what I've told you?"

She nodded. "Maybe it's because I knew him after it was all over. The devastation it did to him."

"That doesn't excuse his treatment of you."

Her father was only aware of what Dakota had said to her in the conference room, not what he had said to her in the hotel room or over the phone. That's what she remembered. That's what she couldn't forget. "I'm not going to let it bother me, okay?" she promised.

"Good, because once we hit the ground, I want to enjoy spending time with your mind too."

Whitney kissed her father's cheek. "I love you so much, Daddy."

When they landed, Armando had someone waiting for him so he said his good-byes on the plane. There was limousine and from the plane's window, Whitney could see only one man standing there. He was big as a house and reminded Whitney of Nathaniel Parker for some reason. She didn't let this bother her, but made a mental note to call Nathaniel once she was in town.

After Armando's departure, Lyle found them transportation to his home, which was a two bedroom flat in the Town and Country Area of Florida. It was a nice single floor home and very spacious. He wasn't use to guest, but he hoped to give her so much more now that she had given him his company back. They had a lot to do and millions of plans to make.

Soon as she was settled, she called Lawrence. He was so glad to hear from her and gave her a quick update on everything.

"The transfer was easier than I thought with Mr. Bellini's assistance. We were able to stop a lot of Eric's plans, but I should let you know, your sister came here the day after you left looking for you. She insisted she was not coming as her father's spy, but I doubt it although there was also a Mr. Heart looking for you, too."

"Did he leave a number?" she asked.

Lawrence gave her the number. "What about your sister?"

"If she calls again, tell her to leave a contact number."

"Will you contact her?"

Before answering that question, she said, "Did she say anything else?"

Lawrence answered begrudgingly. "She said only that she

wanted to apologize and be with you. She felt without her father's presence she could be a very good sister for you."

"I would like to make contact with my sister, Lawrence. Can you help me make it so?"

*   *   *   *   *

Erica wore the same jeans, but found an all black T-shirt in the back of her pile of clothes. The attendant at the gas station had the key out waiting for her to use the bathroom and she thanked him. She washed her hair in the sink and combed it out the best she could and put gel on it slicking it back in a ponytail. That was the best she could do with what little she had. She remembered the five thousand dollars day spas she often went to, who would give her a full work-up from head to toe. She missed that, but doing her own beauty care was certainly educational.

She parked in her usual spot behind the marina and went inside to punch her time card in. Greta wasn't in the office and there weren't any lights on except the ones in his office.

She quietly knocked on Jared's door, but there was no answer. Being that the door was already cracked, she pushed it open and saw that Jared was not behind his desk. Instead, he was passed out on the long couch. There was a bottle of Jack Daniels by the couch half empty and he was snoring so loudly, she could smell liquor on his breath from across the room. He was still dressed in a three-piece expensive suit with his shoes still on.

Kneeling down and picking up the bottle, she made sure the top was screwed on tight. Just as she was putting it back down by his side, he opened his eyes and stared at her. Erica was eye level with him and couldn't help meeting his intense gaze.

He leaned over brushed his lips against hers and deepened the kiss by bringing his hand around her nape, and pressing his tongue past her lips to entwine with hers. The taste of him and the alcohol was an intoxicating swirl of vibrating emotions inside her head.

He pulled away abruptly. "What the hell are you doing?"

Her lips seemed numb for a moment, but she stood up and backed away.

Jared sat up on the couch and looked around as if to check to see where he was.

"I came in early and I needed to know what you wanted me to do? You kissed me."

"Why the hell would I do that?"

She pointed down at the bottle of Jack Daniels. "It's never good to do something like that if you can't hold your liquor."

"Are you trying to give me lessons in morality?"

"I'm just merely pointing out-"

"No need," he growled standing up. "What time is it?"

"Almost eight."

"You aren't suppose to be at work until eight," he noted.

"I'm a little early."

He went over to a small portable bar and poured himself a large glass of tomato juice with a shot of whiskey. She was amazed as he gulped it down and wondered how did he breath.

"Just because you don't have a place to stay, Ms. Thompson, that's no reason to bother anyone else at such an early hour," he sneered.

"I can wait until eight," she said.

"And waste my time and disturb me again." He walked over to a closet and pulled out some coveralls. "Like I told you, the janitor is gone and I need this place spic and span. Start out there with the employees bathroom."

Her eyes widened in horror. "You aren't serious, are you?" "As a heart attack." He tossed the coveralls at her feet. "Be glad I'm allowing you to use those."

Picking up the coveralls, she tightened her lip and bit down on her tongue. To complain would give him an excuse to let her go. She had invested two days of very hard work into this man and would not give him the satisfaction of seeing her complain.

As she was walking out the door, the gray-eyed monster had the nerve to snap, "I'd like to have that completed by the end of the day."

She continued out the door telling herself he was just pissed off because he woke up with a hangover. Before even going anywhere near that bathroom, she found the goggles Phillip had tried to give her the other day and beside them, she found a box of disposable facemasks, which she put on two.

With the gloves pulled as high as she could get them and garbage bags over her shoes, she proceeded to the horrendous smelling tragedy that they wanted to call a bathroom.

The door to the bathroom was tightly shut and she knew why because when she opened the door the smell was ten times worse and she thought for sure what little contents in her stomach would spill out. She tried desperately to think of pleasant thoughts, but the only thing that could come to mind was the kiss. The kiss she wanted to forget. The kiss that was nothing like the one she had given Lethal and was twice as good as anything Dakota Traylor had tried – even though his kisses were pretty good.

Before she knew it, she was halfway done. Once she plunged out the toilet and cleaned the mess up from around it with the cleaning solution from under the sink and a whole gallon of bleach, she could actually take off one of the facemasks. To make sure he wouldn't complain, she did the walls and under the sink just as noon was hitting.

Phillip came by about that time with a fresh bottle of water. "Jesus, girl!" He cried amazed. "You did this?"

She looked around as if she had done something wrong. "What Phillip?"

"This bathroom. Why did you do this?" he asked.

"I'm suppose to," she explained. "Mr. Parker told me to." Phillip ordered her to stay there while he left. A few minutes later he returned with Greta and pointed accusingly at Erica.

Greta's mouth dropped wide open as she looked around in amazement. "My lord, when did you do all this? Were you here all night?"

Erica shook her head and groaned as she stood up against the pain in her back. "No." Kneading her back muscles on her own, she groaned even more at the little relief it offered and wish she did have a few thousand dollars to go back to the day spa in California. She really missed those. "Why are you having a cow, Phillip? Your boss told me to complete this by the end of the day, not including I'm suppose to clean like a janitor around the place."

Greta waved Phillip away. "Mr. Parker told you this morning to do this?"

Erica nodded sincerely wondering what was the problem.

"It's just that, he ordered me to hire a janitorial service that wouldn't be here until tomorrow morning. I don't know why he did that or what's gotten into him lately, Erica. I'll go speak with him. No human should have ever had to endure what was done to this bathroom. At least no underpaid human."

She definitely didn't want that. He might think she was trying to turn his employees against him. "No, Greta," she pleaded. "I don't want to stir up any trouble on my behalf."

"But-" Greta began to protest, but Erica cut her off. "Just don't. I don't want him to think I made a fuss," she protested.

"I'll make the fuss."

"Please, Greta," Erica begged.

Greta relaxed. "You're a much better person than I am." She left out and Erica hoped the secretary would keep her mouth closed.

Phillip came in and ordered her to get out of the coveralls so he could burn them. She did as she was told and waited for him to come back. While he was gone, Jared pulled up in the parking lot

inside of a long black Jaguar that looked as if it had just come off of the showroom floor. He spotted her looking at him and proceeded towards her.

She looked around for some place to duck so she wouldn't have to have a conversation with him. Unfortunately, she couldn't find a place to stay so she stood her ground standing akimbo as he came within arm length of her.

"Taking more breaks, Ms. Thompson?" Jared asked contemptuously.

"I'm taking a breather if you must know."

She noticed he had changed his clothes to another suit just as expensive as the first; looking and smelling good while she knew she smelled like a sewer.

He sighed frustrated as if he hadn't wanted to take a negative or defensive role with her. "I wanted to speak to you about this morning?"

Erica looked as if she had forgotten all about this morning. "What about this morning? Oh, that kissing thing?" Blowing out a raspberry and rolling her eyes around as if he were wasting her time, she snipped, "That was nothing."

Jared stiffened. "I just wanted to make sure you know that is not proper procedure around here. I don't get involve with my employees."

Wanting this conversation to be over, she said abruptly, "Is that all?"

"I drove by the homeless shelter last night and I didn't see your car," he pointed out.

"They don't think people in BMW's are eligible for assistance, I guess, so I parked somewhere and got a few winks," she explained lighthearted. If she couldn't find humor in her whole situation, she would go completely insane. "What were you doing around a homeless shelter?"

He shrugged. "I just drove by. I don't think it's safe for you to be out on the streets at night."

"Is that concern I hear? I'm a big girl, I can take care of myself."

"I'm sure you can, but it's the rest of the population that won't take care of you. I have some lodging upstairs above the office, why don't you crash there?"

Feeling offended by his charity, she said, "I don't want your pity, Mr. Parker. Like I said, I can take care of myself."

Jared looked doubtful about that, but made no more comments toward the matter. "The things I told you to do this morning-"

"I've done it," she said, cutting him off insulted that he would assume she has not followed his instructions.

"Done what?"

"Done what you told me to do," Erica said as if he should know what he said.

He looked over her head to the bathrooms and then walked behind her. "Why is this door open?" he questioned.

Exasperated, she said, "Because I was cleaning up in there like you told me to."

Jared looked back at her as if he couldn't believe what she was saying, and then looked inside of the bathroom as if he couldn't believe what he was seeing. "You did this?"

"Yes." She smiled more to herself, liking the fact that he was amazed at her hard work.

"You shouldn't have," he said extremely perturbed.

Frowning, Erica watched as he came out the bathroom and looked at her as if he were angry with her. "You shouldn't have done it."

Becoming upset, she said, "Next time, when you issue an order, you shouldn't do it in anger." She stormed away before she ended up crying in front of him. Wanting to scream, she ducked in the boathouse to pace off her anger.

Phillip came in carrying his lunch. "Are you ready to eat, Erica?"

She didn't want to remind him that she had no money. "No, Phillip. I didn't bring anything to eat."

"I did. My wife makes all these burritos as if I eat like Mr. Parker. I tell her all the time, I'm too small to eat like that."

"I don't know why you think he eats a lot. He only wastes food," she snipped.

Phillip looked shocked that she would say something like that. "Mr. Parker? Waste food? I've never seen that man waste food and I've known him for a long time."

"Then we must know two different people, Phillip, because just yesterday that man threw away a whole bunch of food."

He handed her two burritos, but she felt bad about taking them. Phillip insisted. "They would only go to waste, Ms. Erica."

Reluctantly she took them, promising to find a way to pay him back, but of course Phillip said it was no problem.

"You've done more around here than any man, Mr. Parker could have hired. He picked a real winner."

Erica wanted to dispute the fact that Jared had not picked her, but Phillip seemed so happy to work for Jared. Instead, she stuffed the burrito in her mouth and pretended her mouth was too full to speak.

"He's been under a lot of stress lately with his present relationship and other mishaps that have happened. You'll have to excuse his strange behavior," Phillip explained. "The man has a lot going on at one time – not to mention the new business venture he is going into."

"So I'm suppose to excuse this as a bad time in his life?" she asked.

"Just come to understand him, Erica. Don't let his foul mood effect you."

Erica didn't want to understand Jared Parker any more than she wanted to clean another bathroom. She couldn't fathom Jared being pleasant to work for. He had been a thorn in her side since she had met him. He was evil, vindictive, spiteful, and hateful.

After lunch, she checked the parking lot to see if the Jag was parked in the same spot, but the vehicle was nowhere to be seen. How a man who ran such a cheap operation could afford a vehicle of that type was a mystery to her. Maybe he did it by not hiring a lot of people and sticking that money needed for his office staff right in his pocket.

Since no one told her any different, she started to clean up around the docks and when she was done, she made the office her last stop. Greta was busy at her desk, when she entered and began to empty the trash.

"What are you doing?" Greta asked insulted.

"I'm cleaning, Greta."

The secretary huffed. "Didn't he tell you to stop?"

"No, Greta and I told you not to say anything to him."

"I only said something after he saw the bathroom. I saw the two of you speaking outside earlier and was positive he would tell you something different."

Erica said, "He didn't and you'll do me a big favor if you could not say anything to him."

Greta looked as if she really wanted to say something, but the hard stubborn look in Erica's eyes made her keep her opinion of herself. "It's not right," Greta grumbled.

Getting back to work, Erica cleaned as quickly and quietly as possible. She discovered there was another bathroom down another hallway near the back of the office and there was another door that had a digital security code so she wasn't able to access it. That it was the only door in the place locked didn't bother her at all being so consumed with her task at hand and trying to forget her back hurt like no tomorrow.

Just as she was almost finishing up the office area - making Jared's office last - she heard someone come into the outer office and froze hearing Jared's voice.

"What do you mean working her like a horse, Greta?" he asked incredulously. "If I was working her too hard, she would have complained by now…why should I keep my voice down?"

At that moment he walked in his office taking off his jacket at the same time. Abruptly stopping in his tracks when he saw her, she knew now he understood why Greta was telling him to keep his voice low.

"What are you doing?" he asked perturbed at Erica. "Finishing up for the day, unless you have another bathroom for me to do around here." She tied up the last trash bag noting his stiff upper lip. Dragging the bag over to a large waste receptacle with wheels and stuffing it in there, she said, "Did you have anything else for me to do before I leave?"

He looked back at Greta who was out of Erica's sight and then looked back at Erica. "I would like to speak to you before you leave for the day."

"Now?"

Shaking his head, he said, "After you're done with everything."

She didn't bother to give him another glance too annoyed to speak to him. It was so difficult, but she had to constantly remind herself that he was her boss when she was so use to speaking her mind in the past not caring what others thought of her.

Just as she was about to leave out the door, Jared called her name. Gripping the door handle and biting her tongue, she cut her eyes at him.

"I hope you won't waste my time and take too long. I'm a busy man."

Stiffly, Erica responded, "I will go as quickly as I can." Yanking the garbage cart behind her, she made it outside, but not before she shot Greta an annoyed glare as she refused to stop and talk with the older woman. Erica emptied out her cart in the large trash receptacles, grumbling to herself about men and their gall. He enjoyed bossing people around. He enjoyed making her life miserable. He enjoyed making her feel like she was a child and in trouble for everything.

By the time she arrived into his office, Greta had gone for the day and the only light on was his office. He was sitting behind the desk with a whiskey glass freshly emptied and staring at the doorway as if he really didn't know what to expect as she walked in the office.

Before coming to his office, she stopped in the bathroom to see how horrific she looked and tried to wash up as best as possible.

"What's the smell?" he asked, crinkling his nose in disgust.

"Probably a combination of sweat, your bathrooms, and cleaning chemicals," she said quite honestly, trying to stand as dignified as possible.

"And yet you still look no worse for wear, Ms. Thompson, he noted.

Suspiciously, she asked, "What's that suppose to mean?"

"It means that during these past days, I've noticed that as much as you hate doing what you do, you continually keep that back straight and head up."

"Is that a compliment?"

Jared shook his head. "Only an observation."

"Of course," she snorted. "It would probably kill you to actually compliment someone."

Leaning forward on his desk, Jared perused her from head to toe, just like he did that first day. Erica became very self-conscious with those smoky gray eyes checking her out now in her horrific state.

"The offer is still open for you to stay upstairs. I don't use it much and I'm hardly ever there," he said.

She shook her head adamantly. "I don't think it would be proper for me to stay there, Mr. Parker. You are my boss."

"Proper? A bed's a bed and any bed is better than the seat you call a bed."

Erica wanted to agree with him, but she remained stubborn seriously convinced the man wanted to find other cruel job position for her to do for him. "I'm sure once I get my check from you, I'll be able to afford something better. I don't want charity."

"How about I deduct one hundred dollars from your upcoming paycheck and so forth after taxes until you find a better place to stay?" Jared suggested.

She still looked hesitant. The idea of sleeping on any kind of bed was better than the lumpy car seat, but just knowing she would be in the presence of him more than the normal eight hours would be stressful on her. Could she mentally take the stress of being in his presence more than she had too?

He decided to sweeten the deal by saying, "I do have a nice bathtub with a jet stream massager."

Her shoulders completely slumped and her eyes rolled up in her head as her body cried out the need to feel that so bad. "You certainly know how to make it difficult for a girl to say no, Mr. Parker, but I just…" Her voice trailed off longingly and then a moment later she found herself nodding her head.

"Good. Go to your car and take out whatever you have to. I'll call for dinner," he said.

"Dinner? I don't think-"

"I insist, Ms. Thompson."

"You'll be taking that out my check too," she stated. "Fifty extra for food."

"I assure you it's not a problem."

"Whether it's a problem or not, I'm not a charity case, Mr. Parker." Plus, she didn't want to owe him one red cent or favors. She

left out the office and quickly went to her car to grab one of her suitcases.

When she returned to the main building, he wasn't in his office, but the door that had a digital lock was wide open and there was a staircase that led up to a large loft. She could hear movement and he was speaking on the phone with someone, so she suspected this was the loft he referred to. There was the futon in front of an electrical fireplace.

With the night being chilly, he had already turned it on and placed a sheet, quilt, and pillow on the edge of the futon. She put her suitcase at the end of the futon and looked around the room. The kitchen divided the room with a large island, which housed a second sink for the kitchen, an indoor grill, plus a black marble counter.

Erica was reminded of Jamison's wonderful cooking every night that she didn't appreciate then, but if she had him now, she knew she would dig right in with thanks up to the heavens.

Jared was pacing the balcony speaking into a cell phone as if he was anxiously nervous about something. She vaguely listened to the conversation about a storm brewing in the Atlantic.

He seemed stressed and when he caught her staring at him, he narrowed his eyes suspiciously. Erica pretended to find the art on the wall of the loft interesting. There were two other doors, but they were closed and she assumed the bathroom and the bedroom lie behind them.

"The bathroom is the last door over there," he snipped, peaking his head in from the balcony to speak with her. Jared had his hand over the receiver mouthpiece and as soon as she went to get her bathroom items, he went back outside and started talking again, but this time with his back to the loft.

Erica wondered if this was a bad night to have company, but he didn't say anything about her being there. She locked the bathroom door behind her and knelt by the tub relishing the cold porcelain against her cheek.

Wanting to laugh and cry all at the same time, she savored the feel of it; even going so far as to press her lips against the cold tub.

A month ago, she would think someone like this was crazy, but now, she didn't care. Running the bath water as hot as she knew her body would take, and then hurried to take off her clothes, she thanked

all her blessings and Lethal for helping her find this place and even meeting Mr. Parker.

Dipping her face in the water to get her hair wet, she stayed under the water for as long as she could hold her breath, and then came up for air, but immediately went back down. It felt wonderful! Exhilarating! Fantastic! All at the same time.

Light knocking at the door stopped her from dipping down in the water a third straight time, and she said in a casually relaxed voice, "Yes?"

"Are you okay?" his gruff voice asked.

She giggled to herself so pleased at her situation wishing she could stay there all night long. "I feel better," she answered lightly.

"The food will be here in about twenty minutes."

"Thank you." She listened knowing he was still standing at the door. After a moment, he walked away and she sunk back under the water.

Thirty minutes later she came out the bathroom feeling very refreshed. Jared was off the phone and sitting at the table. Although his plate was clean, he still sat on the other side of her with his arms crossed. The Chinese smelled delicious, although anything about now smelled wonderful.

Hungrily forgetting her manners as a lady, she attacked the

rice. Just as her mouth was filled, he decided to ask her a question.

"What part of California do you hail from?"

Did he know it was rude to speak when someone's mouth was full of food? Erica had to hold up a finger for him to wait while she hurriedly chewed the food out of her mouth and then took a large drink of water instead of the red wine he had poured.

"Beverly Hills mostly, but since my sister lived with us we lived
in our home outside of Los Angeles, although I was originally born in Detroit, Michigan."

"So you have no ties to Florida, yet this is where you came?"

"My sister will be moving here soon. I'm trying to find her," she
answered. When he didn't speak for a minute, she stuffed more food in her mouth. Again he waited until her mouth was full, before he asked another question.

"What sort of life did you leave, Ms. Thompson?"

Again she had to pause before answering. "Nothing that ever had to do with the word cleaning up. You could say I was a spoil rich girl without a care in the world or at least that's how I chose to live."

"You sound disgusted about your past outlook."

"Well, when reality slaps you in the face, it does a very good job in waking you up," she said metaphorically.

"Can I know why you left California?" He leaned on the table with his palm supporting his straight-laced chin.

Biting her lip, she put her fork down becoming very tired. Her body hadn't had a good rest in days and the work of digesting the food was so exhausting she couldn't eat another bite without passing out. "My father's business interest went downhill causing us to lose everything."

"So you jumped shipped before it sunk?"

Shaking her head and sipping the sweet wine, Erica said, "I was told by a close friend and even my own mother to get the hell out of Dodge before he took me down with him. I think with me out of his grasp, he can't use me to get back at what my sister did to him." Yawning, she stretched and got up from her seat.

Taking her plate to the kitchen, she set it on the counter and paused to gather her strength. "I don't think I can eat another bite, Mr. Parker." Going over to the futon, she tried to figure out how to get the silly thing to lay down, but was too fatigued to even get it to lie down.

"What are you trying to do?" Jared asked from the table.

Another yawn escaped before she could say anything. "I want to lie down. I'm so tired."

He came over to her and laid out the futon for her and even spread out her sheet. She tiredly thanked him and crawled under the quilt.

Jared started to walk towards his bedroom just as she called his name.

"Thanks for everything, Jared," she said so sleepy forgetting etiquette.

If he did respond she didn't know because as soon as her head hit the pillow, she was sleep.

At seven o'clock, Erica awoke to see the place was just getting a hint of morning sun. The balcony faced the east, so it was a beautiful view to see the sun rising. Gathering up some clothes, she lightly stepped towards the bathroom and enclosed herself inside.

Taking a shower, just because, she dressed and went downstairs forgetting the outer door would lock once it was closed and couldn't be opened without a code. Today, she wore some khaki Dockers and a black T-shirt. By this time it was eight in the morning and Greta had arrived.

"Morning Greta," she said stiffly, still miffed about the secretary
opening up her mouth yesterday.

"You sleep well?" Greta asked without the least bit of guilt.

"It was the best sleep I've gotten in a whole week." She couldn't stay mad at the secretary who had been about the nicest woman she had met. Erica had not had a real relationship with her own mother and she kind of liked the motherly bond she had formed with Greta.

"Good, because you have a lot of training to do today." Greta pointed over to a smaller desk that had been situated in the office. "Phillip was instructed to bring this in here this morning."

"Is that my desk?" Erica asked amazed.

Greta nodded eagerly.

Sitting behind it, she immediately noticed when Jared's door was opened she could see right into his office. Hoping his office door stayed close most of the time she liked the feeling of having her own desk. "So my janitorial days are over with?"

"Most definitely," Greta agreed. "You'll be working as my office assistant."

Erica couldn't believe her ears. "Are you sure?"

"Yes, he confirmed it with me early this morning before his flight left for South Carolina."

"He's gone?" she asked amazed.

Greta nodded. "He went to assist in a situation with one of his ventures and isn't due back for about three weeks. He insisted that you make use of the apartment upstairs." Getting a credit card and key out her drawer she handed these items to Erica. "He said to use this to purchase any food or other necessary items and give all the receipts to me."

"I don't think I should take that, Greta," Erica said. The last time she used a credit card, she'd spent over five thousand dollars on Rodeo Drive.

"I can keep it in here if you want. He usually uses a personal delivery service, so we can make use of it," Greta suggested.

Erica nodded. "I think that will work."

"But you will take the key so you can have access to the apartment in case you have to go out at night. The code is the buildings address." She also handed Erica a steno pad and pen. "We'd better get started on your responsibilities around the office. There's a lot to do and learn. Oh yes, I should mention, there is a three-dollar pay raise to this job."

Erica's heart rejoiced and she knew this would definitely help her get her own place to stay. Whitney would be so proud of her.

*   *   *   *   *

Placing the phone down in disappointment, Whitney took a deep breath resigning to the fact that something could be wrong. She sent a message to Lethal for his assistance hoping he would assist her. She had paid him a hefty fee for all his help in giving her information about Eric's holdings and accounts. Whitney had paid off all owed debts from Eric's, her mother's, and even Erica's. Yet, Lethal had warned her to be on her toes because Eric was pretty pissed off.

In the weeks to follow, Whitney was able to find a nice five-bedroom home with a two-car garage for herself while her father lived close by in a condominium. She installed a state of the art security system upon Lyle's insistence and Lethal Heart's recommendation.

Lethal arrived at her home almost four weeks after she had moved in one morning to approve of the installation personally. As they walked around the property, he informed her of Eric's whereabouts.

"As of last week he is still in California trying to repair anything
he has had, but living off people who think he will pay them back. Your request to keep an eye on him has been pretty easy and I will

have my man assign send you up to date reports on a weekly basis," Lethal assured her.

"Do you think you would want to go back and work for him?" she questioned.

He took off his sunglasses and stared down at her with his black eyes sharp. "I go where the money is, and where the right can pay. I do have my subconscious to think about. I'm not as money grubbing as people say I am." Putting back on his glasses, he continued his approval process.

"What about Erica? Have you heard about her?" she asked curiously.

"Yes," he answered, but didn't readily forth come with any information for her.

Whitney had a feeling she would have to drag it out of him. "How is she? Where is she?"

"She's well, if you must know. Are you really concerned about her?" he asked suspiciously. "I'd hate to give you something to gloat about."

Whitney really thought about it, but nodded. "I would like to know how she is."

"She left California and headed to Florida looking for you a little after your birthday. She's in the general area, but I suspect she doesn't have the means to contact you, although she spoke with your lawyer before coming here."

"Do you think she's working for Eric?" she asked suspiciously.

"Going on my gut, I would have to honestly say no, especially once she realized that you were her real sister."

The stunned expression on Whitney's face was evident to Lethal.

"No one told you about it?" he asked.

She shook her head.

"Before you mother met Lyle, she was with Eric. She had his baby, and told your father she had put it up for adoption. She gave the baby to Eric to be brought up in California and came back to Detroit to have you a couple of years later. No one ever told you about the baby because Lyle figured they were not going to see the child ever again and your mother wanted to keep the secret even after you moved in with your stepfather and supposedly step-sister. To

make matters worse, they didn't tell Erica this either." He paused carefully watching her face.

"Does she know now?"

"Your mother confessed to Erica, before taking her own life. Erica was the last one to speak with her." He paused for a moment. "As far as I know, she's really trying to make due on her own considering she was left with nothing."

Angrily, Whitney asked, "Should I feel any pity for her? She was mean to me. She made up lies to scare me. I felt so stupid believing all the crap she made up. She had her freedom and she traveled the world, while I was forced to stay home in a prison."

"She was just a pawn in Eric's game to destroy everything around him all for the sake of greed, Ms. Whitney, just like you were used. Erica's a pretty smart girl, though, and very hard working."

"Hard working?" Whitney snorted in disbelief. "Erica would make Jamison walk three floors up to turn the television when she was too lazy to find the remote."

"Smart people change when the truth is revealed. My sister always says silly things like that. I tend to listen to her since I don't listen to any other women, plus she's so damn bossy I can't help it," Lethal growled sorely. "Your sister's pretty smart."

Whitney knew Lethal loved his sister Onyx very much. Everyone knew this about Lethal. "What does she do?"

"According to sources, she's working as an administrative assistant for a marina in the area," he said rather evasively. "She's doing a damn good job too."

"You've talked to her recently?"

"Not in the past couple of weeks. I'm suppose to get in touch with her over the car she wants to sell."

"The BMW?"

"Yes, it's been her home."

Whitney couldn't help but feel a little pity for her sister. "How much is it?"

"Street value is seventeen, but with the extra miles, you're looking at something lower."

They walked through her home to where she had converted the lower two bedrooms into an office and a den. Going over to her desk, she wrote out a check and handed it to Lethal. "Will you be charging a finder's fee?"

He chuckled. "Well, I'm nice, but not that nice where I just give out information for free. Everybody knows I'm all about getting something in my pocket for myself.

"Can you make this an anonymous donation?" She had written the check out to Lethal.

"I could, but course that's much more than the car is worth." "I'm sure after your finder's fee, it should suffice. If you could have one of your agents monitor her I would appreciate that. If more is needed to supply you with, then I assure you I'll make arrangements with your financial staff."

He tucked the check in the breast pocket of his black silk shirt. "No worries, I've got it covered. Before I leave for the Carolina's tonight, I'll make sure I take care of this," he promised.

Walking a few steps away from him, she said, "There is one more thing I need for you to do, Mr. Heart."

Lethal waited patiently for her request quietly.

"I'm sure you're aware that I was married for a short time after my departure with Eric," she said.

"Armando and I spoke about a month ago about everything before he went on that vacation that went bad," he said.

Whitney frowned. "What do you mean gone bad?"

"Didn't you hear?"

"I seem to be out of a lot of loops."

"After a bad storm in the Atlantic, the yacht he was traveling on went off course and radar lost track of it four hundred miles off the coast of the Bermuda Islands. When the vessel was found two days after the storm, it was at the bottom of the ocean, but only the bodies of the captain and engineer were found on board."

Whitney gasped shocked by what she was hearing. How could this have happened to such a promising young man! According to what she had heard he was a good friend with Dakota. Did Dakota know what was happening? "Are they still looking?" she asked.

"The search party was called off yesterday for bodies by the Navy, so the family has hired me to send a dive team on the eastern side of the Islands on an off chance that maybe…" He shrugged not wanting to voice the worst. "What's so strange about it was that the

captain and the engineer died before the vessel sank. Their necks were broken and there were signs of struggling on the captain's part. What makes this even more of a mystery the woman who was suppose to be the attendant didn't make it on board the yacht. We found her admitted to the hospital overdosed on sleeping pills and Tylenol. She'd been there since four days after the ship left port off the coast of Florida near Orlando, but her uniform was gone so whoever was on the yacht had to have been a female."

"You think a female could have murdered the captain and engineer?"

"The wounds were made by someone very strong," Lethal answered. "But her body or any items she carried on board the vessel are not found."

"What makes you think there might be something to be found on the eastern side of the island?" she asked.

"Because amazingly we found the signal to Armando's cell phone still strong floating in some seaweed on top of the water over there. We judged that it couldn't have been the storm that had carried it so far. It was dropped in the area," he said as if she should have been obvious to that answer. "I'll be leaving early in the morning to head for the Carolinas and to relieve the man who has been out there trying to find out what he can." He came around to see her expression. "Don't you worry your pretty little head off about him. The family is doing enough of that, now what were you going to say about your marriage?"

Whitney had to gather her thoughts back together since they had gotten so off track. "I want you to locate my husband."

"Don't you mean ex-husband?" he corrected.

She gave him a "thanks-for-the-reminder" fake smile. "I have some news for him and I would like to give it to him personally."

"What news could you have for him? According to Armando, you were only married for less than a month."

Whitney gave Lethal a long hard look. Why did she have the feeling Lethal knew more than what he was saying? She knew the man was a private dick to everything whether he was being paid or not. He was a man who had to know the truth and who had to solve everything. Yet as meticulous and perfect as he claimed to be, he seemed also to be a nosey man. "I would assume that matter to be private if my information is being turned over to Kenneth Bellini."

"Lady you pay enough to make me shut my mouth to anyone about your business."

"Good, because I don't want him finding out and like I said, I would like to discuss the matter personally with my ex-husband, so could you find that information out for me?"

Lethal rubbed the back of his neck thinking. "I'm going to be pretty busy with this situation for the family, but before I leave tonight,
I'll assign a man in the southern office to get the information for you as soon as possible."

"No hurry, you have about seven months to find him before I'm due."

Lethel didn't need to be told anything else in order to know what she was talking about and it was his turn to be shocked. "It's his?"

She nodded. "I found out yesterday morning after taking a pregnancy test for the second time."

"Are you sure?"

Insulted, Whitney said, "Of course it's his!"

Lethal shook his head and chuckled. "No lady, I meant are you sure you're pregnant."

Whitney relaxed. "Yes, I'm sure, I'm never late and I have been having all the beginning symptoms." She held her stomach firmly. "It'll be due after the New Year."

"I'll get that done for you," he promised.

(Two weeks later)

Erica hung up the phone and looked at the number to be sure of what she saw written down - Whitney's voicemail number and it was local. She had opted to get a calling card instead of a phone not sure if she wanted to have it so easy for Eric to locate her if he tried. Plus she felt guilty about using Jared's phone for anything when it seemed a lot to be giving her a place to stay and a fully stocked refrigerator.

In the month Jared stayed gone, she learned how to clean and organize the place. The door to his bedroom was kept locked, but she was able to know his taste in things by going throughout the place cleaning and dusting.

He had a lot of thick books of fiction of various writers and some of them were personally signed, plus he had large reference and instructional manuals and works of non-fiction. He also had a collection of instructional videotapes and DVDs that she found fascinating to watch, but saw that on the bookshelf where he kept the tapes and media, there was a locked cabinet.

She was able to wash her clothes in the washroom just off the kitchen and she threw out all the ruined clothes. Erica was so happy to be able to wear her good clothes and not get them messed up, although she knew since she couldn't afford dry cleaning, she had to make sure she didn't wash them wrong or dry them wrong. Of course she messed up a few silk blouses, she destroyed an eight hundred-dollar cashmere outfit, and she faded out and shrunk several suits in her effort to wash her clothes.

This didn't bother her at all because she was so happy to be receiving a paycheck for all her hard work she had put in at Jared's company. Having a job was so rewarding to her and she was proud of herself.

The payphone was next to the outside bathroom, so she had a good view of the parking lot in front of the building and saw a slick black two-door Mercedes pull up and a very beautiful elegantly dressed woman get out. Coming from the very upper crust of society Erica could price this woman down from just a glance and she couldn't count any higher than two hundred dollars – this including the fake extension in her hair. Following the woman into the office, she

went to her desk as the woman didn't even acknowledge her walking up to Greta.

"Is he here yet?" the woman asked Greta.

"No, not yet," Greta said grudgingly. "But you can wait in his office for him, Lecia."

The woman looked over at Erica and narrowed her eyes suspiciously. "You're that Erica girl, aren't you?"

Of course she was surprised Lecia knew her name. "Yes, that would be me, but who told you my name?" she asked suspiciously.

"That's all he talked about before he left for the Carolinas." Lecia shrugged indifferently and walked over to Erica's desk. "That's fine with me. I love a good competition. May the best woman win." She winked wickedly and waltzed in his office closing the door behind her.

"Who is that?" Erica asked in disgust.

Hearing her tone of voice, Greta said, "Stand in line, child. The woman makes me sick too. Just because she had privileges with Jared that no other woman couldn't have no matter how hard they tried, she thinks she's something irresistible." Greta sighed despondently. "This is the part of my job I hate the most when I have to deal with her, but I know after the stress he's been going through, he needs some distraction before he gets back to work here."

"He's coming here? He's back?" Erica asked to be sure.

"He arrived in town about five minutes ago and called while you were outside," Greta informed her. "He asked about your progress and I told him how intelligent and extremely productive you are."

Erica smiled modestly. "You didn't have to be so exaggerated,

Greta."

"If you knew how long I've been waiting for some good help around here, you would understand how glad I am to have you here. He even tried her out here to work, and I swear if I heard her complain about another paper cut as if she was going to die, I was going to slap her silly."

Laughing, Erica said, "She couldn't have been that bad." Yet Erica had to wonder if she was living the standard of life that she had been living she was sure she would have acted the same. Matter of

fact, it seemed weird how Lecia reminded Erica of her old self. "What does she do now for him?"

"Didn't you hear me before? Privileges, child, Jared doesn't just allow for anyone. A bad experience with a woman has made it a hindrance for him."

Erica was completely confused. "I don't understand, Greta."

"He was accused of raping a younger girl."

The news completely stunned Erica as Greta continued her explanation.

"They met when he was working here and she was hanging around the docks during her summer breaks. He was twenty-five years old trying to support him and his mother and living from paycheck to paycheck. This was his third job and he worked the swing shift at night on the docks doing the clean up for the morning crew. She would sneak here at night and try to seduce him. She was only eighteen when they started messing around and everyone knew about it except the owner of the company who had forbade her to date any of the dock workers. Well Daddy found out by catching them in the middle of doing something on top of an old pile of ropes and he was furious. Jared was fired immediately and that girl cried rape to save face with her father. Jared was sentenced to ten years, but ended up serving only six months when the appeal to the courts worked and her lies were brought to the surface on the stand. A lot of people say she was blackmailed for things in order to tell the truth, but others on Jared's side only agree that shit will always float to the top." She gave a playful wink to Erica. "In any case, her father had to pay all Jared's past and present legal fees and Jared won the civil case against the family and ended up owning this marina, which is where he made his first million. Every once in a while, that tart or one of her supporters sneaks on the property and messes up something. For example that bathroom was done by one of them. With the Bellini project taking most of his employees over to the Carolinas to get it up and running, Jared relaxed security around here because he thought it was useless to have them, when there was nothing of value here. But her supporters still came around to do damage."

"Why doesn't he just sell this place if it gives him so much trouble? You told me he has five other marinas around Florida and some on the east coast and in Michigan."

Greta shrugged. "The boy's fond of this place and until his father moves out of his place, he calls this home. Like I told you before this is just his personal office that houses his own yachts he likes to keep in the marina. We don't worry while we're here although I always thought the girl was touched in the head if you ask my opinion."

"Does she still live in the state?"

"Her father moved northeast about three years ago, but her whereabouts are unknown. Jared has a restraining order against her, but she doesn't really care about breaking the rules. She thinks she's above them. Kind of like the chick that's in there now." Greta nodded toward Jared's office door. "Lecia has it in her head that if she is at his beck and call like some call girl, Jared's going to marry her even though everyone knows he'll never marry?"

"Because he knows no one can stand to be in his presence very long without going crazy?" Erica teased even though in a way she was somewhat serious.

Greta chuckled. "No because six months in a jail can do a lot to a man convicted of rape. The prisoners don't take to well to a man with rape charges and for six months of his life, he had to fight to live and sleep with one eye open. He was stabbed on three different occasions, branded with foreign objects in the back, head and legs, and he's broken several bones in his body. A man changes after that treatment and he just never trusted a woman again. He thought he could be without a woman until he could get over his mental pain, but a man has needs and that's where Lecia comes into play. He uses her to supply that need, but only to a

limit." "What limit?"

Unfortunately Greta couldn't answer that question because the door to the office opened and Jared walked in out of breath. Erica couldn't help but look him up and down. He was darkly tanned than normal and she could tell he had been outside a lot. She wanted to ask him so many questions, but refrained from doing so with the knowledge that he was her boss. All she knew at that point was how much she had missed him despite his sobering disposition.

"As always, Ms. Thompson, I see you're standing around doing nothing," he said and pulled out a thick stack of files to hand to her. "Go through each and every one of these receipts and sort them

by date and time, then in company order. I need that in an hour for my financial planner."

She took the stack and nodded.

He said a few words to Greta as Erica sat at her own desk and out the corner of her eye watche him. Just as he was about to open the door to his office, Greta sang out, "Lecia's here for you."

Jared instantly paused before going in the office and looked

back at Erica to see her expression. She pretended to be
very indulged into her task.

"How long has she been here?" he asked.

"Not long, but of course she'll complain at the wait,"
Greta answered.

Whether on purpose or by accident he left the door opened
as he went into greet Lecia, who immediately came up to him smiling
and saying something Erica could hear.

Greta stood up and gathered her things. "You can finish those
tomorrow. He understands it's the end of the day."

Shaking her head, trying to concentrate on her task at hand,
she said, "I don't mind. I'll lock up everything if he decides to
leave before I go upstairs."

The older woman gave her a "suit-yourself" shrugged with her
shoulders. "I'll see you tomorrow. Try not to stay too late. I'll lock the
door from the outside, but Phillip will want to be let in to clock out."

Erica did her best to concentrate on the paper work in front
of her, but it was difficult with the sounds coming from the office.
Deciding to take no more, she quietly got up from her desk and started
to close the door.

Glancing in the office to see them still in a passionate embrace
kissing deeply, she watched as he removed her jacket and opened
her blouse. Lecia didn't stop him as his mouth hungrily mauled her
shoulders and chest.

They were oblivious to the audience they had drawn, but Erica
couldn't stop staring to save her life. Tilting her head to the left she
could easily watch as they made their way behind his desk. By this time
his pants were being lowered to his knees and he sat in his chair as
Lecia moved down to her knees.

Spellbound by what was occurring Erica didn't miss a second
as Lecia's head swooped down to nearly swallow Jared's thick

member deep down her throat. Erica's eyes grew wider and wider as
Jared threw his head back and closed his eyes tightly. Lecia
movements became more fervent and the soft suckling moans she
projected made Erica's own chest tighten.

Erica squeezed the door for support as her legs became weak.
Jared must have heard the gasp that slipped out of her lips, because
his head came up and he looked at the doorway. Their eyes locked and
he could almost project the delicious vibrations that were overtaking
his body.

She had never felt so alive as the pulsation in her veins
made her tingle all over. They never broke eye contact and Erica felt
her body defy her as her hand moved to the front of her dress and she
dipped a finger between her legs and rubbed the most sensitive tip.
Those stone gray eyes looked in approval as he was aware of her hands
and she saw the smirk of wickedness grace those beautiful wet
lips of his. He bit his thick bottom lip and Erica found herself doing
the same. Their breathing became one rapidly increasing until Erica could
feel herself shuddering all over.

"Erica," Phillip called from outside the door.

Gasping in shame, Erica stopped herself and ran to the front office door. Opening it, she took in a large lungfuls of air as if she had been choking. Phillip stood by her to see if she was all right, but he didn't make a move to touch her. She didn't want to be touched. Coming outside all the way, she leaned over and emptied the contents of her stomach.

"Are you sick, Erica?" Phillip asked concerned, passing her a handkerchief.

She used it to wipe her mouth and looked back at the office door. Jared stood there with a sick smirk on his face, but a little concern in his eyes. His clothes were straightened up as if he hadn't just been doing anything. If she made accusations against him, it would be her word against his.

"I-I'll be fine, Phillip," she said, still trying to catch her breath
and walked away, going upstairs through the outside steps to get up to the loft. She didn't want to step foot in the office again. Not alone – not with Jared and that woman.

Angered by her own innocence, she went to the bathroom to remove all her personal items and checked the wash room for

anything she could have left in there. Just as she was closing up her suitcase, he came up the inner stairs of the loft.

"You're leaving?" he asked, seeing the suitcase in hand.

Turning away from him to wipe the tears out of her eyes, she nodded. Erica didn't want him to see her cry. She wouldn't be able to explain her tears. She wouldn't be able to explain her inner fears – she never had been able to understand them all her life. "I should have left a long time ago," she said, finding her jacket and putting it on.

Jared came over to her and helped her on with her jacket, but pulled her around forcing her to look up at him. "Where are you going?"

"Anywhere, but here," she said, stepping away from him. "Don't worry, I've got money for a hotel so I won't be sleeping out on the street." She turned to walk away, but he blocked her way.

"Don't."

Terrified to meet his eyes again, she stared at the floor.

"Is this about what you saw?" he asked.

Closing her eyes, Erica blushed profusely. "I just don't feel comfortable here anymore. I don't feel…" It was hard to speak. Her chest hurt, her palms and forehead were sweaty, and her body was becoming racked with the sensations that she had started to feel downstairs just by his proximity.

With gentleness, he lifted her chin up until he could look into her face. "Is this about what you felt?"

It was so difficult to breathe and she felt so dizzy. "I-I should go." Her throat was so dry.

"If I apologize would that make you stay?" He sounded so

tender and earnest.

Erica forced herself to shake her head and moved around him. "There's nothing to apologize for, Mr. Parker. It's just me."

He didn't stop her anymore as she left out. Getting in her car, she drove to a nearby hotel and checked in, then cried into the pillow."

For some reason when Erica was working that morning, all she could do was daydream about standing at Jared's office door and watching Lecia do that to him.

He had not come into the office as of noon and between Greta and Erica answering the phone, Lecia had called about seven times. Greta didn't bother calling Jared's cell phone like she usually did with calls to the office. Instead, they put the messages on the door holder by the office and kept on going with their busy day.

With Jared back and the Bellini's giving him the approval to do the contract, plus some of the employees back on the marina, the day moved faster, but she still took moments to daydream despite the work in front of her.

By the eighth call near noon, Greta started talking about how Jared had met Lecia. "He went to lower Florida on a whim to buy his second marina because somebody was giving it away next to nothing down there, but when he got down there, the owner said he had never made a deal over the phone with Jared. It was really weird," Greta frowned as she thought on this memory.

"So how'd Lecia come into play?"

"Well, it was Jared's first time away from the city and I convinced him to just stay there over night and come home. Next thing I know, he says he meets this woman and she's beautiful. In my opinion, it looked as if she just walked out of the plastic surgeon's office. She was damn beautiful and…" Greta cleared her throat. "She was just too perfect in the beginning and then after a while, her personality really started to come through, but never for Jared. She moved up here and was his beck and call girl."

"How long was that ago?"

"Five years. Since then, Lecia comes and go. Hanging on thinking soon Jared will want more of her, but he never does." A satisfied smirk graced Greta's lips. "I think he knows her true nature. He just gets some sick pleasure out of using her and keeping her on a very long string."

At noon, Erica called the Whitney on the payphone on the outskirts of the marina. "Hey, Whitney. I was shocked to hear you call me and I really want to see you." She paused and took a deep breath so terrified Whitney would think she was full of shit and never want to speak to her again. "I'm not working for him, Whit. I swear. Before I knew Mom took those sleeping pills and stuff, she told me to get away from there, just like you did. I found the dolphin, after she died, and I knew…He used us both and I hate him for that. Maybe not as much as you, because you had to go through some stuff. I'll never be his lapdog or spy again, Whitney, but I do want to be your sister." She hung up before she sounded really stupid.

Before she could get back into her chair at work, her pager went off to let her know a voicemail had been left. So excited, she used her desk phone to listen to the message. It was Whitney wanting to meet her at a local restaurant not too far from where she worked.

Erica had been saving like crazy, but she knew her funds could support a small dinner.

Jared came in when it was quitting time and walked straight into his office on his cell phone. He was bombarded with people asking him questions and he constantly barked orders for Greta. He paid Erica no mind, but Erica was in such a joyous state about meeting with Whitney, that she didn't mind helping Greta get some of the things that Jared needed done before they left.

When Greta and Erica were leaving, Jared came out his office despite the fact that there were ten people in there waiting for him.

"You're leaving," he asked.

Both women turned to look at him, but it was Greta that answered, "Yes, we are. Was there anything else you required?"

Jared looked from Greta to Erica and then reluctantly back to Greta. "There's nothing that I require, but I have a message for Erica from Lethal Heart."

Erica gasped.

"Do you need me to stay for that?" Greta asked.

"No, Greta. You may leave," Jared said.

When Greta was gone, Erica felt slightly uncomfortable in his presence again even though he was standing five feet away.

"What message?"

"So you know Lethal Heart?"

"A little. He worked for my father in California."

He narrowed his eyes suspiciously and took an envelope out his pocket. "This is for you, but he stated you were not to open it until you called the number on the front of the envelope."

She quickly took the envelope and stepped away from him again. "I'll open it when I get to the motel and use the payphone there to call him."

"No, you'll use your desk phone. I insist."

Biting her lip nervously, she moved around him keeping the five feet distance and sat at her desk. When she picked up the receiver and started to dial the number, Jared went back in his office to give her privacy.

"Heart on the line," Lethal's deep timbre voice said.

Her eyes tingled so happy to hear from him. "Mr. Parker gave me the envelope."

"About damn time. I had to call that asshole up three times today. Things never change with Jared Parker!"

Erica had to wonder how long had Lethal and Jared known each other for him to say that statement. She didn't ask though. "What's with the envelope? Can I open it now?"

"Yes, I'll hold."

Carefully, she opened it, not sure what to expect. Pulling out the check written to her for twenty-five thousand dollars.

"What's this for, Lethal?" she asked, barely able to hold the phone.

"I sold your car," he said. "Don't spend it all at once and don't go thinking you can just up and quit your job and live off of it, okay. In this day and age, that can go pretty fast, so invest it wisely, Erica."

She would! This was her chance to start over!

"Take the check and leave your keys to the car in the envelope on your desk. I've made arrangements with Jared to have the car cleaned up and detailed so his man could drop it off to the seller. Anything you have in there, Jared assured me would get right back to you, so don't worry about doing any cleaning of it before handing it over tonight."

"Thank you so much, Lethal!" she exclaimed.

"Of course I should let you know I did take out my finder's fee."

Erica didn't doubt that and she knew Lethal was just letting her know that he didn't mix business with pleasure. She could understand that. "It's still more than enough."

"That's what I said, but the buyer insisted on paying that amount."

"If you were here, I'd kiss you."

"I'll take a rain check on that, Erica. Have a good night."

The line went dead and Erica replaced the phone on the holder and stared at the check for a moment.

Some of the people left out of Jared's office. Not wanting to be alone in the office with Jared Parker, she hurriedly put her car key into the envelope and put the check in her purse promising herself to find somewhere to cash it tomorrow and find a new cheaper car that would be within her budget.

Lethal was right, it wasn't much. She would often spend that amount on her New York shopping sprees for a weekend, but with her budget now, she was positive this could be a great deal to fall back on if an emergency arise. This check represented security for her and she was so grateful to have been able to get something like this.

Following Lethal's instructions to leave the envelope on her desk, she left out the office as quietly as possible and then decided to walk home from work.

Just as she was getting to the end of the walkway from the

marina, she heard footsteps running toward her. Jared stopped short of three inches from her out of breath, with this strange look in his steel eyes.

"Where are you going?" he demanded.

Erica really wasn't sure how to answer this, so she decided that honesty was the best policy. "I was going to meet my sister for dinner. We haven't seen each other-"

"I want to see you," he cut her off abruptly.

Staring into those beautiful gray eyes, Erica found herself partially caught up in this man's strange behavior. She forced herself to look away and regained her equilibrium. "I don't know how long I'll be. Whatever you want to speak to me about, Mr. Parker, you can speak to me about at work."

"This has nothing to do with work, Erica, and when did we move back to last name basis?"

Glaring up at him, she seethed, "You made that choice when you let that slut-" She stopped herself. He wanted her to confess that she was…what? Jealous? Jealous of Lecia? Jealous that he allowed another woman to touch him like that? No, Erica was jealous, she was

disgusted! Calming down, she finished her sentence, slightly rephrasing it. "…You let me watch you and Lecia do that."

"I didn't tell you to stay and watch it," Jared stated.

"You left your door open," she accused. "But it doesn't matter, Mr. Parker. You're a grown man and you're just my boss. You do what ever you have to do to get by and I'll do whatever I have to do. I left because I didn't feel comfortable around you after seeing you do…that."

"That? What the hell is that? You're saying it like the whole act was disgusting," he said offended.

"This is not the time nor the place to discuss this."

"Then come into my office." "No."

"Come upstairs."

"NO! I will not enter that building alone with you anymore and if you continue to harass me I swear I'll quit. Damn the consequences of being broke again."

Jared conceded and walked away, but she could tell he was very pissed off.

When she got to the motel room, she changed into a nice dress that was comfortable, but not over extravagant. Since the restaurant wasn't too far, she caught the bus.

She arrived early at the restaurant, but that was fine with her and she sipped on water while she was waiting.

"Erica? Erica Thompson?" a surprised voice said behind her.

Looking over her shoulder, she gasped. "Dr. Howell? Wow! What are you doing in Florida?" She stood up and hugged the man.

"I barely recognize you, but when I saw that nose, I just knew that was my artwork."

She blushed almost forgetting how he had repatched her nose after a horrible skiing accident when she was twelve. "And I'm still grateful for you mastery to this day, Dr. Howell."

He answered her previous question. "I was checking in on one of my patients."

"Really? I thought you were only licensed in the state of California. I didn't know you traveled the country."

A waitress came by in a hurry and with Dr. Howell standing in the way blocking the path, the water bumped him slightly. His case

bumped open and papers, photos and other stuff fell out. Erica knelt with the doctor to pick up the papers. Instantly her eyes fell on a picture of Lecia and then a very beautiful exotic woman too.

"That's my case," the doctor said taking the pictures away from her and putting them in her bag.

"But she was beautiful before," Erica said.

"I said the same thing, but she said she wanted a whole new look because she resembled her cousin too much. Isn't that the silliest?" He didn't wait for her to answer. "She flew all the way to California to have me do it, but she called me recently and said she wanted her breast bigger. This time I'm thinking it's now only to attract a man. She gave me certain specifications for her face and body. I should have known then, but I was just so honored that she thought my work was so special I did it any way."

Erica could only nod as she wondered why Lecia had her face redone and did Jared know this?

"My flight leaves soon," the doctor said and handed her a business card. "Keep in touch when you can. You look so different, Erica. Beautiful, if I might say so myself."

She took the card and smiled gratefully, "Thank you, Dr. Howell."

"He's right, you do look different," a familiar voice said behind her.

Turning around, Erica gasped at seeing Whitney standing behind her. Shrieking in delight, she forgot they were in public and hugged her sister.

Whitney hugged her back so grateful to see a familiar face and really feeling like she had a sister.

"You look different yourself," Erica said as they finally sat down.

"I had to change appearances, but my color to my hair is coming in faster than I expected and I'm getting a little of my thickness back." She flustered a bit, but Erica was too enthralled at seeing Whitney.

The waiters brought menus and Erica looked at the prices immediately, which was a first. In the past she had never cared about how much things were. She'd order food just to order it and sometimes she wouldn't even touch it.

Now with only fifty dollars in her pocket, Erica didn't want to overspend and become embarrassed in front of Whitney.

"I insist you let me treat you, Erica," Whitney said. Shaking her head, "No, Whitney. My small job has afforded me to have some luxuries. We'll do dutch this time and then next time I'll let you treat me."

Whitney conceded and ordered first, while Erica had time to find something cheap on the menu.

When it was her turn to order, she said, "I'll have the side salad with blue cheese dressing."

"That's all," Whitney and the waiter asked at the same time.

"I'm not all that hungry," Erica lied. "That's why I insisted on Dutch. I'd just be wasting food if I ordered anything more." In truth she was hungry. She had not eaten breakfast or lunch that day and this salad was just going to be teasing her for more, while Whitney ate a full course meal.

When the waiter left, Erica decided to change the subject all together and insisted to know, "How's everything, Whitney? You must tell me how you did it. Even Lethel couldn't figure it all out and that's pretty amazing."

* * * * *

Whitney regaled her sister with her adventures from California, to Chicago, but she left out about her meeting Dakota, getting married and the divorce.

Erica listened with an attentive ear and looked proudly upon her.

She had never seen Erica's face so full of life and there was definitely a change in the shallow sister now. When she was done, she insisted that Erica tell her everything that had happened since leaving California.

"Oh, it's all so boring. Lethal was instrumental in getting me the job I have now," Erica said evasively. "I worked so hard, that my boss gave me a promotion after a couple of days." She pulled her hands over her lap thinking Whitney had not seen the brittle nails and the calluses that were just now healing.

Erica then told Whitney about the night their mother died and Whitney found herself almost crying in public. They found a way to console each other and actually grow stronger.

Whitney was glad that she had reconnected with her sister. Very glad.

"Do you know that Dakota Traylor's here in Florida?" Whitney announced after dessert.

Erica gasped remembering that name very clearly and a look

of guilt swept over her. "How'd you know this?"

"He's one of the partners in one of the clubs I've invested in. Like I told you Nathaniel was a big help in getting me back my father and he turn down the money I wanted to give him, but he said he would accept it if I helped him to get his business together. He bought out a bunch of clubs and he's really good at running them. Well, Dakota is really good at making the profit." Whitney paused. "I don't know if he'll be coming after you or not, but I've been keeping my eye discreetly on him."

"I don't know if he'll even understand that I was just a pawn for Eric? I know he'll be pretty pissed at me. So pissed he probably wouldn't accept my apology for all I did to him and his company." She looked solemnly at her sister. "I'm sorry for everything, Whitney."

Taking her sister hand in her own, Whitney smiled. "I know, Erica. I know."

It was past midnight before Whitney dropped Erica off at the hotel. Looking quite wary from the long day, Whitney asked if she would be fine. Erica nodded with a yawn and proceeded to get out the car. Whitney touched her arm drawing Erica's full attention back inside the vehicle.

"I know we've never been as close as sister's should be, Erica," Whitney said. "We both had our jealousies about each other."

"Then that sounds almost normal to me," Erica teased sleepily.

Whitney smiled in meek agreement. "But I hope in the upcoming months we can find a way to connect like normal sisters do."

"What's coming up in months?" Erica asked worriedly.

Whitney took a deep breath and looked at her stomach. "I'm pregnant."

Erica gasped and excitedly asked, "How? When?"

Blushing, Whitney said, "It's a long story and we've talked so much tonight I think I'll save it for another night." A yawn escaped her lips.

"I'm too young to be an aunt."

Whitney threw her head back and laughed. "I'm too young to be a mother."

Erica bit her tongue for her selfish remark and was glad Whitney didn't take anything to heart. "When are you due?"

"After the new year. I was wondering if my sister wouldn't mind being my companion." The look on her face changed to serious. "I know my father won't be as understanding as another woman would."

She felt honored Whitney wanted her to be her companion. "What about the father of the baby?" she inquired.

Coldness overcame Whitney. "He doesn't know yet. I haven't

told him."

"Are you going to?"

Shrugging, she said, "I'm trying, but…" Her voice trailed off and then spoke as a new thought, she said, "It's weird, I know in my heart I could do anything in the world accept speak to that man again. I'm angry with him, but at the same time, I feel…" She was lost for words.

"You love him?" Erica asked.

"I don't know."

Hugging her sister tightly, Erica kissed her cheek tenderly. "I love you."

"Well, now I think I can sleep tonight," Whitney teased.

They giggled together like little girls.

"How about tomorrow I pick you up after work, if your boss isn't too mad at you or I. We can drive over to Clearwater to check out one of the clubs I'm investing in," Whitney suggested.

Looking very wary, not too excited anymore at the outlook of bumping into Dakota, Erica shrugged, "I don't know, Whitney."

"Trust me, he won't be there. I've specifically told Nathaniel it should be just me and him."

With that assurance, Erica nodded, "Pick me up tomorrow after four."

Tiredly, Erica made her way up to her room and was too exhausted to take a shower – as much as she loved them. She pulled off her clothes leaving on just her slip and crawled into bed. When sleep was just about to welcome her, the pounding on the door startled her. Thinking maybe something happened with Whitney as she was trying to get out the bad neighborhood, Erica didn't bother dawning on anything before she ran over and threw open the door.

Jared stood there looking very upset at her. Clothed from head to foot in a dark brown Pelle Pelle jogging outfit, if she didn't know him so well, she would have mistaken him for a giant street rogue. He didn't bother to ask her permission to come in, but picked up the bag by his foot and entered the room.

"Close the door," he growled.

"I don't think this is appropriate at all," she protested.

Putting the bag carefully down on the table, he turned to her with narrowed eyes, "You're right, but if you want all the world to see you in your underwear by all means leave the door wide open for all I care."

Realizing she was practically naked, she quickly closed the door, but didn't move away from it. "You must leave now, Jared."

"Oh? We're back to first names again?" he asked as if her voice had come from somewhere else. "Where the hell did you go?

How long does it take to talk to your sister? What if I had plans?
What if I needed you back at the office?"

Not sure how to take his strange mood, she just stood
there looking dumbfounded and speechless.

"I've decided we won't be having that problem again," he
stated as if declaring war on a small country. Turning to the large
black bag he had brought in, he pulled out a cell phone and handed it
to her.

Coming up to him, not even looking at the electronic device,
she reached up to put her hand on his forehead feeling for a fever.

"What the hell are you doing?" he snapped.

"I was just about to ask you to same thing, Jared."

He pushed her hand away annoyed and placed the phone
on the table. Reaching in the bag again, he placed a charger on
the table as well.

"Are you going to leave now?" she asked.

"NO," he stated emphatically as if she should have known the
answer to that.

In truth she had known because he was too darn obstinate for
his own good.

"I'm going to continue to come here until you stop being
stubborn and move back in the loft," he said.

"So I can watch you and Lecia do disgusting things to each
other?"

"Having sex is not disgusting."

"Watching the two of you is."

"This has nothing to do with Lecia, plus I never had her up
in the loft."

With a look of skepticism, she said, "Next thing you're going to
tell me is that I'm the first woman you've had up there."

Sheepishly, he avoided answering her question by changing the
subject. "This is a bad neighborhood and without you having any
transportation, you don't expect me to insist you stay at the loft?"

"I don't want your charity anymore, Jared, and I don't want
to have this argument tonight," Erica insisted. Her head was starting
to pound from the hungry headache she had started to get before she
laid down. She had thought she would be able to make it through the

night just sleeping and then find something in the morning on her way
to work. "I told you I shouldn't be there anyway."

"And I say you should. All your things are there other than
what's in here. Did you forget you still had all those suitcases in your
car? Phillip spent damn near five hours cleaning and detailing the thing
before Lethal's men came to pick it up."

Erica was grateful Jared took care of her items. "I'll come get
them tomorrow and bring them here," she said and sat on the edge of the
bed tiredly. "Please leave, Jared. I'm too tired to even speak anymore.
Whitney and I have been talking all night."

Obdurately, he took a seat at the table. "I'm staying until you come to your senses, Erica."

Angrily, she crawled under the covers. "Fine, but don't you dare step foot towards this bed."

"This chair is quite comfortable," he said, reaching in the bag to pull out an Italian dinner.

The smell of food made her stomach rumble and she remembered she had only eaten the salad all day. She was so use to eating all the time and now her stomach craved what he was eating despite how tired she was. Sitting up in bed, she watching him practically inhaled the food.

Jared paused for a moment in his eating and reached inside his large black bag to pull out another meal. He set it beside him on the table and began to eat again.

Not even asking permission, she wrapped the blanket about her and sat in the chair next to him to eat.

She really hated Jared Parker, Erica told herself as she hungrily ate the vegetarian spaghetti in a rich wine sauce.

*   *   *   *   *

Pounding his pillow, Dakota lied there in the darkness trying his best to sleep. He had a long day tomorrow in getting the first facility up and running by the scheduled opened date. Yet as hard as he tried he couldn't get a wink of sleep.

Her name whispered in his mind, his nose remembered her scent, and his ears longed to hear her voice.

Sitting up in bed, Dakota ran a hand through his hair frustrated at his lack of sleep, but mostly frustrated because no matter how he tried to deny himself, he still wanted Whitney Canton. He knew the possibility of ever having her again was zero. Now that she knew the truth about him and his destruction to her father's business, Dakota knew Whitney would want no part of him.

Getting out of bed, he went to his drawer where he kept important papers. The envelope he received from Bellini law firm in Chicago was still unopened. Picking it up, he ripped the top off and pulled out the papers inside. It had been a quick divorce and he knew Kenneth would make sure every I was dotted and every T was crossed.

She probably turned to Kenneth for comfort. She probably was now making love to him.

Possibilities of what they could have shared if they had stayed together continued to flow through his mind keeping sleep further and further away from him elusively. What should he have done differently in order to keep her?

Something dropped out the bottom of the papers and he picked up the two torn pieces of the check written out to him. Kenneth was facetious in his quest to irritate the hell out of Dakota. After dumping the check and divorce papers back in the bureau, he slammed the drawer and stormed back to the bed.

Damn, Whitney! He could live without her. He would live without her.

Dakota just didn't know if he really wanted to.

*   *   *   *   *

Awakening alone the next morning, Erica took a long shower before heading to the office. Greta had just arrived and was busy on the phone. Jared's car was nowhere to be seen, but Erica was only slightly relieved that he wasn't there. Their late night session had really gotten to her and she wasn't sure how she should feel when Jared was around and they weren't in the privacy of her room.

He talked a lot last night. She found out the problems he was experiencing and how he was very worried over Armando Bellini being lost at sea. The body hadn't been found, but the family was not giving up hope. They hired Lethal to take over and look for the body even after the Navy called off the search. He was also stressed about other things going on in his business life, but nothing bothered him more than his father trying to come into his life and start up a relationship with him all over again.

Jared was deeply depressed about what his father had done in the past and how much his father had hurt his mother. Yet, his mother was so easy to forgive and forget, but Jared couldn't. He spoke about the poverty they had suffered while his father lived a life of pimping in California. Yet he never sent Jared's mother a dime while she had struggled with four jobs and trying to raise a son all by herself.

Erica had fallen asleep against her will in the chair across from Jared, but awoke when he carried her to the bed and tucked her in. He started to sit back in his chair, but she called his name.

Jared only looked over his shoulder as if he didn't want to show her the front of his body.

"Aren't you going to lay down?" she asked sleepily.

"In the chair, Erica. I know you don't want me to lay down with you."

Moving over to make room for him, she pulled back the covers and patted the space beside her. "Come lay down, Jared," she ordered.

He took off his shirt and shoes before joining her in the bed. She pulled the covers back over them and laid on the pillow facing him. Their eyes met for a long time before her eyelids became heavy again and she was fast asleep, but safe in knowing he was there beside her.

Somehow during the night, their bodies came together wrapping around each other for warmth and security.

It was one of the best sleeps Erica had in a long time.

"Are you going to concentrate today or not?" Greta asked startling Erica from her daydreaming.

"Concentrate," Erica choose, shaking off the feelings that she remembered from the night before.

"So, are you going to tell me why Jared is so concerned with your state of mind today?"

Erica frowned. "How do you know that?"

"Because he called and told me not to tell you he called, but he asked a million and one questions about what you were doing, how you were feeling and so on."

"I wouldn't know why he wanted to know," Erica said nonchalantly.

Greta looked slightly suspicious, knowing Erica wasn't telling her something. "I'm just as confused, but even more confused as to why he was making calls from Lecia's house so late in the day. Usually if he goes there, he never stays around so long."

Erica stiffened, but she was not going to let Greta see her break down and show jealousy.

After lunch, she was able to get a lot of work done, because she forced herself not to think about Jared.

Lecia arrived at the office a little after three in the afternoon. Erica noticed immediately she was carrying the large black bag Jared had with him last night and had taken with him this morning.

Instead of going to Greta's desk, she came over and dropped the bag in the middle of Erica's desk. "Jared left this at my place when he left this afternoon. I would have brought it sooner, but I was so exhausted from that's man's lovemaking." She performed an exaggerated yawn and smiled dreamily. "He sure can wear a girl out if you know what I mean." Lecia winked at Erica wickedly.

It took everything in Erica not to jump up from the desk and backhand the slutty tart. Gripping the desk to control her temper, Erica forced a smile through gritted teeth. "I'm sure he'll he glad you returned his property. You didn't happen to bring the money he left on the nightstand too to wave that in my face." Slowly standing up and leaning over the desk, she viciously snarled. "How much do you charge, Lecia? Five, Six hundred? Or is it some kind of flat rate for more than an hour?"

Lecia only smiled falsely. "Jared gets discounts since he likes to hit it so often."

With a flip of her fake yak hair, Lecia turned and strolled out the office.

Erica rushed into the bathroom too angry with herself by stooping to Lecia's level. She wasn't sure how much time had passed, but enough time passed for Greta to knock on the door and let her know it was nearing the end of the day. Throwing cold water on her face she came out the bathroom to see Greta packing up and leaving.

"I'll be leaving a few minutes early, can you lock up?" Greta asked.

Nodding, Erica went over to her desk. Phillip came in shortly after Greta left to clock out and Erica was glad to see Whitney pull up. Phillip wished her a goodnight and Erica grabbed her things to rush out the door.

Just as she was locking the office door, Jared pulled up and jumped out of his car. It looked as if he had rushed there. He was out of breath and looking a bit panicked.

"You can't leave. We have to talk."

Angrily, she sneered, "All you ever want to do is talk, Jared. We have absolutely nothing to say to each other. Why don't you talk to Lecia some more? You've been doing it all morning." Although she hadn't meant for her jealousy to come out like that, it had and there was nothing she could do about it. She tried to walk around him to Whitney's car, but he blocked her way.

"I want to say something to you, I've been trying to say to you all morning."

"Jared, no! We aren't going to say anything to each other. I don't know what you want or why you even bother to show you care, because it means nothing to me. You mean nothing to me."

He backed away, but refused to show in his face how much her words had hurt him. Erica knew they had. There was a hint in his eyes, and she could feel it in his soul, but he didn't show it. He wouldn't show it. Not in front of her. He couldn't trust his emotions to anyone. Not even her.

Stepping around him, she started for Whitney's car until Lecia's car pulled up burning rubber on the parking lot's dark surface, but it wasn't Lecia who jumped out the driver's door.

A very beautiful exotic looking woman about Erica's height jumped out holding a riffle and aiming it at Jared. "You self-righteous son of a bitch!" she screamed. "I'm going to put a hole through you for everything you did!"

Whitney got out the car, but made no attempt to cone around and stop the woman even though she was closer. Erica looked back at Jared who stood only perturbed at the woman.

"What the hell are you doing in Lecia's car?" he demanded to know.

The woman cocked the gun. "You stupid bastard. My cousin seduced you in order to get you where we wanted you and we almost had you."

Disgusted, he said, "She never had me. That's why I broke it off with her this morning. I don't want her. I never wanted the tramp."

Lecia got out the car. "Put the gun down, Natalie."

Erica looked over at Whitney, who was picking up her cell phone to call for help. Looking back over to Natalie who held the gun aimed at Jared's chest, she assumed this was the woman who was stalking Jared.

"If this has nothing to do with me," Erica said. "I'll leave you three love birds alone."

"No!" Jared and Natalie said.

The gun was now pointed at Erica.

"What does this have to do with her?" Jared asked protectively to Natalie.

"You broke it off because of her. Everything would have been fine if she hadn't come. You think I'm not going to make her pay for destroying my plans to destroy you."

Erica lost her temper. "I had nothing to do with anything!"

"Yes, you did!" Lecia said, coming around the car.

Too angry to speak to Lecia, Erica didn't care that there was a double-barreled shotgun aimed at her. She turned around to walk away.

The riffle went off and Erica could feel wind whizzing by her face. Turning back around, she couldn't believe Natalie had the audacity to shoot at her. Neither could Natalie for that matter or Lecia. The shot had destroyed the front door of Jared's business and it was a good thing no one had been in there.

Everyone seemed a bit dumbstruck for a moment, but Erica was quick to react as she charged for Natalie and knocked the gun out her hand.

Natalie tried to fight, but anger was behind Erica's punch as her fist connected to Natalie's face several times until Natalie fell to the ground unconscious.

Lecia barred her claws and charged at Erica, but was soon lying on the ground next to her cousin in a coma.

Erica winced, shaking her knuckles hoping she hadn't broken anything. Jared warily stepped up to her and took her hands gently in his to examine her knuckles.

"They don't look broken," he said, reading her thoughts. "Thank you. I owe you for that."

Snatching her hands away from him, she sneered. "You can return the favor by staying away from me, Jared."

"Erica-"

"I mean it!" Getting into Whitney's car, she slammed and locked the door.

Whitney got in with her.

"Just drive, please," she ordered Whitney.

"I'll take you back to the hotel. I don't think we should leave him here to try to explain this mess to the police," Whitney said.

Erica really didn't care what Whitney decided to do; she just wanted to get away from Jared Parker.

Whitney dropped Erica off at the hotel, but immediately returned to the marina. Erica retrieved some ice from the machine in the motel's hallway and surrounded both her knuckles with ice, hoping she hadn't broken anything.

Lying down in bed, she waited for her sister to come knocking, but soon fell asleep. Whitney arrived later on that night with the police who questioned her about the incident. Neither cousin had said they would press charges and according to Jared and Whitney, Erica's actions had been self-defense.

Erica looked at Whitney in confirmation of this and her sister only gave her a nod to go along with the officers.

"So would you like to press charges against these women?" the officer asked.

"No sir," she said.

When they were gone, Erica asked Whitney, "What was that all about?"

Whitney smiled relieved. "Jared threatened to press charges against Natalie for violating a restraining order if she didn't say it was their fault and convince the police they had struck first."

Warily, Erica asked, "Why did he do that?"

Her sister shrugged. "Maybe he loves you?"

Erica doubted that, but she would not have this conversation with Whitney at this moment. Going over to the window and watching as the police drove away, she looked across the street to see Jared's car. She knew he was in there and she knew he was watching her.

"Did he say anything to you?" Erica asked Whitney.

"He said he wanted to talk with you after the police left."

Erica looked back at her sister who didn't look upset by all this. Whitney was handling it as if something like this in her life happened every day. "There's nothing to speak about with him, Whitney."

Gathering her things, she said, "I'll be back in a couple of hours, Erica. I don't think it's safe for you to stay here anymore by yourself and if you won't stay with him, then you can stay at my house."

"You've been talking with him?" Erica asked as if she had been betrayed.

"Because he cares about you Erica. He doesn't want you to be harmed."

"Well, he shouldn't have…" She almost let it slip. What happened between Jared and her should not be said to anyone. Erica couldn't tell anyone or they would think…

"What, Erica?"

"Like I said," Erica said, looking back out the window. "We have nothing to talk about."

Whitney looked a bit bothered by Erica's stubbornness. "Have your items packed to leave before I get back. I'm going to get your other items from the loft and have them delivered over to my place." "Thank you, Whitney," she said, moving away from the window not at all liking the warm chill that started to move down her spine.

He was staring hard and she didn't like the way her body was reacting to his visual perusal of her. Erica hated that she could feel him even when they were far away from each other. It was as if they had this invisible connection that no one could feel except for them. Did he feel her fear of him? Did he know about her jealousy?

She hoped not. She didn't want him to know she was jealous of the fact he had spent the morning making love to Lecia.

Sitting on the bed, she was still emotionally exhausted from the day's events and decided to lay down for just one more moment

before getting up again to pack her things. There was a light knock on the door and she assumed it was Whitney, but she should have checked because the visitor at the door was not wanted.

Eric stood there looking as cool and casual as he could possibly look. Clicking his tongue, he saw her state of disarray and brushed past her into the room uninvited.

Frozen to her spot, her eyes and mouth were wide open in terror.

"You look like the cats been doing a lot of dragging, Erica," he said. Holding out his arms, he ordered, "Come and give Daddy a hug."

Erica wanted to scream, but she was too scared to do anything.

He knew her fear of him was great. She was very aware of his power because she used to watch people cringe in fear when she told them who her daddy was. She remembered the respect she garnered by being his daughter.

Now she was on the wrong side of his favor and he had come personally for retribution. Did he know she was on the enemy side?

Jesus, Whitney please don't come back here now!

Staying close to the door, she shook her head in defiance.

He sat in the nearest chair. "You look terrible. Why don't you let me fly you to California tonight and treat you to a nice massage? Or better yet, I know this great place in Orlando that can do wonders for you. How about it, baby?"

She shook her head again reluctantly. A back massage sounded so good.

"Aren't you going to say something, Erica?" He sounded a bit piqued, but Erica knew she couldn't careless.

Again she shook her head.

Taking an envelope out of his inside breast pocket, he placed it on the table. "This is for you, baby. I came down here to make sure you were okay."

He was lying, but she wasn't going to tell him that.

Eric walked over to his daughter and tweaked her nose like he use to do when she was a little girl. "You are missed, baby." He pressed his cold lips to her cheek, but Erica still didn't say anything. "I

love you."

Biting her lip, Erica stared at the wall over his shoulder too terrified to look into eyes like her own. She was terrified that the evil consuming his soul would be able to touch her own.

"I left a little present for you on the table. Use it to help yourself out, Erica. I'll be back tomorrow to take you somewhere nice, okay? We can start over and it'll be just us and no one else. We'll get all our money back and live the life of luxury we were destined to live."

Erica didn't respond, but stared hard at the wall.

He started to leave and she began to relax until he suddenly turned around and whispered in her ear, "If you happen to know where your little sister is, you'll be a good girl and tell Daddy won't you?"

There was a menace to his tone that made perspiration instantly spring upon her forehead. Reluctantly, just to get him out the door, she nodded.

He smiled triumphantly and left.

Erica closed the door and collapsed on the floor in relief. She had been terrified to death and she didn't want to ever see her father ever again. Getting up, she quickly finished packing up everything she had.

Going in the bathroom to gather all her things, she felt a breeze on her legs. It was then that she realized she had not locked the door to the hotel room. Coming out the bathroom, she stopped dead in her tracks as Jared filled the doorway with slanted eyes and tight lips.

"What are you doing here?" she demanded, relaxing her anxiety. "I said there's nothing to speak about."

Pushing his self from the doorway, he walked into the room and she could tell there was something different about him. He wasn't his usual cool and collective self.

The wave of alcohol hit her even before he opened his mouth. "There's a lot to speak about."

Disgusted, she said, "You're drunk, Jared."

"Not drunk enough to know you think I did something I didn't." By now he was arm length from her and she had to look up to see his face and those beautiful eyes filled with confusion and anger.

"There's nothing to talk about Jared." She put the last of her items in her hand into the suitcase and closed it.

He demanded to know. "Where the hell are you going?" "Away from here and away from you," she answered in a cool voice.

Jared grabbed her shoulders and pulled her to him. When she was close enough, he wrapped his hands around her waist despite her feeble protest. "No," he said softly, kissing her forehead, cheek, ears, and neck.

She could feel those warm tingling feelings overcoming her and she gave into his mouth liking the taste of the liquor on his breath. Their tongues entwined in an arousing dance making the fires he had already started in her flame up even more.

Her arms moved around his neck as the kiss deepened and his hand moved up her skirt, while his other stayed on her back.

Before Erica knew it, she was lying on the bed under him and his hand had made a path between her legs. Her eyes widened in fear as she felt him slip a thick digit between her soft womanly folds and press deep into her moisture.

Pushing away from him, she shook her head terrified. "No Jared. Stop," she said breathlessly.

He groaned and tried to deepen the kiss some more holding her hands down and trying to force her face to stay still, but Erica was frantic now.

She didn't want this! She didn't want to be touched like that! Writhing underneath him, she screamed out her fear.

Jared was slow to react to her attempt to get away holding her down in his drunken state to try to see what was wrong with her.

Bringing her leg up, she kicked him in the groin. His reaction was immediate as he rolled off her. Erica sprung off the bed and ran into the bathroom locking the door behind her.

Jared was sluggish in his attempt to follow her, but once he made it to the door and realized it was lock, he pounded hard upon it. "Open this damn door, Erica!" he demanded.

"No!" she screamed hysterically. "Get away! Get away from me, Jared!"

There was silence on the other end. She began to become alarmed and pressed her ear hard to the door. There was a shadow moving underneath the floor. He seethed a vicious curse to himself.

"Erica," he said with his tone of voice almost normal. "Erica, open the door, please."

He didn't sound drunk anymore, but Erica wasn't fooled. Men were nothing but monsters disguising themselves in the form of human. Shaking in fear, she covered her face with her hands and cried as Jared continued to demand for her to open the door.

The other side became silent again and Erica listened as Jared pressed against the door. He slowly moved down to where she was crouched at on the other side. For some reason she could actually see him placing his hand on the door and leaning his head against it. She did the same on her side, putting her hand exactly where she knew his hand would be.

"Please," he whispered. "I just wanted to talk, Erica. Open the door."

She closed her eyes in emotional agony, but she was too scared of him and herself. "Go, Jared," she said quietly. "Just go away and never come back."

There was another moment of quietness, before he angrily hit the door where her hand was, splintering the wood on his side. She backed away from the door scared he would kick the door in drag her out and rape her.

"Jared, what are you doing here?" Whitney asked on the other side of the door.

Jared walked away from the bathroom door and Erica could hear them talking, but couldn't tell what they were saying. The hotel door closed and smaller footsteps came to the door.

"Erica!" Whitney called. "He's gone, Erica. Open up. Hurry, please."

Erica swung the door opened and flew into Whitney's arms hysterically crying, but relieved her sister had come for her.

(One year later)

Erica watched Whitney check the window again for the hundredth time before going back to her usual pacing. The bundle Erica was holding wiggled a little and cooed a lot. Erica was drawn back to the baby and cooed back.

"Your momma's a nervous wreck," she said using baby talk.

"I'm not a nervous wreck. I just can't stand waiting for people to let me know if I have a choice to do whatever I want to do." She paced harder. "We can't stay here, Erica."

"I know this," Erica said obviously. "But stressing out when this has happened to us three times this year is not going to make it any better. Eric has his sources and you know he was going to find us eventually."

Whitney sat on the couch next to Erica. "Are you scared?"

Nodding, Erica leaned her hand over on her sister's shoulder. "I'm scared of what he might do to you mostly."

"You don't think he will do anything to you?"

Erica shook her head. "I never took his money Whitney. I left it there on the table. He should have found it the next morning. Either that or a maid made a very nice tip."

The phone rung and Whitney hopped up and answered it. The exasperated look on her face when she heard the voice was a clear indication to Erica exactly who it was on the other line. Whitney lied, "No she's not here, now quit calling." She hung up the phone and glared at Erica. "You know who that was."

"I know, but I'm not talking to him, Whitney."

"He knows I'm lying. He knows you're here. I'll tell Nathaniel to quit giving out my information to his son."

A cell phone went off in Erica's room, but Erica ignored it.

"This is crazy," Whitney said. "Why won't you talk to him?"

Erica hadn't said anything to Whitney in the past year about this, but it looked as if Whitney wasn't going to stand being a wall between her and Jared much longer. "You really want to know?"

"Yes! I can't stand you not wanting to talk about this and Jared seems about as lost as I am about your reasons for not wanting to talk to anyone about it."

"He raped me, Whitney," she blurted out.

Whitney gasped shocked. "That night? And you didn't report him Erica?"

Standing up, Erica sighed. "I couldn't, Whitney. That whole day was so messed up. I just wanted to get out of there."

Whitney calmed herself. "Are you sure, Erica? He forced you to have sex?"

Erica slumped on the couch and began to recount her version of what she remembered to her sister. "He came over, he was drunk, but we kissed. I did let him kiss me, Whitney," she admitted guiltily. "I did enjoy that, but then his hands…his fingers." She tightened her legs together. "I tried to stop him, but he didn't stop and he held me down on the bed and continued to try to kiss me even though I tried to tell him no."

"Were you screaming no, or was it something else?"

"It was a breathless resistance at first, but when he didn't and I felt…I yelled. He should have stopped, Whitney. He knew I didn't want that."

"But you kissed him, Erica."

Incredulously, Erica cried, "Are you taking his side? Does that give him a right to continue when I told him to stop?"

Whitney shook her head. "A drunk man has a hard time trying to understand what you're saying or what is going on, Erica. He probably wants to say sorry."

"He probably doesn't want me to send his butt to jail for rape."

"If you haven't done it in a year, Erica, I don't think that's what he's really worried about. Especially since you've put a restraining order on him and sent him to jail for violating the thing twice. I think you should just speak to him," Whitney persisted.

"No!" Erica said adamantly. "I don't want to speak to him ever."

Whitney sighed. "I'm just tired of him calling."

"Then why don't you get a restraining order against him so he can't call the house at all."

"I won't do that, because he's been nothing but nice to me, Erica. De loves him." Whitney tried to reason with Erica. "There's no justifiable reason for him to do what he did to you, Erica, but has he ever made advances like that before?"

Erica had to be honest with Whitney and shake her head. "But I told him to stop, Whitney."

Agreeing with her, Whitney said, "I'm sure you did, but like I said, a drunk man is nothing to contend with. Maybe he knew that, Erica. Maybe he wants to apologize for his actions. At least meet with him. See what he wants."

Terrified, Erica shook her head desperately. "You meet with him," she insisted. "You find out what he wants and then come back and tell me."

Whitney gave her sister a crazy look. "I'm much too busy to meet with him, plus it's not me he wants to see."

The phone rung again and Whitney jumped up for it. "Hello?… Yes, we're alright…Nothing?…Yes, I will. Thank you, Lieutenant." She hung up the phone and sighed tiredly. "They checked the package they found near the car and said it was nothing, but they think they can pull prints off of it. Hopefully it will lead to Eric or maybe his people. Either way he said to continue to have security until they can find out everything."

"Lethal shouldn't mind," Erica said.

"As much as I'm paying him, he shouldn't." She picked up the phone again and dialed Lethal's number. Erica went over to the crib to check on the baby. De was fast asleep. He was unaware of the danger they were in on a constant basis.

Ever since leaving the hotel room a year ago, Erica had been Whitney's "companion." They had left the country for a while. Whitney wanted to drum up more business for her father, while she still had the free time to do so without worrying about the baby. They returned a month before De was born and Whitney had enough things to do, including having the baby to keep her hands full.

Erica was there for her sister through everything. Watching Whitney bring the baby in the world was more difficult on Erica then it seemed on Whitney. Several times the doctor had to revive Erica during the labor with smelling salts, but dazed and confused, she saw

the beautiful boy child with the most precious face of all. They loved the boy instantly and vowed no harm could ever come to him.

Whitney never talked about his father. It was a sore subject with her, but every once in a while, she let things slip about the father.

Getting off the phone, Whitney stood by Erica and looked down at the baby. Dreamily she said, "He looks just like his father the first time…." Whitney stopped herself and turned away.

"Why do you do that?" Erica asked.

"Do what?"

"Never talk about him."

"Because he's a subject I don't like to talk about." "Then you know how I must feel with Jared."

"No, Erica. The man who gave me that child is someone no one wants to know."

"But you married him," Erica said remembering the partial story Whitney had told during her pregnancy in Rome, but Erica had not heard the whole thing, yet Whitney refused to speak anymore about it.

"Like I told you before. It was against my will."

"Even so," Erica said, "You tell me all the time how you enjoyed being with him. Sex wasn't a bad thing with him."

"It wasn't, but the other part of him was a terrible thing," Whitney said.

"What other part?"

"His personality. He was sarcastic, cruel, and vengeful." She looked away from the baby and began to pace.

"So if you saw him today, you wouldn't like him."

"I have seen him lately," Whitney confessed. "And I think he's ten times worse with women."

Erica couldn't believe this revelation. "So he knows about De and he hasn't come to see him."

"You think I would be crazy to tell him about my son, Erica?" Whitney asked incredulously. "You think I want that man around my child."

"It's his child too."

"He would be a bad influence on De. Look at the boy, he's already picking up bad habits from Jared and he's not around him that often. That boy eats anything you put in his mouth."

Erica couldn't help but smile at that familiar trait about Jared she remembered well about him. "De is too young to pick up habits."

"He's influenced by males around him very easily. I don't want him around his father," Whitney said adamantly.

"Whitney, he has rights and you should tell him about the boy."

"He probably has a million bastards out there from the way he's been passing himself around lately and he doesn't care about any of them."

Erica knew her sister was just finding excuses not to talk to the man. "Just talk to him."

"He's cruel, Erica. He's so cruel." There was so much hurt in Whitney's voice. "Plus Daddy will have a heart attack if he finds out I was even thinking about contacting him."

"Why?" Erica asked. "I would think Daddy Lyle would be happy." Lyle had become a true father to Erica. Forgiving her for being in on Eric's plan and understanding she had been a pawn in Eric's game for revenge against Lyle.

"Because he hates him for what he did."

"To you?"

"No, his company."

Erica frowned not understanding. "What does De's father have to do with Lyle?"

"Because De's father is Dakota Traylor."

A shock wave hit Erica like a slap in the face. "You mean the Dakota Traylor?"

Remorsefully, Whitney nodded.

"He thought you were me, didn't he?" Erica asked remembering the story Whitney told her about meeting De's father. "He was going to hurt you because of me, wasn't he, Whitney."

Again Whitney nodded. "But once he realized the truth, he agreed to the divorce and he was repentant, but he didn't know that you were really my sister. I didn't realize the connection either until Daddy told me everything."

"And you weren't going to tell me?" Erica asked hurt her sister could keep something from her like this.

"I didn't want you to worry. Every time I brought up his name you broke out into a sweat and acted like you had the hives. I didn't want that to bother you, so I figured since I'm keeping my identity a

secret from him anyway with the business, you don't have to find out," Whitney explained. "I wasn't trying to be deceitful, Erica. I was trying to protect you."

"So you've been watching him all this time and never once let him know about his son? Whitney, that's deceitful. Whether he's a bad person or not, he's got a right to know about De. He's got a right to know the truth too. Whitney you've got to tell him."

Whitney narrowed her eyes at Erica. "Alright. If you talk to Jared, I'll talk to Dakota."

Erica huffed in frustration. "Whitney-"

"I mean it, Erica. You first."

"I'll do it if you find out what he wants first and I won't meet with him alone. You'll come with me in somewhere open and public."

"Jared's not going to kill you. He just wants to talk."

"I don't trust him to be alone with him, Whitney." She paused for a moment and then said softly, "I don't trust myself."

Whitney smiled at Erica. "I'll see what he wants."

The phone rung once more and Whitney picked it up. "Yes, Jared I did lie," she said.

Erica stiffened and listened to the one sided conversation.

"She doesn't want to speak to you….yes, I've told her that you want to speak to her, but she still doesn't want to speak to you…fine, tomorrow at my office." Whitney hung the phone up and looked at Erica with a lot of exasperation. "He's very insistent, Erica. I just don't see why you don't understand that he loves you."

Spitefully, Erica said, "He's incapable of love. He just knows how to piss a lot of people off. He's an unemotional jerk who couldn't show real feelings to save his life."

"I'll admit Jared's not a very outgoing kind of person, but what he lacks in personality, he does make up for in body and looks."

Erica groaned. "If you start on that sexy trip, I'm going to scream, Whitney. I still haven't changed my mind about it all."

"Are you going to tell him about yourself and your fears?" Whitney asked.

Erica shook her head. "That's not something he should know."

"Just like Dakota doesn't need to know about De?"

"That's not the same."

Whitney clicked her tongue. "If I have to tell Dakota about De, you have to tell Jared about that."

Erica conceded. "Fine, but I don't have to talk to him until you meet with him."

"He'll be at my office tomorrow."

As an after thought, Erica added, "Maybe before you spring that big news on Dakota, you'd better let him know you're his investor. I'm sure that will give you a lot more leverage in the situation, if he's as mean as you say he's become."

"It would also make you look great when I spring on him that you're my sister, too," Whitney teased.

Crinkling her nose worriedly, Erica said, "Maybe we better keep that information to ourselves until a better time."

Dakota noticed Nathaniel before his partner spotted him. The frantic look on Nathaniel's face made him look much older and Dakota wondered what Nathaniel could possibly be more stressed out about now?

Everything was going so well with their clubs. Since the New Year, they had been hitting capacity every day of the weekend - Even Sunday nights. During the week the club was booked almost two years in advance for activities.

Nathaniel had gotten so many gray hairs in this past year, but Dakota couldn't tell if it was from the stress of the hard work they had put into the business or the quick success they were experiencing.

Dakota had decided to stay even after the time he had told Nathaniel. Not because Nathaniel had begged him to stay, but because in his heart and soul, he really didn't care about getting revenge on Erica anymore. What was done was done and it was all in the past.

When Nathaniel finally found Dakota in the VIP section surrounded by three lovely women catering to his every whim, he looked almost panicked. Dakota got the hint and sent the women away to give them some privacy.

"You're not usually out so late, Nathaniel," Dakota noted. "Maybe you should have a drink? Is it women trouble?"

Nathaniel shook his head to both questions and handed Dakota an envelope. "I have the monthly bonus check for you."

Dakota raised a curious brow. "You usually mail these to me.

Why do I get special delivery today?"

"Because we need to talk," he said, looking around nervously.

Feeling a little unease at Nathaniel's behavior, Dakota suggested, "Let's get to my office and talk in private."

Nodding, Nathaniel said, "That sounds even better."

When they were ensconced in privacy, Nathaniel took off his jacket. He was sweating up a storm and it wasn't even that hot in the club tonight.

"What's going on, Nate?" Dakota asked becoming worried.

"Have you done anything lately to anyone? You know, caused some mess you just haven't told me about?"

Frowning confused, Dakota said, "I haven't done anything that could warrant your paranoid state right now."

Nathaniel became serious. "Dammit, Dakota, there's obviously some shit you did, because I got a call from the investor tonight telling me they want to see you."

This was a shock when the investor had avoided Dakota like the plague all year. Even when Dakota had demanded to see whom his mysterious investor was, Nathaniel had constantly told him there was no chance in hell he would ever know who it was. Yet now… Had he done something to cause ire with this investor?

"Did they say why?" Dakota asked.

Nathaniel took a handkerchief and wiped his brow. "Lately there's been some trouble since coming back in the country, but I didn't think…" He huffed as if he couldn't believe this was happening. "She just has some kind of trouble on her back and it's been occupying her time."

Dakota wanted to point out that this was the first time Nathaniel had let it slip the investor was a female. He knew there was nothing to really worry about because there was no woman who could resist his charms – except one, but Nathaniel didn't know about that one. Even Dakota didn't want to think about that one.

"It's been really bad lately, but she just up and called about an hour ago and asked that you come to her office tomorrow at noon," Nathaniel said, digging in his inner coat pocket and passing Dakota a business card.

Looking down at the card, he frowned at the address. The Canton Towers near downtown. He hadn't been to that building in years and knew it housed many other businesses other than the one he used to work at. Even the suite number was on a different floor. Last time he worked there Lyle Canton only had the upper two floors. This suite was located on the second floor.

"What can you tell me about her?" Dakota asked already planning his seduction strategy.

"She's different."

"You act like she's the queen bee, man. This is a woman, Nate."

Seething, Nathaniel pounded his fist on Dakota's desk to make his point. "She's not one of them sluts you jump in and out of bed with

man. She's cool, but she's the bitch of all bitches. She did me a favor in loaning me this money, but when it comes to business she's damn good at what she does. I've seen her cut the legs off a man while he's still standing and didn't lose a bit of sleep over it. She's in the business to make money and if she thinks you aren't doing your part to put greens in her pocket, she'll cut you off and make sure you never get back up."

Dakota didn't feel so calm any more. Nathaniel looked terrified. "Do you think this meeting could affect our business, Nate?" "I'm just saying don't go in there flying that charm shit around. She knows what she wants and it ain't cats like you, trust me. You may not know her, but she knows you and your lifestyle disgust her."

"So why the fuck she even gave you the money?"

"Because like I said, I did her a big favor when she needed something important done. I helped her old man. She didn't mind giving it out like that because she doesn't like owing people. Just remember, she still holds the rights to this place and if you piss her off she could likely sell those rights to the highest bidder and you know we'll never get a deal like this and the freedom like this from anyone. Don't mess this shit up, Dakota. Just keep in mind, she's different." With that, Nate left the room and Dakota looked down at the card again.

The last woman who was different in his life, he married her and he had a hard time getting her out of his mind to this day. Now he would meet someone else different? What were the chances that this one wouldn't remind him of Whitney Canton?

* *   *   *   *

Whitney braced herself as Jared came into the office and walked straight up to her desk. He didn't bother to ask to be seated and her chair protested his weight.

Jared was probably the only man who knew her well enough to just come in her office and act as if they were lifelong friends. He had come by many times and had come to know Whitney as good acquaintance. Whitney didn't have to put on the tough façade with Jared. He knew she was going through an uphill battle in her business life because she was so young and also a woman. There weren't a lot of women who did well in the import/export business, but

she was an exception to the rule because of her hard nose style and "bitchiness" that everyone knew her by.

Often they spoke about business. Because she was close to his father they had a connection on that level. Jared was still on the outs with the man, but she was like a negotiator and made things a little bit easier between the two men. Jared could almost tolerate being in the room with his father for over thirty minutes.

They stayed away from the subject he really wanted to speak about most of the time, but today was different. Today, she had given her permission and Jared looked eager. It was the first time she had seen him actually look like something really mattered when all the other times he had come to visit her he looked absolutely bored with life.

Jared was so on edge he didn't know how to bring up the subject.

"Jared, what do you remember about that night?" Whitney asked.

"That's the problem. I don't remember much. I know I came over there to talk. I wanted to let her know I was free and clear of Lecia, but when I sat in that car and started drinking I knew she was pissed off that she had to get in the middle of that."

"That's not why she was angry with you that day, Jared."

"It wasn't?"

Whitney shook her head not believing how the two of them had allowed a little misunderstanding get in the way of being together. "Lecia came to the office earlier and suggested that you had been with her all morning long."

"But I hadn't. I went over there to speak with her about breaking it up, she became this whole mess of emotion and I got out of there with the quickness forgetting my stuff I had come over there to get."

"That includes," Whitney added, "The black bag you came over with."

Jared's face showed understanding as Whitney continued.

"Lecia set that bag right in front of Erica so there would be no misunderstanding as to where you were all morning and mentioned in so many words you were definitely not just getting waxed." Whitney winked wickedly.

He didn't look too happy about that.

"But that's neither here or there. Erica has almost forgotten about that part of the day. Now tell me what you remember from that night."

Shifting his weight uncomfortably, Jared said, "She came out the bathroom. We started talking and next thing I know we were kissing on the bed and I was…" He looked at her with narrowed eyes as if she made him admit something he didn't want to admit. Shifting again uneasily, he said, "In my drunken state of mind, I'll admit I was slow to realize she wasn't grinding against me for pleasure, although that is what I thought, but in truth she was fighting me. I was shocked that she was so frigid and maybe I held her down in a clumsy effort to calm her, but she started to become hysterical and screamed. I didn't know what was happening and she ran in the bathroom and locked herself inside."

Whitney shook her head at the mess all this had become. He didn't know the truth and if he had, would he have done that to Erica? Likely not. "Jared, I convinced her to speak to you, but I think you should use some precautions. She thinks you practically tried to rape her."

Jared's eyes went wide and the frown increased in his brows.

*   *   *   *   *

Dakota pulled up in front of the Canton Towers and paid for parking. Security seemed extra tight for a Sunday at the building and the malls that were opened on the first floor impressed him. The place looked as if it were making some money and he was somewhat glad that after the destruction Eric had put Lyle through the old man was able to get back on his feet again.

Going over to the elevator, the guard looked at him warily, but his name was on a special list and after verification by a phone call the guard allowed him to get on the elevator. There was even a guard present inside the elevator to make sure he went exactly to the right floor.

"What's all the security about?" he questioned the guard.

"The boss lady's had some threats and after the top three floors were set on fire, she isn't taking any chances. Twice this year we've found bombs on the upper floors."

"Despite the threats people still seem to come here and shop."

The guard smiled proudly. "That's because the boss lady gets things no one else can get and people know she won't cheat them."

Before Dakota could ask any more questions, the elevator door opened and he was instructed to follow an older woman down the hall to double doors. There wasn't a secretary, but the door was cracked partially.

The older woman said, "You're a bit early, but at your appointed time, just knock on the door."

He nodded and checked his watch. He was twenty minutes early and stared at the door wondering who was behind it. He could hear some voices, but couldn't make out what they were saying.

*   *   *   *   *

Checking her watch, she knew this discussion with him was running over. Jared was very inept at a woman's emotions.

"Alright Jared, I think I have the solution. Why don't you pretend that I'm Erica and you have five minutes to tell me what you want to say."

"But you're not Erica."

Coming around the desk in exasperation, she stood in front of him. "Its called pretending, Jared! Stand up and spit out exactly what you intend to say to her."

Reluctantly he stood up and rolled his eyes in annoyance. "This is not going to work."

"You've tried everything else, Jared, I would think you would be open to suggestion."

Staring hard at her, he tried to force himself to say something. After a few moments he shook his head. "I can't, Whitney. I can't pretend."

Reaching up and cupping his face, she tenderly ordered, "Close your eyes, Jared."

He obeyed.

"Now pretend you're back at your marina again and you're getting out your car. Erica's not angry with you and you have something to tell her that's really important to. Remember that day.

Remember driving up and seeing her. I saw the look on your face and I knew you had something really important. Say it—"

"I love you," he burst out. Jared's eyes opened and he looked down at Whitney, but she knew he wasn't seeing her. His arms came around her waist and he said, "I woke up this morning and saw you lying beside me and I knew I wanted to be with you."

Whitney smiled. "And?" she prompted him with encouragement.

"I'm sorry for everything I did to hurt you. I would do anything to make it up to you."

Throwing her arms around his neck, she kissed his cheek. "That's it, Jared."

A throat cleared at the doorway and both of them looked in that direction.

The shocked expression on Dakota's face made Whitney realized she was still in Jared's arms and that position they were in looked very intimate. Nudging out of Jared's thick arms, she stood in front of him as if she could protect Jared – as if he needed protection.

"Dakota Traylor, I'd like you to meet a friend of mine, Jared Parker," she introduced.

"I know who Jared Parker is Ms. Canton," Dakota gritted out, stepping up in the office.

Erica had designed the office so that one had to step up into. It gave the main desk a feel of more power, especially since Whitney needed to look as powerful as possible. The dark blue in the office along with the mirrors made the space in the office more than what it was, prompting a look of wealth. The bookshelf was a nice touch and the furniture in the office went fine with the status Whitney chose for people to see.

"I was just leaving," Jared said.

"Wait, Jared," Whitney said, going around her desk and looking at her appointment book. "I have tomorrow night free, how's your schedule?"

"For what?" Jared asked.

"To come to my home for dinner."

"Tomorrow? So soon?" There was a bit of anxiousness on his face.

"Like I said, I had to pull some strings."

"Yes!"

She smiled as he left Dakota alone in the room with Whitney.

They stared at each other for a long moment. Dakota's fist tightened and opened repeatedly as if he had an imaginary stress ball in his hand.

Grumbling, he said, "I think they showed me to the wrong office."

Whitney came from around her desk so there was nothing between them. He had yet to come up the three steps to make her level with him, but he was tall enough. She didn't think she would remember so much about him, but she did and she had to suppress a lot in order to make it seem as if she was feeling nothing. Forcing her business façade to come to the surface, she said, "You're at the right office, Mr. Traylor. You are just a little early."

He scowled. "You're the investor, Whitney?"

She nodded. "Nathaniel came to me after he did a favor and I loaned him the money on good faith to pay back. I didn't know you were his partner at that point. I didn't ask any questions about what he wanted until afterwards when he turned in the paperwork to pick up the check. I saw your name and I told him I wanted secrecy. I didn't think you would perform as well knowing I was giving the money for the operation. I had given my word on the loan and I wasn't going to take it back out of a vendetta for you. Nathaniel showed me he could do this project with or without you, but he chose to have you with him. I didn't make this a point."

He came up the stairs and she didn't move from her place. She was very aware he could reach her in three long strides of his long legs. "All this time you've been the investor?" he asked warily as if she were going to spring something else on him.

"Yes," she said with a short nod.

Narrowing his eyes in distrust, he asked, "Why are you revealing yourself now?"

"I've come to the conclusion, you should know."

He shook his head. "Don't give me that bullshit, Whitney." "Don't curse," she ordered.

"I'm not scared of you. You've got all these other people believing you're some hard nose bitch. I just think you're a spoiled rotten cold woman who couldn't careless about-"

"You don't know me," she snapped, cutting him off.

"I know enough to say you've got something else up your sleeve and if you think I'm going to let you use me to get what you want you've got another thing coming." He turned to leave, but the clicking of her tongue and tapping of her shoe stopped him.

Turning around to face her, Whitney smiled wickedly. "Alright Dakota, you want to know the real reason why you're here?"

Coming forward until he was only a few feet away from her, he nodded. "Yes, I want to know what you want."

Moving around the desk, she pointed to the chair Dakota had previously been sitting in. Reluctantly he sat down and waited for her. Her brain was working a mile a minute and she tried to think of something that could just annoy the crap out of him just as he had done to her. How well did he think he knew her? How well did he think he could figure her out?

"Until the loan is paid off, the club is mine, correct?" she asked.

"You know the terms. I didn't make them, Nathaniel made them," he sulked.

"Are you saying the terms are not favorable to you, Mr. Traylor?"

"I would rather wipe my ass on that piece of paper you're holding over us, Ms. Canton, if you want my honest opinion."

"Then pay me what is owed to me and you'll have your club."

"Trust me, I've been using whatever I have to give you what you should have."

She looked at her books. "Oh yes, and in about three years you should have all that to me, shouldn't you, Mr. Traylor?" she asked triumphantly.

He stiffly sat there as if answering her was going to kill him.

"So for three years, your butt is mine and anything I think I can do with." Leaning forward she asked just to rub salt on the wound she had opened, "Is that right, Mr. Traylor?"

Gritting through his teeth, he said, "Basically. Why now Whitney? You had this power a year ago. Why didn't you surface then to rub this power in my face?"

Leaning back casually she said, "I've been too busy to really care what you did, Mr. Traylor."

"Don't you think your interference in my life will affect the business which will affect your money?"

"No, I don't. I know you care too much and you've put in too much hard work to allow yourself to let the business become affected." Sitting back and resting her ankle on the corner of the desk, she could see his eyes were occasionally checking her out.

"Are you going to tell me what you want?"

"How about we strike a deal, Mr. Traylor?"

"I thought you and Nathaniel already had a deal."

"Aren't you even willing to negotiate something better?"

He thought about it for a moment before agreeing. "Only if it's better than the one we have already."

Smiling wickedly, Whitney said, "Oh you'll like this deal." Her phone rung and Whitney was glad it was business. Being a cruel bitch was so difficult around Dakota. Yet, the distraction gave her an idea of how to get to Dakota. Writing something down on a Post-it note, she placed it in front of him not giving him a chance to even touch her. Putting her call on hold, she said, "Come here Thursday and plan to be away until Sunday."

Frowning with distrust again, Dakota asked, "What does this have to do with business?"

"No questions until Thursday, Mr. Traylor." Picking the call up, she waved Dakota away as if he were pesky fly. She even had the audacity to turn her back to him and continue her phone conversation clearly dismissing him. When he slammed the door to her office on his way out, she smiled clearing knowing she had piqued his anger.

Now all she had to do was come up with a way to torture Dakota Traylor without getting on his bad side. What could she do?

Whitney arrived at home late. Even though it was a Sunday, she had a lot of work to do. Once she had De, Lyle pretty much decided he wanted to enjoy the rebound success of his company and spend more time on the road. He traveled to drum up more business and for pleasure. Not seeing her father as much didn't bother Whitney. With all the technology that was available, they were constantly in touch on a daily basis.

In addition to his business travels, Lyle was trying to find out who was funding Eric. Someone had to be doing it in order for the man to have traveled to Florida and secretly set up to harm Whitney. Eric was on a vendetta, because even if harm came to Whitney, Eric wouldn't receive a dime of her money. Everything would go back to Lyle and a trust fund set up for her son, plus custody of her child would go to her father.

Erica had insisted that nothing be reverted over to her for the safety of Whitney and De. She didn't want to give Eric any reason to use her for anything. Many times Erica had insisted leaving Florida to see if that would get Eric away from Whitney, but it had been Whitney who insisted on Erica staying. She was the only family Whitney had and they had become great friends. Erica had changed so much since being away from her father, although her view on sex was so distorted that it was starting to drive Whitney mad.

Thinking of sex, Whitney poured herself a glass of wine in the quietness of the house. Erica had left the fireplace going low to take the chill off the room knowing Whitney was going to work late.

"Did you really think I would be asleep?" Erica asked at the doorway of the living room, carrying a tray of freshly made hot chocolate.

Whitney faced her sister with a knowing grin. "Is De asleep?"

Erica stretched and sat on the sofa. "I'm waiting, Whitney. You know that boy is fast asleep. He can't make it past eight."

Sitting next to her sister, Whitney took a deep breath. "I spoke to Dakota today."

"Forget that for now," Erica said impatiently, making Whitney laugh.

Whitney knew what her sister wanted to hear about. "Fine, Erica," she chuckled. "Jared came to the office and we talked about you and your feelings. Did you know he's unaware of the fact that you think he raped you? He is sorry though for anything he might have done."

"Did he say it?" Erica asked with a measure of disbelief.

"Yes."

Erica rolled her eyes heavenwards. "Men will say anything to get what they want, Whitney."

"Is that so bad that Jared wants you?" Whitney exclaimed.

"In that way, yes, when I don't want him like that."

Whitney was getting frustrated. "I like Jared, Erica. He's become a good friend and I think you're letting the past get in the way of a very wonderful future."

"Practice what you preach, girl," Erica said in a melodious voice.

Offended, Whitney squinted her eyes and asked, "What's that suppose to mean?"

Erica stood up and poured herself a glass of wine before answering her sister. "It means, the past deeds Dakota has done prevents you from making a future with him. I know there's a great guy somewhere in him and you know this too. You wouldn't talk so much about the time the two of you spent together if you didn't think he was great, Whitney. And don't bring the fact that Lyle would disapprove. He knows you wouldn't just get involved with Dakota for nothing and he would just trust and eventually accept Dakota as his son in law."

"This discussion has nothing to do with Dakota and I don't think we should even compare Dakota and I to Jared and you. They are two different men and Dakota will never be as wonderful as Jared is."

Erica snorted. "Jared is not wonderful. He's an unemotional selfish ogre who gets his rocks off by making other peoples lives uncomfortable."

"That's where you're wrong, Erica, and you know it." Whitney pointed out, "He loves you!"

"Ha! That man wouldn't know love if it smacked him upside his head."

"You're still going to talk to him. You promised."

"I will, when the time comes."

"The time will be tomorrow night here for dinner."

"So soon?" Erica exclaimed.

Whitney smiled. "He said the same thing. I think the sooner you guys get together, the sooner a lot of confusion about the past will be cleared up."

"Will that go for the same between you and Dakota?"

Whitney rolled her eyes heavenwards. "Like I said, you can't compare Dakota to anyone or anything. The man stands in a class by himself."

"Whitney, I will admit Dakota is pretty messed up and I'll admit I'm partially to blame for it by stringing him along like I did and using him. He had to be pretty angry and crazed to confuse you with me and drag you to the altar, but don't you think you had a hand in his insanity by what you did to him?"

"NO!" Whitney vehemently denied. "I did nothing to him."

Erica sucked her cheeks. "Oh really? When a man is willing to careless about the hate in his heart and spend twenty four hours with you just to see if he wants to be with you forever, you don't think considering the possibilities and making him feel bad about even considering it were wrong?"

"That doesn't make any sense, Erica," Whitney said.

"He wanted to consider staying married to you, Whitney," Erica insisted. "He wanted to spend more time together. What could it have hurt to consider something like that?"

"I was too young to be married and he promised a divorce. You know I couldn't afford to have him there with me. I couldn't have someone close that Eric could control."

Narrowing her eyes suspiciously, Erica said, "Or someone who could control you?"

"That's not true, Erica."

"I call them like I see them, Whitney. You felt something strong for him. I see it when you talk about him. I hear it in your voice. You change and you were scared of that. You were scared of losing your freedom, but that man wouldn't take it away from you. He loves you."

Whitney bit her tongue, trying not to argue with Erica. Going into her feelings for Dakota or why she knew she couldn't be with him always made her feel awful. She didn't like the way she felt when she thought about it. She didn't like how things had turned out between the two of them.

Speaking of how things had turned out, she said, "Aren't you even the least interested in what happened when I met with Dakota?"

Erica nodded looking very interested. With a ghetto slang, she asked, "Did you tell him he's your baby daddy?"

Whitney chuckled at her sister's silliness. "I only let him know I was his investor. I felt getting that point across to him was important?" "Why?"

Shrugging picking up a cup of hot chocolate, Whitney said, "I had to put myself in a position with him to throw him off. He runs over women with the disregard of a careless speeding driver and women are just rabbits in the road."

Erica winced at the description. "I'm not going to sit here and go tit for tat with you about Dakota. I will agree when I met him, he was a lighthearted charmer who did feel that women had only one purpose in life, and his charms affected me in some way. He is good at what he does and that is to please a woman, but if you want him in the palm of your hands, you have to be good at what you do." Taking a sip of her own hot chocolate, she thoughtfully added, "And use what's already in him."

Frowning, Whitney asked, "What if what's inside of him is all bad?"

"Then use it, but what I'm trying to say is, that man had something inside of him for you. For a man like that to feel something for a woman is pretty powerful and can't be forgotten."

"So he would have something inside of him for you too?" "But I think once a man like that meets someone better, it cancels the feelings for the last person out."

"You sure know a lot about other peoples feelings, Erica," Whitney pointed out. "Why don't you use some of that relationship philosophy on yourself and Jared?"

"Don't go changing the subject, little sister," Erica insisted, finishing up her brew and setting the cup back down on the tray. "Now if you don't mind I am going to retire for the night."

"You will be cooking tomorrow, right?" Whitney placed her cup on the tray.

Erica groaned. "Do I have to, Whit?"

Whitney nodded. "I want him to see how wonderful you can cook now. And no arsenic in the food, big sister."

Muttering something under her breath, Erica proceeded to the kitchen to dispense with the tray and cups while Whitney pondered what to do with Dakota as she stared into the fire.

Coming from the kitchen, Erica asked, "So no other meeting is planned with Dakota? All you did was lay down that you're the investor?"

Whitney shook her head. "If you must know, I asked him to strike a deal with me."

Erica became excited. "What kind of deal?"

"That's the problem. I don't know. I was on the fly with this thing and my mouth kept talking while my brain came up with absolutely nothing. I asked him to meet me at the St. Royal Thursday and plan to be away until Sunday. I have no idea what I'm going to do with that man."

Snorting, Erica said, "You know exactly what you're planning Whitney and I can't believe you?!"

"What?" Whitney asked baffled.

"Oh, don't give me that innocent look, little sister. You plan on having sex! No one invites someone to a luxury suite for four days with plans to just talk."

Whitney blushed profusely. "It could have been a subconscious plan."

"Oh please," Erica said, not believing a word her sister said. "As much as you use to talk about it in detail while you were pregnant and as much as you curse his penis while you were in labor, I know you're still horny for him, Whitney."

"If you know so much Erica, then tell me what should I do?"

Faking a large yawn, Erica said, "How would I know? I don't read minds. Good night, Whitney."

* *   *   *   *

Dakota tossed his keys in his basket as soon as he walked in the door of his apartment. He was so deep in thought he didn't realize there was someone else in the apartment until it was too late.

"Dammit Crystal, you scared the shit out of me!" he bellowed.

Clad in only a Frederick's of Hollywood clear evening gown, Crystal's small body seductively came up to him handing him his usual shot of Absolute straight.

For the first time in a long time the taste of alcohol didn't appeal to him now and looking down at Crystal's body, he found himself in a state of confusion because it wasn't what he wanted now. As much as he tried to fight it, he knew what he wanted.

Drowning the drink down, he gruffly thanked her and went over to the couch. "You shouldn't have come, I'm really tired," he said.

Crystal put the glass down on the bar and came over to him. "I came because I knew you would need some relief. You haven't called upon me in about a month and a half. Nate told me you had to see the investor. Well?"

Sighing, he rubbed his eyes partially oblivious to the fact that she knelt in front of him and began to unbutton his shirt and loosen up his pants. "She's become a bitch."

"She? I never imagined a woman doing that?"

"I never imagined it would be her."

Crystal looked up into his eyes and he knew there were no words needed in order to let her know whom he was speaking of. She had known him for a long time and when she had come into his life three months ago, he had welcomed her as a way to relieve himself of his sexual tension. She knew this was a short termed arrangement just like before and was never jealous of it.

Crystal enjoyed sex and Dakota enjoyed Crystal's way of pleasing him, but they were friends. He didn't love her and he knew she was a woman who never wanted to settle for just any man although she remained faithful to Dakota.

"How?" she asked, pausing her undress of him.

He shrugged wishing for another drink. Maybe that could calm his nerves down. "She said she owed Nate a favor and didn't let the fact that I was Nate's partner stop her from giving him the money. I find it all bullshit and now she's decided to strike up a new deal with me."

"Have you told Nate?"

"I mentioned that she wants another meeting this Thursday at the St. Royal."

Crystal pulled away looking hurt. "She wants you to meet her at a hotel, Dakota?"

"Yeah. Why does that alarm you?"

Standing up, she said, "That doesn't alarm you?"

"You don't know her the way I knew her, Crystal. She wouldn't use sex in order to get what she wants. She's turned into a hard nose business bitch." He took her hand and gently pulled her down to her knees in front of him. "Don't you want to try to take my mind off of her?"

Crystal smiled honored he should asked and proceeded to try with her mouth.

Dakota did his best to relax, but he knew Crystal was in for a long night when all he could think about was Whitney Canton.

⋆ ⋆ ⋆ ⋆ ⋆

Erica looked at the time and hurriedly closed the oven after getting the Swedish Stuffed Hen out and setting it on the counter. She had yet to put on her makeup and the dessert was taking an overly long time to chill, but if she left it in the freezer through dinner,
she was sure it would be fine.

Looking at her main course masterpiece, she smiled to herself.

Whitney gasped coming in the room. "It's so large! It looks delicious," she said.

Erica did a dramatic curtsey. "And you know this, girl," she said exaggerated.

Laughing at her silliness, Whitney came over to the stove in awe. "You've got talent in this room, Erica."

The doorbell rung and they looked at the clock together.

"He's on time," Whitney noted, which was the same thing Erica had been thinking. "I'll put the bird on the table and get the door while you go put on your make up and meet us in the living room."

Erica rushed up the stairs. Her nerves were a mess and her attempt to apply liquid eyeliner took five tries before she didn't look like she had two black eyes. Coming to the top of the stairs she could

hear Whitney speaking, but Jared's voice was low and she couldn't discern what he was really saying.

Moving down the stairs, Erica's heart beat excitedly as she descended one step at a time in her approach to get to Jared. His back was to the doorway and this gave Erica a chance to take him all in, before he realized she had come in the room.

Yet once his name seemed to whisper through her mind, it was as if he had heard her and turned suddenly to take her in. He started to step forward, but stopped himself.

"Erica," he said stiffly, keeping his emotions in check.

She nodded and moved around him quickly to stand next to Whitney.

"Erica's made a wonderful dinner," Whitney said. "She took one gourmet cooking class early last year with me, and that was it for her. She couldn't stop herself. You'll love it!"

Jared's eyes were on Erica as he said, "I'm sure I would."

Whitney carried on lighthearted conversation to keep the tension in the room low. Erica tried her best to ignore the fact that Jared's eyes didn't stop looking at her. She refused to meet his gaze too terrified of what she might do.

Erica was glad when Whitney suggested they adjourn to the dining room to eat. Everything was on the table except the main course and dessert.

"Jared, would you do us a favor and get the dish on the stove," Whitney said. "I seemed to have forgotten to bring it in." She pointed to the kitchen doorway and he went through that door.

"Would you at least talk to him!" Whitney seethed when the sisters were alone.

"About what?" Erica asked truly confused. "I don't know what to say to him."

"Anything?! Ask how his business is going."

"I already know that."

"Erica! He's here and this is your opportunity to talk to him!"

Erica looked distraught. "I-I don't know what to say, Whitney."

"If you don't, I'll embarrass you." "You wouldn't dare!" Erica sneered.

The door to the kitchen open and Jared came in the dining with the bird in hand. He set it down in the middle of the table where there was a space open.

"Jared, why don't you sit in my seat at the head of the table," Whitney insisted.

This would place him right next to Erica and she knew if she moved it would be a clear indication to him she didn't want to be next to him. It took all of her strength not to move away and the warning look in Whitney's eyes kept her there.

"So Jared," Whitney said fixing plates, "I have a business situation that I would like to pose to you."

"I usually don't discuss business at dinner, but I'll make an exception for you seeing it's not any business of mine, Whitney,"

Jared said casually, but his eyes were back on Erica.

"I have a loan which I'll like to be without, but I don't want the
people I've loaned to think I can throw away money like that."

"How much is the loan?" he inquired.

"A quarter of a million is owed, plus I have stock options." "That's
quite a lot of money to just throw away." His shifted his
weight around the chair. "Is the payoff worth every penny?"

"I wouldn't say every penny if you want to put a value on the
person, but the power over the person would be worth it."

He frowned looking at Whitney clearing trying to figure out
what she was up to. Erica narrowed her eyes at her sister not
believing she was asking this of Jared. "Why don't you tell Jared what
you're really up to Whit, so he can better understand that you're as
evil as they come."

Whitney chuckled at her sister's disgust. "I want sex for the
loan, Jared."

His brows shot up, but quickly came back down and he
actually had the audacity to look as if this was not a problem to him.
"Are there any other conditions? Emotional tie ins?" he asked
seriously as if they were discussing a regular business deal.

"There's one small one, you could say," Whitney answered.

"And if this is offered, do you think it would be well received?" "I
think it would be highly considered. According to Erica, he
still could have some feelings for me."

"So this wouldn't be just regular sex, though."

"For me, yes, and I believe after the person he has become,
it would be just sex for him. We had a small emotional bond in the
past, but I think now he would be able to handle walking away from it
once I am…fulfilled."

Erica's cheeks bloomed in embarrassment not believing
Whitney was discussing this subject at dinner.

Jared continued, "I would assume this man is to your liking
and that even after this fulfillment, you wouldn't want him anymore?"

Whitney hesitated. "Well, I would want to be on friendly
terms with him for other reasons. Our business would be concluded
though once I'm given what I want."

Keeping a business mindset, Jared said, "I would put the
offer on the table, keeping the stock options that way I could tie in
with my personal reasons for keeping the relationship open."

Erica really wanted to wipe that satisfied look off Whitney's
face, but she bit down on her tongue to keep herself in check.

"What about getting him to where I want him with sex?"
Whitney asked.

"What do you mean?" Jared asked.

"I mean I want him to…teach me."

The room was quiet and Erica felt herself shrinking in shame.
How could Whitney just talk to him like that as if they were
discussing the weather.

"Isn't there a book you could buy? I'm sure that would be cheaper and you wouldn't lose so much money," Jared pointed out.

Whitney laughed. "Isn't he funny, Erica?"

"I wasn't aware he had a sense of humor," Erica said sourly.

Jared glanced over at her sharply, but returned his attention back to Whitney. "In that manner, Whitney, I suggest you have to be brazen with your request. As casually as you talk to me about this, you have to do the same with him. As if your proposal or your request is not out of the ordinary."

"And you think he would like it?" Whitney asked.

"It depends on the man," he said rather evasively.

"Would you like it if a woman asked you to teach her to make love?"

Again the room went silent, but that was because Jared was trying to chew the food out of his mouth. It seemed like a perfect

deterrent for him to pause in the questioning. Looking over at Erica, he said, "I wouldn't mind being the teacher."

Erica felt the room spinning and she hoped it was because of the wine and not the stopping of her heart. That smoky look in those deep gray eyes had her body shivering on its own. Her throat felt parched and she took extra sips of her water. "I think I should check on dessert," she suggested hurriedly, getting up from the table and practically running into the kitchen.

The doorbell rung, but Erica knew it was for Whitney since she knew no one to call on her, so she didn't bother to answer. She took an overly long time in the kitchen before taking the double chocolate ice cream cake back into the dining room. There was a caramel cream sauce to accompany it, which she hadn't put on the top of the cake yet.

There was another male voice coming from the dining room and Erica pressed her ear to the door to try and discern whom it was.

"Lethal," Whitney introduced, "I'm sure you know Jared Parker."

"I know him," Lethal said stiffly.

"Well, let me get the file, Lethal. I'll be back in a moment," Whitney said and excused herself out the room.

"Where's Erica?" Lethal asked Jared.

"She's in the kitchen getting dessert."

"Doesn't she have a restraining order against you?" There was humor in Lethal's voice. "I don't have to take you in custody, do I?"

"I was invited. Whitney is trying to help."

"Help with what?" Lethal asked viciously. "What I'd like to know from you is why Erica had to go so far to make sure you didn't come near her?"

Jared stood up and rightly so. The tone in Lethal's voice didn't sound friendly and Erica hoped they didn't fight because of her.

"It's all a misunderstanding, Lethal."

"What kind of misunderstanding? That you tried to put your

paws on her without her say so?"

"I didn't hurt her," Jared denied. "Whatever she believes, I wasn't trying to hurt her."

"Then what the fuck were you trying to do?"

"Like I said it was a misunderstanding."

"Well, maybe this whole shit was a misunderstanding. I sent her here because I thought I wouldn't have to worry about her being in this kind of situation. When did you start liking respectable women again, you son of a bitch? You swore them off after Natalie."

"I didn't think I'd like her so much, Lethal, but I do. I love her."

"Fuck that shit. You wouldn't know love if it smack you in the face, Jared. You pride yourself on making peoples lives miserable, especially women like Erica. You don't deserve her, you self righteous son of a bitch!" Lethal sneered shoving Jared. "Now tell me why she thinks you pawed her ass."

"Dammit, Lethal. I didn't. We kissed. I was drunk and I didn't realized she didn't want me anymore, until she was damn near hysterical!" Jared insisted.

Lethal's rock hard fist connected to Jared's stomach and Jared lost his balance falling against the wall by the door. Erica backed away slightly, but cracking the door a little, she could see the two of them standing there; Lethal grabbing the front of Jared's shirt ready to strike him again.

"Didn't you fucking learn your lesson about your drinking? Isn't that why you got in this shit in the first place because of Natalie, you shit?!"

Jared held up his hand defensively. "Wait, dammit! Wait!"

Erica was sure if they really went at it, Lethal could kill him, but Jared wasn't trying to put up a fight.

"Why the hell should I wait, you ass? Don't you get it! She was raped before." Lethal's fist connected again with Jared's stomach, knocking the wind out of Jared's body.

Lethal stepped away just as Whitney came back in the room. "What are you doing?!" Whitney cried at Lethal going to Jared to see if he was okay.

"I'm just making sure this asshole knows who the fuck he decided to mess with. Next time a lady tells you no, you'd better be sober enough to listen or I'll come here and personally break every fucking bone in your body," Lethal threatened.

Whitney glared up at Lethal. "He hasn't touched a drop of alcohol since that day, Lethal. He swore it off!"

"Good, then I'll gladly kill him sober. Why'd you have to try to help them out, Whitney? She's perfectly fine away from him. He doesn't deserve her," Lethal grumbled angrily.

"That's not for you to judge and I just want this misunderstanding resolved, Lethal," Whitney scolded him.

Jared had a little of his breath back in his body, and gasped out, "I didn't know about…" He coughed.

"The past is the past," Whitney said. "Erica has a little more healing to do from it, but even I know it's not your only objective of being with her, Jared. I'm sure she knows this too."

Jared used the wall to hold himself up, still in pain from the punches. Angrily he asked Lethal, "You wanted her for yourself?"

"Let's just say I like some things about her. She's come a long way and she doesn't need some cold asshole like you messing up her life," Lethal answered. "I don't want her to get hurt."

"I don't plan on hurting her anymore, but if I have to I will fight
for her."

"Not in my house," Whitney declared. Looking back at Lethal, she ordered, "Why don't you meet me in the hall while I clean up in here."

Lethal gave him a warning look before he left out the room.

Erica stepped back from the kitchen door covering her mouth in shock. The sauce on the tray had gotten cold so she went back over to the microwave to warm it back up deep in thought about a lot of things. She knew her fear of sex was because of the past and she had seen a psychologist for a while and felt she had gotten over what had happened to her. Her fear of Jared came because her father had told her for so long that the feelings of enjoying sex were bad and that she was to blame for the rape. Guilt had a way of tearing ones mind apart and distorting their feelings.

She was only eleven when it had happened. One of her father's men cornered her. Touched her. Stuck his finger where it shouldn't have been despite her protest.

Gripping the counter, she forced herself to push away the horrible memories. No, it wasn't her fault and Eric shouldn't have made her feel like that. Her father had used that incident as another way to control her. Make her feel as if she was nothing. Distort her

own view of herself and men in general just so he could always keep her under his thumb.

Taking a deep breath, for the first time in her life, Erica had a clear understand and a full memory of the whole incident. She had purposely pushed it out of her memory after it had happened because it made her feel dirty and stupid, but now… Now she understood that she had not incited his lust. She had always been afraid of the bodyguard because he stared too long and he was always watching. He took advantage of the situation once he had her alone.

It wasn't her fault. And it wasn't fair to make Jared pay for the past.

Stepping back into the dining room, she noticed Whitney had cleaned off the table and placed the dishes over on the side table that was usually used for buffet meals. There were only two place settings at the table and Whitney was no where to be seen, leaving her alone with Jared who had turned his chair around to face the kitchen door as if he were expecting her.

Standing as she came in the room, he asked, "Do you need some help?'

His offer to be nice to her was pretty alarming and she didn't really know how to react to him. He wasn't the same mean Jared to her, but when she really thought about it, from the time she had met him, he had been very nice to her. Even though she hated his charity and hated her need to have his kindness in her life, the little things he had done to annoy her to death, balanced out his exterior that everyone else saw.

Shaking her head, she proceeded to the table and placed the cake in front of him.

"You made this?" he asked.

Nodding, she asked, "I should go find Whitney. I know she loves this dessert." She started to leave again, but he blocked her way.

Forcing herself to look up into those eyes, she heard him barely whisper, "Don't leave, Erica."

Her heartbeat accelerated as she felt his proximity do things to her senses. He smelled so good. She missed that about him. She missed their talks and their closeness.

Most of all, she missed his touch.

Clearing her throat, looking away at the cake, she said, "I didn't add the icing to the cake yet. I should apply it before it cools down."

"I'll do it," he offered.

They turned to the cake and she passed him the rubber spatula to dip in the caramel sauce. Watching him try to maneuver the difficult thick caramel around was almost amusing in itself and he seemed to get more caramel on his hands than on the cake.

"Wait," she said before he began to attack the cake again with a second dipping. "Let me show you." Taking the spoon from him, she dipped in the sauce and with ease spread the caramel a little at a time without destroying her cake or getting any on her hand. She could feel him watching her intently. Passing the spatula back to him, she said, "You try."

Jared tried, but he just couldn't master the artistry she had with the sauce.

Taking his hand with the spatula, forgetting her nervousness, she maneuvered his wrist to create the short strokes that were able to apply the sauce on the cake. When they had to do the backside, she leaned over to give him more room and he ended up leaning over her to watch as he let her use his hands to accomplish covering the cake.

Erica was concentrating so hard on what she was doing with his hand and the cake, she forgot about him being so close until he moved his thigh to gain a better posture between her legs and his other hand rested on her hip. She stopped and looked behind her to him. He wasn't even looking at the cake. He was looking at her. All she could do was look in his eyes and then at his lips, as they seem to draw even closer to her.

"I love you," he said.

Erica broke eye contact and looked down at the cake, fighting the tears welling up in her eyes. "I think you can do this on your own now." Unnerved she felt her cheek to make sure she hadn't allowed her emotions to get the best of her.

"Did you hear me, Erica?" he asked in a whisper by her ear. "I said I love you."

Closing her eyes, she pursed her lips together as if she was trying to wake up from a dream.

"I don't want to be a part from you, Erica." He nudged her to face him and she did looking up at him.

Shaking her head, she said, "I can't be with you the way you want to be with me, Jared. I'm not Lecia or Natalie."

"I don't want them, I want you."

"But I don't…" Erica couldn't even say it. "I don't do what you want."

"What do you think I want?"

"Sex!" she exclaimed frightened. "I can't…and I'm so scared. You wouldn't be happy with me."

"Sex isn't everything, Erica," he reasoned. "You're thinking too much."

"But you're a man Jared. You'll have needs that I can't…and I don't think I could handle sharing you with someone like you did-"

"I didn't sleep with Lecia that morning, Erica. I went over there to tell her how I felt about you and that I wanted to cut all ties to her to
be with you."

"But she said-"

He cut her off, "I don't care what she said. The truth is despite how you feel about sex; I want to try to help you overcome all your hurt and pain if you would let me."

Erica knew she was a lucky woman to have met someone like Jared. She knew despite his coldness and his ability to hide his emotions so well, there was a man with a passion that could light up the whole world. On top of all this, he loved her. "I won't make any promises, Jared, but I will try."

The desk called Whitney to let her know Dakota was on his way up. She sat down in a chair all the way across the room to finish up a call from Europe with her father. Lyle was wondering why she had ordered all her calls be transferred over to the St. Royal guest suite.

"I'm just taking a small vacation, Daddy," she said evasively. "The office security situation is taking a toll on me."

"Do you want me to catch the red eye home, honey? You know I will."

"No, Daddy," she insisted. "I'm fine. Just give me a couple of days and I'll be back to new again."

"How's everything else though? Is De and Erica fine?"

The door to the hotel room opened and Dakota stepped in.

"Everyone's good. I'll see you next month in Washington, right?"

"Most definitely. I love you, sweetheart."

"I love you too." She hung up the phone knowing very well Dakota had been listening to her conversation and that he looked a little up in arms at the last endearment.

"There's a bar to your right, Mr. Traylor. Please pour yourself something to drink," she insisted. Her eyes took in his strong broad shoulders, lean waist, and thick powerful legs. She remembered so much about him unclothed lying underneath him…She was feeling a bit parched herself.

She had to keep telling herself, 'be the bitch! Be the bitch!' Dakota had seen her in her innocence and now he was seeing a different woman. In order to keep the upper hand, she had to keep the persona of the hard nose bitch that wasn't scared of anyone.

"I'm not thirsty. I just came to find out the terms and leave, Whitney," Dakota growled still very close to the doorway as if he were scared to step in the room.

"Then have a seat," she ordered, pointing to the soft leather covered white sofa in the middle of the room. "I don't bite."

Rigidly, he walked over to the sofa and sat down on the edge as if to relax would kill him. Stepping over to the matching chair in front of the sofa with the coffee table between them, she sat down with an heir of authority.

Nodding to the papers in the middle of the coffee, she said, "Those are for you, Mr. Traylor. New bank papers and partnership papers drawn up for our agreement."

He snatched the papers up from the table and quickly read over them. She knew when he got to the part that was questionable by the way his expression changed from happy to distrust. "This is too good to be true, Whitney. You're willing to lose all that money?"

"Don't worry about the money, Mr. Dakota. The stock payoff I keep will be well worth it."

"But the value of the stock you have won't be worth a damn until five or more years from now. You're willing to wait that long?"

She was impressed with his knowledge of the value of his company. "Like I said, it will be worth it in the end." Picking up a pen, she handed it to him. "Are you going to sign the papers?"

Dakota looked down at the agreement hungrily. This was what he wanted. This was what he had dreamed for. He would own his own business again. She could see the passion in his eyes of a man about to accomplish his dreams.

"What's the catch, Whitney?" he insisted.

"Didn't anyone ever tell you never look a gift horse in the mouth?" she asked.

"Yeah, but I always follow the rule beware of people coming to me baring gifts." He tossed the thick stack of papers back on the coffee table in front of him. The smack of the papers hitting the wood was sharp and cold. He demanded to know, "What's the catch?"

Sitting back amused that he had so much distrust for her, she said, "The catch is I won't sign the papers until there's a verbal agreement worked out between us. That is why I brought you here."

Narrowing his eyes in suspicion, he asked, "What agreement, Whitney?"

Standing up and going over to the bar, she fixed a straight shot of Absolute and another glass of only club soda. Taking a moment to drink the club soda, she was able to compose herself again, but didn't move from behind the bar as she spoke to him. "I won't lie to you, Dakota. I've watched you work this past year without your notice and I've watched the man you've become." Looking at him, she shook her head. "It hasn't been pretty."

"If you didn't like what you were seeing, you didn't have to watch," he sneered standing up. Most likely he was probably perturbed at how she was being evasive about the agreement.

Whitney didn't let his negativity unbraid her. "Yet as much as I've tried to go on with my life, there's this curiosity inside of me and amazingly, this…how should I put it…innocence and obvious lack of knowledge about being with others."

"What the fuck are you trying to say?" he growled impatiently.

She poured herself another glass of club soda needing another moment to get the nerve to say everything to him all the while remembering Jared's advice to keep her own self-control. "Can I ask why you never went after the girl who broke your heart, Mr. Traylor?"

"What the hell does that have to do with the agreement?"

"Just answer the question," she demanded bitterly.

This threw him off a bit and his voice was rather calm as he said, "Because it didn't matter anymore."

"But you wanted to hurt her so much. Why didn't you ever just take the money you made from the club and find her?" she asked.

"Is that why you were watching me?"

"You're changing the subject. You haven't answered the question."

He came over to the bar and picked up the shot of Absolute. Downing the drink quickly, Dakota set it back down on the bar and she quickly poured him another one. "Like I said, Whitney, I didn't matter anymore. I was putting the past behind me."

"So you don't hate her anymore?"

Crossing his arms over his wide chest, he said, "Let's just say I don't care to hate her anymore. I figure she's going to reap what she helped Eric sow sooner or later and I didn't feel like being the judge and the jury anymore. Plus my attempt to get her back was completely fucked up when I met you."

"You aren't going to get revenge against her then?" "I don't give a fuck about Erica anymore," he said. Whitney wondered if he was cursing because she knew it bothered her and he wanted to annoy her. Coming around the bar, hoping he didn't move away from her, she asked, "And me? Do you still hate me, Dakota?"

"No," he barely whispered. "I can't hate you, Whitney.

Whitney turned away from him. "Even if I tell you I would do it again. I would sacrifice everything to get my father back his company."

"I can't hate you for wanting to do the right thing for him. Lyle was a very upstanding man. I still respect him despite what I did to him." The room was quiet for a moment. "Is that why you're doing this, Whitney? You want revenge against me for what I did to your father?"

Shaking her head, she said, "This has nothing to do with that. I've worked my butt off creating a new success for my father's company. Eric let the company go to waste, but I think I've done a pretty good patch job."

"You've done well. I've heard many accolades about the success of Canton Imports."

Facing him, she asked, "You've been watching?"

"Somewhat," he said evasively. "I wanted to know what happened so I've been watching the stock every once in a while. Whitney, you haven't told me the agreement."

Licking her lips, she said, "I want to be able to start a relationship with me other than business, but I'm not very skilled at it. You know this. I pride myself on being an expert at things I'm taking on, but in the past year, I've found that I'm lacking in certain skills, so I figured if I had someone to teach me how, then I wouldn't be so unsure of myself."

He frowned so hard she was positive his face had to hurt. "Are you seriously asking me to sleep with you, Whitney?"

Stepping away from him to give them some room, she said, "I'm asking you to teach me what you know about making love, except from a woman's perspective. I figured since you were so instructional before about other things, you would be the only one who would be understanding to my situation."

"And this shouldn't bother me?"

"No, it shouldn't," she said going over to the chair.

He followed behind her with his glass of Absolute. "Why shouldn't it?"

"I see the way you handle those women at the club. I see the way you don't care. Why should it matter with me?"

It looked as if he wanted to say something, but held his tongue. Sitting across from her, he looked down at the agreement. "Once I instruct you, then what?"

She smiled knowing he was giving in to the idea. "If by Sunday, I feel that you've instructed me properly, I'll sign these papers and overnight them to my lawyer to be certified. The club will be yours in a shorter amount of time than you expect once my bank receives the rest of the money and that's only to cover the lawyer fees, loan installment fees, and so forth. It equaled out to only fifty thousand," she assured him.

Rubbing his brow deep in thought, he said, "I need to think about this, Whitney."

She looked deep in his eyes to try and see what he was trying to think about, but he kept his expression tight. Her cell phone rung and it was a business call. Her assistant was letting her know there was a package at the hotel's front desk for her to sign. "I've got to sign some papers in the lobby," she said. "Would that be enough time?"

He nodded.

Grabbing her purse, she left out of the hotel room and closed the door. Had this been the right decision? Would he still be there when she came back?

         * *   *   *   *

Dakota looked down at the papers and rubbed his brow hard. She was taking full advantage of him on this matter. To refuse her would make it seem as if he didn't want her. Yet he had to wonder why had she really chosen him? Had she really watched him all this time? Could he really just teach her and walk away from this with signed papers and not want more from her?

This was crazy! He told himself going over to the sink behind the bar and dumping out the contents of his drink. Leaving the glass by the bar, he went back over to the papers and picked them up. He hadn't slept a wink after Crystal's unsuccessful attempt to please him with her mouth four nights ago. Repeated hot showers had not helped him in his effort to relax his mind or his body.

Now that he knew what she wanted, he couldn't believe how easy she was making it for him to have his dream, yet the payoff would either make him a better or worse person.

The knock on the door to announce her return almost startled him. Signing where he was supposed to quickly, he bade her entrance and prepared himself to get Whitney Canton out his system for good.

* * * * *

Whitney took a deep breath before entering the room very prepared for anything. He wasn't in the front room when she came in, but the papers were still on the table. Going over to them, she could see he signed them, and her breathing fluttered a bit knowing what that meant. He would agree to her terms? Had it really been that easy? Or should she be wary of what was to come next? She was actually putting herself into Dakota's hands for a whole weekend. She would have to be susceptible to all he could teach her. There was a knock at the door and she went over to see it was the room service she had ordered while she had been down at the desk.

A light meal had been ordered with Merlot to drink. After signing the slip, she let the attendant out and locked the door securely. The overnight case Dakota had brought with him was no longer by the door and she assumed he had gone into the bedroom. Walking over to the bedroom, there was a different atmosphere. Looking over at the bags she had brought to the room that was filled with candles and different aromas, she could tell they had been touched instantly.

He lit candles around the room, pulled the bedspread down, and there was water running in the bathroom.

Proceeding to the bathroom, she stepped in cautiously not really knowing what she would see, but once she saw the bath water in the large tub, and the candles all around, her breath caught in her throat. Fear and excitement combined filled her and she knew she would really enjoy what was to come. Behind her, Dakota wrapped his strapping arms around her waist and whispered in her ear, "Be prepared to learn, Whitney Canton. There will be a test later on."

Whitney's entire body shuddered at the expectation.

Turning her around to face him, Dakota guided her fingers to the buttons on his shirt commanding her, "Undress me."

In her anxiousness, she fumbled at the first two, but by the third, she had her breathing well under controlled and moved down to his pants quickly to disperse with them. Once undress, Whitney looked him over and her eyes danced in arousal at just the sight of his magnificent body. Even in his state of semi-hard, his tool was a beautiful sight.

Grabbing her arms and pulling her roughly to him, Dakota molded her body against his and kissed all over her face except her lips. It was his turn to undress her and wherever her clothes disappeared from, his mouth was sure to taste. She wasn't embarrassed over her nakedness with him and she was so glad her silvery lines from pregnancy had almost disappeared. In his eyes, she could see she was beautiful and that meant so much to her. Briefly she wondered if he would be able to tell she had a baby almost six months ago.

Starting at his chest descending, she touched him everywhere with her hands wanting to remember every inch of his powerful body. Teasingly, she would use the tip of her tongue on his stomach, waist, and inside his thighs. Moving behind him, she started upwards pressing her lips to the back of his calves, thighs and knees. She tantalized the perfectly sculptured bottom, nibbling the dark caramel skin like it was candy. His back was a playground of nerves and she liked how he tensed and relaxed from her exquisite massage. She could see his legs start to tremble and his manhood grow even more.

Whitney was dying to taste him, but he purposely avoided touching her lips until he was done giving her his own oral massage. He ordered her to kiss him and dipped his head to give her small statue length a chance to reach him without straining her tiptoes too much. Moving her arms around his neck to steady herself on her toes, she ensnared his lips in binding osculation that sent hard electrical charges to her brain. The delicious taste of him, combined with his wonderful tongue had her body easily ready for anything that was to come.

He kept his arms behind his back making her do all the work, but it was a labor she didn't mind.

Without breaking the kiss, Jared moved down to the edge of the tub and she followed him into the sitting position by moving astride his hips. He took her hand and guided them to his shaft showing her how to build up his passion even more. Moving his hands under her soft bottom, he nudged her to lift.

"Slowly take me," he instructed in a whisper of passion.

It was odd hearing that from a man, but the sense of power the words evoked inside of her, made it all the more stimulating. Swirling the tip around her womanhood, she tormented the sensitive peak with so much expectation.

Dakota gripped the side of the tub and threw his head back at her mercy. Her sheath grasped his shaft in a strong hold. He cursed vehemently and she slowed her motions.

"Am I hurting you?" she asked worriedly, forgetting her own initial discomfort of his entry.

He gasped a few times before shaking his head in answer to her question. "You…feel tighter than before." Dakota buried his face in the crook of her neck. "F-feel so good, Whitney."

Smiling with confidence that her secret was safe and that he liked what she was doing to him, she pulled out all stops gyrating and riding him. She could see he was trying so hard to maintain his control, but when Whitney realized how sensitive he became the more she teased him, she used her hands and mouth to keep him titillated. Her own body was a flurry of moisture as she felt her own orgasm building. As she surrendered to her explosion, she brought him along for the ride and they held each other close as they became one.

Dakota planted small kisses on her breasts as she tried to control her breathing. He tenderly rubbed her back and waited for her to find her equilibrium.

A strange frown came over his face and she asked,

"What?" "Your breast," he said. "They feel heavier."

She returned his frown. "Are you sure it isn't from mistaking me from all the other women you've had?"

"My memory is very good, Whitney, and I remember your breast very well."

Blushing she tried to get up, but his hands were around her waist and she still had him embedded inside of her. Teasingly, she said, "Maybe they're just full of excitement now." Nuzzling at his

collarbone knowing it was one of his hypersensitive spots, he was soon letting the matter go and indulging in the rest of her body, but she notice how he seemed almost worshipful over her breast size. She hid her relief and did her own indulging.

They made use of the bath water and he showed her how to bath and massage a man. Getting his release initially made him very relaxed and he was able to show her a lot more without getting too aroused, yet occasionally he was able to maneuver himself deep inside of her. She never knew taking a bath was so exciting.

When the water had become cold, they adjourned to the large bedroom and he had a renewed sense of strength and stamina as his mouth explored her body from head to toe. Whitney was shown how to please, while she was being pleased and the new experience sent her over the edge in multi-orgasms.

As the night began to turn to day, they finally slept exhausted.

* * * * *

Since there was no call from Whitney, Erica assumed everything was fine. She checked on De before retiring to her own room making sure the intercom from the baby's room was on high and the security alarm was on very sensitive.

Turning on a late night movie, she paid little attention to what was on the screen. Her thoughts were more on Jared and how he had stayed most of the night with her. They talked so long about everything that night he had come for dinner, and she had fallen asleep in his arms. He left in the early morning with Whitney and had left a message on her phone he had to leave town for a week because of the Tornado storms in Miami where one of his docks were.

She understood, but she missed him.

The phone ringing by her bedside startled her. "Whitney?" she asked answering it.

"No," Jared said on the other line quietly.

Erica could hear raining and a lot of yelling in the background, but Jared didn't seem at all connected to what was going on around him. "Where are you?"

"Deep in some serious shit, but that's not important," he said as if it didn't matter that his sentence had alarmed her.

"What's wrong?"

"Nothing for you to be concerned with, Erica. I called because I thought you missed me."

Touching her chest feeling emotional about the bond they shared, she said, "Yes, Jared, I'll admit I miss you."

"Good, I miss you too."

Erica chuckled realizing it wasn't in Jared's nature to be emotional and when he did have to discuss how he was feeling he made it seem as if a person should already know, but with him being so darn evasive about showing his feelings, it made it so frustrating. Teasingly, she said, "And if you were here with me right now? What would you do to show me how you feel?"

He was quiet for a moment on the other line and if it wasn't for the background noise, she would have thought they had gotten disconnected. "Hold you all night."

His answer touched her. "I wish you were here, Jared," she said forlornly, allowing her depression to come to the surface.

The line disconnected and she figured he had lost his signal. Calling his cell phone back, the recorded voice said the number she was trying to reach was out of calling range.

Giving up, she laid back down in bed and prepared herself to go to sleep.

* * * * *

Four hours later, the buzzer on the gate awoke Erica abruptly out of sleep. Checking the camera, she couldn't believe that black Mercedes sat there and she pushed the electronic gate to open. By the time she made it downstairs in her bed robe opening the door, Jared was getting out his car-soaking wet. The storms had yet to hit Tampa, but she had a feeling he had driven all the way from where he was to her home as soon as he had gotten that phone call.

Running in his arms despite his drenched appearance; she squealed her happiness to see him.

Cupping her face, his lips molded against hers and she didn't draw away, but cherished the sweetness of him.

"Can I still hold you?" he asked.

She smiled avoiding his question and pulled him in the house. "You're going to catch your death of colds, Jared. Why didn't you change clothes?"

"I'm fine." Yet a sneeze escaped belying his true state.

"Did you bring a change of clothes?"

He shook his head as she handed him some tissue and took his coat. Jared wiped his face and she insisted he come upstairs to her room where it was warmer in the home.

Using her bathroom to remove his clothing, she waited on the bed for him to come out. She found a large terry cloth robe Lyle had left over for Jared to wear.

Coming out the bathroom with the robe on, Jared was drying his hair with a towel. Her eyes were wide at the sight of his bare chest. His muscles were defined and wet. Jesus, he looked so…

He looked down to see if there was something wrong and then looked back at her confused.

Erica got up from the bed, feeling as if the room had gotten especially hot. "You shouldn't have driven all this way, Jared."

He moved up behind her. "You never answered my question from downstairs, Erica."

Forcing herself to stay calm, she busied her hands with straightening up her collection of figurines on her desk, by her window. Jared moved his hands around her waist and held her hands. His smooth chin rubbed against her cheek. Erica closed her eyes feeling as if hot flashes were all over her body even down to her toes.

"It's not bad to feel this way, Erica," he said.

"I shouldn't feel this way, Jared."

"Even if I feel the same."

Turning to him, she asked, "How do you know how I feel?" she asked suspiciously.

He pulled her gently in her arms and whispered in her ear, "Hot, feverish all over."

Erica couldn't believe he had hit the mark like that. Innocently, she asked, "How do you make that feeling go away?"

"Do you want it to?"

Confused she pushed away from him and sat back on the bed. "I don't know what I want, Jared. I just know I do like you." Looking up at him, she bravely admitted, "I love you."

Kneeling down in front of her, he leaned in and softly let his lips press against hers. She closed her eyes and languished in the feel of his mouth as he suckled her bottom lip. Parting her lips, she allowed him to take a kiss deeper.

He bent his head sideways and she like how his tongue pulsed inside of her mouth, sending shivers down her throat making the tingling inside her belly grow to a smoldering heat.

Jared broke the kiss leaving her breathless. "Let me put out your fire, Erica," he murmured sensually in her ear.

Every nerve in her body cried out to allow him to have his way. She wanted to quench the yearning he made her feel and knew Jared would be a wonderful lover, but…

Shaking her head, she closed her eyes as if she were in pain. "No, Jared. I can't."

A defeated groan could be heard deep in his throat. "You won't be sorry, Erica. I won't hurt you."

"I know, but…" She couldn't explain the fear in her. As much as she wanted him and loved the way he wanted her, she couldn't put aside the fear to allow herself to feel what he could allow her to experience.

Jared didn't press her. "I'll leave, Erica, if you want me to."

"No, I don't. Can't you stay, please?"

The brief look of pain crossed his features. "Yes, Erica. I'll stay."

The smell of burning bacon awoke Erica and she jumped out of bed and rushed down to the kitchen. Through the fog of burned grease and smoke, she could see Jared making a mess in the kitchen.

"What are you doing?" she asked.

He placed a tray on the table in front of her and looked as if he had defeated the Russian army single handedly. "Breakfast."

De was sitting in a high chair, trying to figure out how to get a banana in his mouth, but was becoming frustrated because he couldn't get his hands to work the way he wanted them to.

Erica picked up the baby and the bottle and placed De in the playpen nearby. Just as she was checking the diaper, Jared said, "I already changed him."

She couldn't complain. He had done a wonderful job at taking care of De, but that breakfast needed serious help. "Thank you. I must have slept hard. I hear anything from the speaker."

"I turned it off so you could get some rest. I know I kept you up."

He had washed his clothes and was now wearing them although they were filled with grease stains. Pulling a chair out for her to have a seat, he said, "Are you going to eat?"

"What made you cook breakfast?" she asked sitting down.

He sat on the other side of the breakfast nook table after fixing his plate. "I left my credit cards in my suitcase down in Miami and I didn't want to wake you up."

Staring at the almost burnt toast, over fried bacon, scorched eggs with cheese and the dry grits, she chuckled. "For a man who loves to eat, how can you possibly not know how to cook?"

He shrugged. "I was too busy trying to support my mother

rather than know what she did in the kitchen. Most times she brought home food from the places where she worked — restaurants, hotels, homes she cleaned to make ends meat and so forth. Once I was old enough all I was able to do was boil a mean pot of water."

Erica forced herself to eat the food knowing he had worked so hard to make it, not wanting to hurt his feelings. To get her mind off the taste, she asked, "Are you returning to Miami today?"

"No, I've booked a flight for tomorrow morning to California. I might swing back over to Miami if something comes up tonight there, but I doubt it." He was almost finished with his food. "Did you have any plans?"

"Nothing, except to hang around here with De."

"I take it Whitney's getting her monies worth this weekend?"

She flushed. "Whitney's activities aren't for me to discuss, Jared," she said, trying to keep the disgust out of her voice.

"Does her activities include Dakota Traylor?" he asked.

Frowning she asked, "How do you know about him?"

"He came to the office the other day when I was leaving, but that look on his face was too personal for business. That man was clearly jealous of me."

"And you know Dakota from your father?"

"Yes, he comes by when I'm visiting my mother to talk with my father, and on occasion him and I have spoken." He looked inquisitively at her. "He mentioned you."

Erica looked a little guilty. "I'm sure Whitney's told you about the relationship we had."

"Whitney told me something about the things you did in the past, and remarked on how much you've changed." Tilting his head to the side, he said, "You've changed a lot, Erica. The person Dakota describes doesn't come close to the person you are today."

"Yeah, but I still feel like I have the burden of my past on my shoulders, Jared. I was selfish spoiled rotten girl, who thought doing those things for her father could actually be good. I thought if I helped my father's evil cause he would love me more and respect me more, but in the end I learned that Eric Thompson only loves himself and money. He doesn't care who he hurts or who he uses. I think I'll hate myself forever for doing what I did to Dakota and Lyle. I don't think I'll ever forgive myself for what I helped my father do."

"Dakota has gotten over it. Lyle certainly holds no grudge. And the lies you told Whitney certainly doesn't bother her today considering where she is and what she is doing."

Huffing in exasperation, she said, "I don't want to even think about what she could be doing right now."

He pushed his plate away empty and sipped on his orange juice. "Can I ask you a personal question, Erica?"

Warily she nodded.

"Do you ever plan on having children? Starting a new life and family away from your sister?"

Looking longingly at De who was on his way to dreamland, she said, "I don't know. I don't think about that in my life right now."

"Will you work for your sister forever?"

Shaking her head. "I've wanted to get back to working and she's encouraged me, but I wouldn't know where to start looking."

"And working for me is out of the question?" he asked.

Avoiding his eyes, she said, "I don't think it's appropriate." "Why?"

"Because of…this. Our friendship."

He shrugged as if it were no big thing. "But it's only friendship.
I think you would make a perfect personal assistant until something better comes along. You know what I like, you already know how I work, and you'll be ready on a moments notice since I spend most of my free time around Whitney and with you."

Erica was fully aware their relationship would be no problem to him when he was conducting business, but it was her own mental stability that would be a problem to the relationship. She could keep their friendship in check, but knowing she would be around him more and more made it difficult to be able to keep her emotions out of the whole thing.

Although he had been looking for a new assistant for the past six months with his other one and decided to take a job in Orlando af ter getting married. "Maybe you should find someone else," she suggested. "I don't think I would make a great assistant for you Jared."

"Are you my friend, Erica?" he asked as if it meant a lot to him. "Yes, Jared, but-"

He cut her off. "And friends do help friends in need?" "You're using our friendship for selfish reasons," she pointed
out offended.

"I'm just making a point that to some degree you shouldn't be so selfish," he retaliated.

She started to argue more, but pursed her lips together in a muse. Maybe she was being selfish. "How long did you have to think this over?"

"All night actually. Especially as I drove here, but all night long
as I watched you sleep, I thought about how it would very convenient if I had you closer to me."

Suspiciously she asked, "Why? What is it of me you want?"

Indifferently he said, "Only friendship. Right Erica?" She didn't think she liked the way he was thinking. Jared
Parker had something up his sleeve and the scary part was that he was losing sleep over it. "So why didn't you sleep all night? I'm sure

you were exhausted."

"I was, but…I was rather uncomfortable if you must know." "Are you trying to talk about my bed?"

He shook his head. "I was talking about my body."

She didn't want to go into that subject and found something else to talk about, but in the back of her mind, she had to wonder what Jared was up to and why was he so determined to try to deepen their friendship. Any other guy would have given up on her a long time ago. Erica would take his job offer. She would find out what Jared was up to and see that he was just like all the other men. "I won't be able to take the position until next week. Whitney and I have already started looking for nannies and we've settled on a particular older woman, who we think we can have to take care of De."

"That's fine." He cleaned off their plates and looked down at his shirt.

"Why don't you go home to change and stop back by here before you leave out of town?" she suggested.

He had a look that clearly told her that wasn't his plans. Politely, he said, "I have a meeting to go to in town, and I want to get packed for my trip if you don't mind." For some reason he was stiff and distant. Going to the doorway of the kitchen, he stopped and looked back at her. "I had hoped coming here and showing you how much I missed you would…change things between us, Erica, but maybe…maybe I have to do more."

"What is it you want from me, Jared?"

He didn't answer that question, but there was a look of frustration in his eyes.

She watched as he let himself out and she wondered what was really on Jared's mind. Checking on De, she covered the baby up before going upstairs to her room. Jared had hung the bathrobe

on the back of the bathroom door and taken a shower. She must have been pretty tired or he was especially quiet when he got out of the bed.

Looking around the room, she checked to see if anything had been tampered with. It wasn't that she did not trust Jared. He wouldn't take anything, but he was up to something and she wanted to know if there was maybe a clue as to what he was up to.

At her desk, there was faint handwriting on the notepad. She noticed a piece of paper had been torn off. Checking her garbage, she saw nothing new in there, so she went into the bathroom to check the pockets of the bathrobe.

Inside was the paper from the stationary on the desk and Jared's handwriting of a California phone number. Picking up the phone, she called the number and hung up immediately when Jamison picked up the other line and said, "Thompson's residence, how may I help you?"

Her first reaction was to call Whitney and alert her, but Erica didn't have all the information, yet knowing that Jared was in connection with Eric Thompson was still enough to be cautious about.

Whitney didn't need the stress, so Erica decided to call someone who could help her. Lethal Heart.

* * * * *

Whitney had gone to her office and come right back to the hotel room. While at the office, she checked her messages. Erica had called a little after one on Friday to assure her everything was fine and not to worry about the baby. Although there was a weird inflection in her voice, she also mentioned they would really look into getting the nanny to start work by next week because Jared had offered her a job as his personal assistant.

"Whether or not I take the job, I still would like to get back to work. Call me tomorrow when you check in at the office again, because I really want to speak to you about Jared."

Whitney figured it was personal, but the edge in Erica's voice really piqued her attention, yet since her sister didn't seem as if there was anything to worry about, Whitney wasn't going to worry.

Dakota was still there and it was as if they had never left that hotel room over a year ago. He seemed to be relaxed although there were times when she would catch him staring at her deep in thought.

Saturday morning, she awoke to see him lying on the opposite end of the bed staring at her. Stretching contented, she sat up slightly and asked, "What time is it?"

"Eleven," he answered.

She allowed a yawn to escape. Last night had been marvelous lovemaking and she knew this experience would certainly go in her diary.

"I think we should talk, Whitney," he said bothered.

"What's to talk about, Dakota?" she asked imitating his stiffness and the relaxing again. "We're both getting what we wanted, aren't we? Is your conscious actually bothering you?" She knew that was a challenge to his carefree lifestyle.

"No, but this just seems too easy. What happens after this weekend between the two of us?"

"We go our separate ways. I keep my stock in your company and watch you make money for me, and you can do whatever you want in your life."

"And you wouldn't care?" he asked.

Lying, she said, "No, I wouldn't."

"And if I wanted more?"

Rolling her eyes heavenwards, she said, "There can't be anymore. My life is still complicated. I still have Eric trying to come after me."

"You think I would complicate things by being in the picture?"

"Dakota, I don't want a deeper relationship with anyone."

"Except of course Jared Parker, the meanest son of a bitch this side of the Mississippi," he sneered.

Whitney realized what he was after. He was interested in the relationship between Jared and her. "Jared's a good friend to me, Dakota."

Narrowing his eyes skeptically, he questioned, "What kind of friend?"

"You're jealous," she accused him.

He looked insulted. "I'm not jealous of that cold hearted bastard. I'm just inquiring on the depth of your relationship."

"Depth of relationship? Does it matter what our relationship is about?"

"It matters if you're going to crawl out of bed with me and go right back to bed with him. The fact that I'm preparing you to be with him matters a whole hell of a lot."

It was her turn to get a little perturb. "Is that the type of woman
you think I am, Dakota?"

He was aware of her upset, but obviously it meant little to him. "If this was a year ago and I was bedding some sweet innocent girl who didn't know anything and was scared to even think about laying with a man, then maybe I would think you wouldn't be that type of girl. Yet the more I spend time with you Whitney, the angrier I'm becoming because I know you aren't that sweet innocent girl who I made love to. You've changed."

She tightened herself not wanting him to see how much his words had hurt her. "I've matured a lot, Dakota. I've grown a lot in the past year. A lot of things have come into my life that have made me different, but I'm still that woman you knew." Getting out the bed she drew the sheet around her and went into the bathroom slamming the door behind her.

*   *   *   *   *

Dakota watched her leave the bedroom and enclosed herself into the bathroom. Popping a peanut in his mouth, he stared back at the spot she had just left and wondered if his simmering for the past two hours about his feelings for Whitney had any affect on his callous words to her.

He thought by now she would just open up to him and profess her love; say she didn't want this weekend to end. Dammit, at least once she could have admitted her feelings for him in a little way. How could a woman make love like there was no tomorrow and still remain noncommittal to him? Unless she had a true love – A true love like that bastard Jared Parker.

The more he thought about the angrier he became until her beautiful eyes opened and she gifted him with that smile that tore his heart to pieces because he knew in less than a day she would be gifting that smile on someone else.

Hell yes he was jealous and very angry with himself, because he knew that Whitney Canton would never be out of his system. Never in his life would he have imagined that he would be hung up over his ex-wife.

Any other woman he didn't give a damn about. Any other woman he wouldn't care if she dated a million men other than him, but this was Whitney. This was the woman who had somehow gotten under his thick skin and entwined herself in the strings of his heart. He realized now that he had never loved Erica this much. He was just pissed that he hadn't had his way with her, but even after he had taken Whitney he found his body still couldn't get enough of this woman.

To make it worse, it wasn't just sex with Whitney. She made his body experience a spiritual pleasure he had never experience with anyone else.

Some how he had to get her to bind herself to him again. As her husband, he could have her all to himself. As her husband, he could have more time to make her love him.

The door to the bathroom opened unexpectedly and Whitney came out fully dressed.

"Where do you think you're going, Whitney?" he asked standing up bare as the day he was born.

His nakedness certainly caught her eye and she smiled wickedly, but caught herself and became that cold hard bitch he had just called her in so many words. Her facial expression was searing and detached.

When she spoke, he could tell whatever he had said had pissed her the fuck off. There was enough iciness in her voice to make the room grow very cold. "As much as I would love to stay and listen to you tell me how much I've changed, Dakota, I think our agreement we have has been fulfilled by you and we don't need to go on."

Dakota bit his tongue fighting the urge to take the words back. Why should he when it wouldn't matter? She was just looking for an excuse to leave him - To get the hell away from him. He cursed his own weakness for her for allowing himself to be used by her.

"Why'd you make me?" he asked bitterly.

Grabbing her coat and purse, she said, "It's a free country Dakota. I didn't make you do anything you didn't want to do."

"Why me? Why did you choose me?" he demanded to know.

Flippantly she said, "I told you Thursday, I was comfortable with you."

Turning his back to her, he said, "I hope to hell you're done with using me, Whitney. I hope to hell you stay the fuck away this time."

"Was that your objective? To keep me away?"

Lying, he sneered over his shoulder, "Yeah, is it working? Will I have to deal with you anymore other than business?"

Quietly, she said, "No, Dakota. You've shown me this wasn't a good idea to begin with. This place is free until Sunday. Leave when you feel like it."

When he heard the front door close, he slumped on the bed and ran a frustrated hand through his hair thinking, 'What have I done?'

Gripping the steering column trying to maintain her control, Whitney wasn't sure what she wanted to do. Scream her frustrations was a good thought, but she would lose control of the wheel and run off the road.

The distraction of her pager going off was perfect and she answered the nine-one-one at her office.

By five o'clock she was mentally tired and ready to go home, but entering her home, she could sense there was something not right by the emergency bags at the doorway.

"Whitney! I'm so glad you're home!" Erica said rushing down the stairs wringing her fingers nervously.

"What's going on?"

Erica burst into tears, which made Whitney worry more.

Repeating her question, Whitney also asked, "Is it De?"

Shaking her head, Erica sobbed, "It's Jared. I just got off the phone with Lethal and he confirmed that Jared's been taking flights for the past year to California."

"Why does that upset you? He's been exploring some investment options."

"Is that what that lying pig told you?!" Erica sneered vehemently.

Whitney was taken aback by Erica's upset over Jared. "What made you call Lethal?"

"Jared came over last night and when he left this morning, he forgot to take this out of the robe pocket he wore." Erica handed Whitney a piece of paper from her own stationary, but with Jared's handwriting of a California area coded number. "When I called it, Jamison answered announcing Eric's residence."

Whitney gasped, "No!"

"Yes!" Erica retaliated. "He's got to be the one spying for Eric all this time."

"But how? Does Lethal know? I mean he's the one that referred Jared to you. I trust Lethal."

"He's trying to find that out, but he told me not to alert you until
we have all the facts." Angrily with gritted teeth, Erica said, "Lethal

doesn't want to believe Jared could be the one funding Eric's campaign to sabotage Canton Industries and trying to kill you!"

"I don't want to believe it either. When did he say he would call back?" Erica asked.

"He's checking on Jared's cell phone records and he has a man out in California. How can we not believe it could be Jared?" "Erica, I think you're just upset and you're allowing your feelings not to see that it can't be Jared."

"He's a man, Whitney. They will stick together."

"I don't believe that about Jared. He's been nothing but on our side from the get go."

"Obviously your feelings for Dakota are getting in the way of your safety," Erica said.

Whitney refuted, "That's not true, Erica!" She began very offended by the reference. "My minds clear about Jared and I think you're just upset over the fact that you can't sort out your feelings for him."

"Don't you see!" Erica exclaimed. "Maybe it was my intuition telling me not to trust him."

"Maybe you're just trying to find a way to avoid what you need to face."

Throwing her hands up in exasperation, Erica said, "My past has nothing to do with this deceit that's going on."

Whitney huffed in frustration. "I don't want to believe what you're trying to tell me, Erica, but I was coming home anyway because there was a fire at the office again. I spoke to the Lieutenant and he said we should probably get out the house as soon as possible."

The phone rung and Erica rushed over to pick it up. Pushing the speakerphone, Lethal's voice came over the line as Erica let him know Whitney was there.

"What did you find out, Lethal?" Whitney questioned.

"Too much," he said with a lot of disappointment in his voice. "He's been making phone calls to California for the past year along with his flight schedule. That number in particular that Erica gave me has been called extensively in the past six months to and from his cell phone. Judging by the lengths of the conversation he had to have been speaking to Eric personally."

Erica whined a frantic sob.

Whitney sat down to gather herself. "Do you think what Erica thinks, Lethal?"

He was quiet for just a moment, and then answered with a poisonous venom to his voice, "I don't want to, Whitney and that son of a bitch better have a damn good reason before I break every bone in his body with my bare hands."

"What about the flight?!" Erica demanded to know.

"I have an agent at the airport waiting for Jared to land tomorrow morning. We found out also that he uses the same car company every time he's in California and that there's been pick ups at the address that phone number goes to. Eric's got a few warrants for arrest and I'm going to light some fires just to see if I can find out more or get this address in the hands of someone who could round him in."

Whitney asked, "What do you suggest that we do on this end?"

Erica nudged Whitney. "Tell him about the fire, Whit." "What fire?" Lethal asked.

Infuriated, Whitney explained, "There was a fire on the first floor of the building deliberately set in the room right below the server for my company. It was more like an explosion that occurred. It's a good thing that I had your company fire seal that room a month ago or we would have lost some very important information, but that side of the building will have to be closed for a long period of time and that's crunching into my profits."

"This is no time to discuss business," Erica said. "I'm going to wrap up De so we can get to a hotel."

Lethal agreed. "You better go, Whitney. Leave your phone on so I can keep in touch and make sure you check in on my line when you're settled for the night."

"Thank you, Lethal," Whitney said and hung up.

Erica rushed out the room, while Whitney grabbed a few files out her desk and stuffed them in her briefcase. Just as Erica came downstairs with De, a loud explosion startled both of them and sent the entire household alarms off. Whitney screamed for Erica, who confirmed her safety with the baby in the front foyer. They met in the living room and Whitney accessed the panel that hid the security

cameras. Erica pointed to the monitor that patrolled the front gate, which was now mangled, from the explosion.

"Get to the car!" Whitney ordered, going for the foyer to grab all the bags. Erica was going to the garage using the kitchen exit instead of going out the front door.

Passing Erica her phone and instructing her to call the police, Whitney had to use the manual pulley in order to open the garage since the sensors shut down with the alarms going off. Once the doors were up and Erica had the bags in the van they used for emergencies, Whitney took De who was crying.

"Get in the passenger side and I'll put him in the seat," she ordered her sister.

Erica turned to go around the van but let out a shrill of terror before she passed out at Whitney's feet. Looking in the direction that Erica had been headed in, she was a bit startled to see Dakota standing at the doorway of the garage looking not at all pleased at

Erica's unconscious body.

"What are you doing here?! How did you know where I lived?" Whitney demanded to know.

He looked up at her with an even deeper frown as if she was the one who should be explaining things. "I made Nate give me your address because I don't think we finished talking this morning. What the hell is going on around here? As soon as I pulled up the gate exploded!"

Holding De close to her chest protectively as Dakota stepped over Erica's body coming toward Whitney, she said, "This isn't the time or the place. Like I said before my life is complicated Dakota. Eric's out for vengeance."

"Is he out to kill you?"

"I don't know what he's trying to do, but he's scaring us. Did you see anyone around, Dakota?"

"No, Whitney."

He looked down at the baby who was grasping Whitney jacket for dear life. "What is she doing here?!" he demanded to know.

She could hear sirens in the distance, but she still didn't feel safe at the house. Going around the van as he followed her, she hurriedly put De in his seat quickly and closed the door so the tinted windows covered the baby from Dakota's perceptive eyes.

"You might as well know now, she's my sister, Dakota. I will swear that I didn't know she was or that she had anything to do with you when we met, but we've just recently come together and bonded especially during my pregnancy." She walked around him hurriedly back to Erica and shook her violently.

Erica moaned.

"Get up!" Whitney demanded.

Slowly, in a daze Erica opened her eyes, and first she locked eyes with Whitney to show great relief.

"Is this all? Is this why you were afraid of being with me?" Dakota demanded.

Erica screeched in fear. Whitney helped her sister up straining from Erica's terrified condition putting all the effort on Whitney. "This isn't the time, Dakota." Once she got Erica into the passenger side she rushed over to the driver's side.

Just as she was about to get in, Dakota grabbed her arm. "Why didn't you tell me you had a baby?! Is that the relationship between you and Jared?"

Trying to wrench away from him, she cried, "You don't know anything about my baby or me, Dakota! Just leave it be."

"Leave it be?! Why couldn't you tell me the truth about everything?" he demanded.

Angrily Whitney finally snatched away from him vehemently sneering, "So Eric could use you again? You think I wanted that? And what about my father, Dakota? Did you forget he still has yet to forgive you for your part in destroying his life and his company? Just face the facts! We will never be able to be together. NEVER! Now leave me alone! I don't love you! I don't want you in my life! I never want to see your face again."

Obviously her words were enough to get him to back off, because he allowed her to get in the van and moved aside as she took off using the back driveway to get off the property.

Erica handed Whitney a Kleenex because unknowingly Whitney had begun to cry. "It wouldn't have worked, Whitney," Erica said feeling her sister's upset. "Do you think he'll ever find out about De?"

"I don't think Dakota Traylor will ever want to speak to me ever again, Erica," Whitney said.

"And if he does try? Will you tell him?" Erica asked hopefully.

Whitney cut her sister a hard glare and sarcastically said taking that familiar ghetto tone Erica took every once in a while, "Yeah sure, Erica. If I ever see Dakota Traylor again, I'll make certain I tell him he's my baby Daddy."

They checked in the St. Royal's penthouse suite under a different name. With the St. Royal being one of the Bellini owned hotels, it was easy to have Kenneth make private arrangements for her and he didn't mind doing so at so late of an hour.

Once they were settled, Erica insisted to go and speak with the Lieutenant in Whitney's place. "You need your rest," Erica said. "I'll call you every hour on the hour if you want."

Whitney wanted that. Through the night she found out Lethal had caught a flight from Detroit with a list of the area bomb experts who could have had the expertise to pull off the explosions at her office and home. She also found out, shortly after they left the house, that several charges were activated at the house, which was consumed in fire. What the fire didn't destroy, water damage was inevitable.

Despair set in fast for Whitney. She loved that house, but most importantly, Eric was endangering her son's life. If something happened to Whitney, De would grow up never really knowing his father.

When Erica came in to crash on the couch at six in the morning, Whitney took the opportunity to get down to the hotel's workout room. For two hours she overextended herself, but although her muscles cried out from the stress, her mind was like a hyper child never wanting to rest.

Arriving back at the room, she was surprised to see Erica up and about.

"You should be sleeping," Whitney scolded.

"Just like you should have been last night?" Erica questioned with sarcasm.

Whitney chuckled guiltily. "So what's new?"

"Last I heard from Lethal was that he was waiting for California time to get in touch with his man, who started following Jared as soon as he touched ground at the airport."

The sadness in Erica's face was evident. Whitney was very sure Erica had been so close to falling for Jared and trusting him. "I think we are making a big thing out of this, Erica. I mean if you really think about it, why would he offer you a job, if he has no intentions of employing you."

"One of his many tactics to get in my pants," Erica said as if she were some kind of sleuth figuring out the biggest crime of the century.

Whitney's eyebrows shot up in bewilderment as she looked at her sister. "Where did you get that ridiculous philosophy, Erica?"

"Oh come off it, Whitney. You don't think he's capable of saying anything just to get into my pants?"

"I think the need for psychiatric help could definitely do you some good right about now, Erica."

Angrily Erica said, "He's been deceiving us for the past year, Whit? How can you take his side?"

"Because I won't believe it until someone shows me some proof. I don't feel I'm taking any side. Not until I know for sure, but you've been so quick to judge him Erica when you don't really know the truth."

Stubbornly, Erica huffed, "Action speaks louder than words."

"Well I'm going with my gut until someone proves to me something different."

Snorting, Erica said in a melodious voice, "Seems to me, following your gut ain't telling you to do the right thing anyways."

Offended, Whitney asked, "What's that suppose to mean?"

"It means, if you hadn't followed your gut feelings you wouldn't have had your legs spread for the past days."

Whitney gasped at her sister's vulgar innuendo. "Just because-" Before she could scream at her sister for her remarks, there was a loud knock at door.

They both gasped in fright and moved closer together terrified at who could be knocking at the door.

"Whitney, I know you're in there!" Dakota bellowed on the other side of the door.

The sisters looked at each other confused.

"How did he know I was here?"

Erica blushed. "W-Well, I sort of thought I was doing you a favor. I didn't know he was still in the room."

"What are you talking about Erica?"

"I thought since all our things were gone in the fire, you'd want the clothes you left in the company's hotel room. So I called down while you were in the workout room and instructed the staff to have them bring up your things. I thought he would be gone by now."

Whitney rolled her eyes around in immense frustration. "How could you, Erica?!"

"I didn't know."

Dakota knocked harder on the door. "Whitney, you can't avoid talking to me!"

"Get away from my door!" Whitney cried.

He yelled some more, but Whitney was too busy glaring at Erica. "You did this on purpose. Now send him away!"

Erica looked terrified. "You don't expect me to talk to him, Whit. Plus you promised. You promised to speak to him."

De started crying from being awakened by the noise.

Whitney started to go get the baby, but Erica stood in her way.

"You get the door, I'll get the baby," Erica ordered and before Whitney could agree upon it, Erica rushed in the bedroom and locked the door behind her.

Whitney huffed as she swung open the door to catch Dakota in mid swing of another round of pounding. "Why are you stalking me, Dakota?"

He nudged past her without being offered a formal acquaintance of entrance. "I don't stalk, but we still have a lot to talk about, Whitney. I don't think this is over and that silly attempt you made to get me to stop coming after you was useless."

"I can see that," she said.

"I don't care about the baby, Whitney. I still want to marry you and if I have to prove to your father, I'll treat you right, I will. I'll do whatever it takes to get his forgiveness for the past mistakes I made in my life. If I have to fight Jared for the right to have you as my wife, then I will!"

"You'll fight Jared for what?"

"Dammit Whitney, I love you. Can't you see that?"

"You loved Erica too," she said defensively.

"Not like this. It's not the same and you're using something else to throw in my face to get away from the truth you're trying to hide from. Eric will never use me again and you know this. I'll love

your son just like he was my own. You have no more excuses. I want the real answers, Whitney. I want to know why won't you let us be together?"

At the top of her lungs, she yelled, "You want answers? Fine Dakota, I'll give you answers. My baby is not Jared's son, he's yours!"

Taken aback by this statement his voice became very soft. "H-How long did you know about this?"

"Three months after Chicago," she said, calming down a little. "You're the only man I've ever been with Dakota."

"Why didn't you tell me sooner?"

"A baby would have complicated your life and…" Her voice faltered a bit, but upon clearing it and gathering her courage, she said, "And our relationship."

"What relationship, Whitney? How was I suppose to know you had gotten pregnant?" he asked strained. "You said you didn't want anything to do with me. You didn't want me involved in your life. You made up your own complications. I figured if things had gotten to that point there was nothing to stop you from aborting the baby."

"I thought about it," she admitted honestly. "I seriously thought about it, Dakota, but…" Taking a deep breath. "I didn't think someone else should pay for the mistakes I've made."

He looked truly hurt by her words. "I was a mistake?"

Shaking her head she decided to put all her cards on the table. "I made the mistake in allowing myself to be selfish and not giving you a second chance. I know the person my father described and the man I knew were two different people. If Erica could change, I knew the same was true for you. I did love you, Dakota, but I was scared of my feelings and what I would sacrifice if I allowed them to come to the surface. I was scared of loving you because I felt I would be sacrificing something."

"But now?" he asked.

Stepping forward to him bravely. "You're right. I made up the complications. I could be with you and you would be able to be a great father to our son."

He was overwhelmed with emotions. "Our son? Can I see him?"

Whitney heard the bedroom door unlock and knew Erica had been listening to the whole conversation. Going into the room, Erica

had the boy held out and waiting for Whitney. Shooting her sister an "I'll get you back later" glare, Whitney took the wiggling boy who cooed in happiness to see his mother.

Going back to the front room, Dakota immediately looked over the boy. De didn't cry at the sight of a stranger. They looked at each other with the same colored eyes and Whitney smiled at the adoration on Dakota's face.

"Was it bad?" he asked her concerned.

She flushed honored he was worried over her health initially. That meant so much to her. "I think I put a few roots on you during labor, but once it was over and I saw how beautiful he was, it all didn't matter. I loved him." She kissed De's cheek lovingly.

Dakota actually had the nerve to look a little jealous. "Can I hold him?" he asked her tenderly.

She carefully passed the vivacious child over to Dakota just a little apprehensive as Dakota weighed him in his thick powerful arms and held the baby as if the child would break.

"Thank you," he said, after gazing at the child for a long moment.

"For what?"

"For giving me this wonderful baby."

Her heart sang with joy.

Erica tried to hear more, but she knew Whitney was purposely keeping her voice low. Biting her lip, she cracked the door open and smiled seeing Dakota hold De with so much pride and love in his beautiful eyes. Jealousy didn't even enter her heart - Only joy that her sister would be so happy with Dakota.

Longingly, she closed the door to give the new family a chance to be together alone. Erica thought about Jared, but for the hundredth time bit her lip not wanting to even dream about what she knew would never be. Why did he have to be the one who was betrayed them?

"What?!" Whitney screamed. "That gives you no rights at all, Dakota!"

Forgetting her fear of Dakota, Erica rushed out the room to see what was Whitney so angry about.

"He's my son too, Whitney, and I deserve to be apart of his life!" Dakota refuted, not even paying attention to Erica's presence in the room.

Butting in on the argument, presuming that Dakota wanted parental rights, Erica said, "But I thought that's what you wanted, Whitney. You didn't think he would ever find out that De was his son when you named the boy after his father."

Whitney narrowed her eyes at her sister and Dakota looked proud.

"This isn't about parental rights, Erica," Whitney sneered. "He wants me to marry him or he threatened to take De away!"

"So you'll marry him," Erica said simply.

"If he wanted to marry me, he could have just asked me!" Whitney cried insulted.

Dakota looked shocked as if the answer couldn't have come to him in a million years. "So you'll marry me?"

"You haven't asked me properly," Whitney pouted.

Dakota got ready to kneel, but hesitated because he still had the wiggling De in his arms. Erica rushed over and took the baby and then quickly stepped away wishing she had a camera as Dakota got on one knee and took Whitney's hand.

A voice cleared at the doorway and Whitney's shoulders slumped as Lethal's presence ruined the moment.

"Was I interrupting something?" he asked innocently, coming in the room giving Dakota the once over apprehensively.

"No, Lethal," Whitney said with disappointment. "This is Dakota-"

"I know who that is, Ms. Canton. I've been watching the bastard long enough to know who he is."

"I take it since you're not in a good mood, you don't have anything to tell me," Whitney said.

"Oh I have something to tell you alright." Lethal looked Dakota up and down as Dakota stood to do the same for Lethal. With long strides, Lethal entered the room, closing the door behind him and plopping a file on the table in front of the couch. As usual he wore tight black jeans and a black silk shirt along with his black Stetson, which he took off as he came in.

Erica still thought he was sexy as all get out, but it was hard trying to picture herself with him when there was too much of Jared on her mind.

Lethal proclaimed, "We know who your bomber is, we just don't know where he's at."

Erica picked up the file and leafed through it. "So we're safe right now?"

"No," Lethal said disgruntled. "Eric's still out there going under a different name, but when I passed his name around to a couple of contacts in the government, I received returned calls from the DEA, ATF, FBI and the IRS."

Dakota whistled. "That's almost the whole damn alphabet."

"That's almost the whole damn government, you could say and they all wanted to know why the fuck was I looking for their criminal. They all want their hands on him for different reasons."

"Like what?" Whitney asked frightened.

In a very deadly serious tone, Lethal said, "Due to my security level with the United States government, I'm unable to release that information."

"So we should leave Florida?" Erica asked.

"No." He tossed his Stetson on the table and rubbed his eyes in frustration. "I've already fixed the problem of your whereabouts, Ms. Canton."

"How?"

"As we speak the press is getting a release about the body of Whitney Canton, being found in the fire at her home." He looked over at Erica. "Your body and the baby's body have yet to be recovered."

"Will it be believable? The bomber was somewhere close last night," Whitney pointed out. "Which is why he retaliated against the house, right?"

"It is assumed you were still in the house, because both of your vehicles are still there. The van was always kept in the back garage for emergencies," Lethal explained. He would know because he had made the suggestion to do this. "The bomber must have assumed you two were in the house and when the police were called he decided to finish the house up before they came."

"But I was there last night and I didn't see anyone," Dakota said.

Lethal gave him a wary look. "When were you there?"

"We left him at the house as we took off from it," Erica said.

"When did you arrive?" Lethal asked Dakota.

"I heard the explosion from the main street and when I pulled up I saw the gate ruined," Dakota answered not at all nervous about the suspicious glare Lethal caste his way. "I ran inside the gate forgetting my safety trying to find what the hell was going on and there were other matters on my mind. Although…" His voice trailed off, as he was deep in thought. "When I went by to ask Nate about the address, he was adamant about me not going over there. He said I should wait to speak to you."

"Why?" Whitney asked.

"I don't know," Dakota said pretty bothered the more he thought about it.

"That's it!" Lethal said. "That's the connection I've been looking for."

"What connection?" Whitney asked completely perplexed and scared.

Erica wanted to go to her sister and comfort her, but she didn't want to get to close to Dakota. Even though she knew he wouldn't hurt her while Whitney was present, she didn't want to call out too much attention to herself to him.

"I gathered all the information I was given from each agency, but of course none would give me in-depth details about their specific

reasons for wanting Eric. And for the life of me I was trying to figure out how the hell did Jared end up in all this bullshit," Lethal said angrily yet with a sense of relief.

Erica looked over at Whitney and then asked Lethal, "So what's Jared's involvement?"

"Due to my security level with the United States government, I'm unable to release that information," Lethal said in that same deadly serious tone. "But I can let you know when I met Jared in prison, he has always been the type of guy that does right by people. He may be an unemotional asshole, but he's true to his word and his friends. He did some work for the government which in turn hired me to help him out with his case."

Curiously, Erica asked, "What work for the government?"

"Due to my security level with the United States government, I'm unable to release that information," Lethal said repeated like a robot.

Erica was getting really tired of hearing that.

Frustrated, Whitney said, "So when will we find out if we should trust Jared?"

"Trust no one right now, Whitney. You're dead remember?"

"But he knew I was alive?" Whitney said to Lethal pointing to Dakota.

"That's because you had your bags removed from the hotel room and delivered up here. I figured it out without any assistance and I was at the house and saw you leave. Obviously no one else saw you leave."

Whitney glared over at Erica knowingly.

"And I ordered the delivery. If anyone has any questions, they would just assume I was gathering the last of your items," Erica said defensively.

"But you said the bomber had to be in the vicinity," Whitney said to Lethal.

"Yet not close enough to see you leave the house. From the way the bomb was built, the detonation could have taken place in the five-mile radius," Lethal pointed out. "That would give you time to leave the premises before he got there to see what his bomb had destroyed and to assume that you were thinking to stay inside of the house for safety. We found footsteps around the place to show he

had just recently planted the bombs and drove away from the scene before police and fire arrived." He looked over at Dakota. "We also saw that you were there in a different car and the footsteps didn't match up to you."

"I didn't do anything," Dakota said insulted that he was being accused.

"Trust me, if you were, you wouldn't have been alive in this room for this long," Lethal said with a venomous look in his eyes. "But now that I figured out how all this shit got started, I think it's best you
stay here with Whitney. Have you had any other contacts with anyone else since leaving the house?"

Dakota shook his head. "Like I said, I was too concerned over other matters to take notice what was really going on."

"Good!" Lethal smiled wickedly. "I think I have a plan to draw Eric out of hiding."

"What?" Whitney, Erica, and Dakota said simultaneously.

"Due to my security-"

"Lethal!" They all cried cutting him off.

"But I thought Eric would be in California now?" Erica said. "Especially since Jared's flying out there this morning, right?"

"Eric may be, but knowing that Whitney's dead will have him on a flight to Tampa ASAP," Lethal speculated and walked up to Erica with that wicked look in his eyes. "And you're going to help me catch that bastard."

"I am?" Erica asked, holding De closely, her voice a little shaky. "What am I going to do?"

Lethal lifted his Stetson and set it back on his head in a cool calculating cocky manner. "Set a trap for your father."

Erica looked over at Lethal warily. She was terrified at the thought of facing Eric, but this was the only way to save Whitney and Erica would do anything to save her sister and De. If Eric got his hands on the little boy, it could mean trouble for the Canton Industries again.

"We're here," Lethal said, pulling up in front of a gray building with no name on the front of it. He escorted her inside after entering a security code to unlock the doors and down a dim lighted hallway. After scanning his hand for identification, the door opened to a brightly-lit tan conference room. A woman of lithe stature stood up from the end of the conference table looking very disgruntled. Her black eyes seem to size Erica up quickly leaving a murky shudder down Erica's spine.

"This is your bait?" the woman asked Lethal in a sneer. Dress in a tight leather black outfit, the woman's shoulder length hair was swept up in a super taunt ponytail. She wore no jewelry or makeup, but she was beautifully exotic looking as she walked up to Erica. The woman had to have stood at least five foot four, but the heels on her knee high leather boots were about four inches to give her added height.   "This is his daughter," Lethal said proudly.

Again the woman sized Erica up. "This is little Erica Thompson." She smirked with malevolence. "Oh this is too sweet. She still stuck on you?"

Becoming insulted that the woman was talking over her head as if Erica weren't there; she spoke up, saying, "Why don't you ask me?"

The woman glared at her viciously. "Because I was speaking to my brother."

Lethal stood next to Erica. "Erica, meet my sister, Onyx Heart, a queen of bitches."

"I'm not stuck on your brother…anymore," Erica said knowingly.

"Oh yeah," Onyx snorted. "You got the hots for Blankman."

Erica frowned up at Lethal who explained, "That's her nickname for Jared." He winked with assurance at her before addressing his sister. "You find out anything."

Onyx went back over to where she was previously sitting and put on a telephone headset. "Del was in Cali watching Blankman the whole time. He met up with Eric's lawyer who gave him a package. DEA was all over their asses so Del didn't step in."

Lethal growled, "Del wouldn't step in."

"In any case," Onyx said ignoring her brother's agitation, "Jared promptly got back on the plane and is due to arrive in Florida with the package in…" She checked her watch. "An hour."

"Does he know about the fire?" Lethal asked.

Shrugging, Onyx said, "I don't know." Reaching under her chair, she put a silver case on the table. "Here's the stuff you called me about. You want me to rig her?"

"I think she'd be more comfortable with you," Lethal said looking back at Erica who shook her head in disagreement. "You want me to stay?"

"I want you to tell me what is going on first," Erica demanded.

"Once Jared gets in town, he's going to try to find you immediately if I know the bastard. Eric will most likely either convince him to let him see you too or follow Jared until he finds you. Once we draw Eric out, we'll catch him."

Erica looked terrified. "You don't think he might hurt me?"

"Of course not. You're his daughter. Getting you back to do what he wants is his goal. You're all he's got," Lethal said.

Shaking her head, she said, "No Lethal. I won't meet with him…I can't!" Her frustration was evident on her face.

"All you have to do is get the truth out of him, Erica. You can do this. You can show him you're stronger than him and get to him before he gets to the truth about Whitney. We're so close to catching his bomber and all his other contacts and funding," Lethal said. "Erica, you've come this far. You've changed so much. Eric can't hurt you or use you anymore. You're strong enough to face him."

Erica thought about his words and she knew he was right. Plus she did want to help Whitney in anyway possible. "What do I have to do?"

Lethal opened the case to show the communication equipment. "We're going to wire you. Your conversations will be taped. As soon as Jared lands, you're going to call his cell phone from here and tell him to meet you at the marina. You're going to let him know you have the baby and you're scared."

"But I am scared!" Erica agreed. "Do I really have to have De with me?" She had left De at the hotel with Whitney and Dakota.

Lethal answered, "No, we'll get around that. Don't worry. If my assumptions are true, Eric will show his face once a location to meet you is confirmed or he'll follow Jared to the marina."

"And then?" Erica asked.

"That's when you'll get your father to admit all that he's done and his future intentions."

Erica took a deep breath. She could do this if she didn't think about the fact that Jared was involved in all this. How could he do this to her?! "What about Jared?"

With toxin in his voice, Lethal growled, "Don't worry, I'll take care of him personally."

She heard his knuckles crack as his bawled his fist up and she prayed Lethal wouldn't kill Jared.

* *   *   *   *

"Stop squirming," Onyx snapped in her ear.

"How can you tell?" Erica asked.

"Because your damn clothes are rubbing up against the mike," Onyx sneered.

Erica really didn't like this woman, but Lethal was monitoring at a different location and needed Onyx to sit at the office and transmit what was going on. They gave Erica a car with a tracking device attached. She was to drive to the marina, use the code to get into the loft and call Jared from there - all the while pretending she had a baby in the backseat.

No one was at the offices when she arrived and rightly so. It was late Sunday afternoon and usually only Jared could be found at the marina. Soon as she entered the loft, she notified Onyx of her location.

"Do I make the call now?" Erica asked.

"Hold on for a second. Let me confirm with Lethal," Onyx said.

While Erica waited she noticed the door to Jared's bedroom was cracked and thought this was odd since he always kept it locked when she was there. As long as she had lived in his loft, she had never once entered his bedroom.

Just as she was about to peak inside, filled with curiosity, Onyx came back in her ear startling her.

"Lethal said to call," Onyx ordered. "Jared's father met him at the airport and he's just finding out about the fire."

Going over to the phone house, she dialed Jared's cell phone number and took a deep breath.

Jared answered his line in a calm cool nature even though she was sure he had Caller ID and could see where she was calling. "Jared speaking."

"Jared, this is Erica," she said nervously.

"How long have you been there?" he asked his tone clearly piqued, but he was ever so cool as if he didn't want anyone else to know exactly whom he was speaking to. "I just got here. Can you come here?"

In the background she heard a male voice ask, "Who is that?"

Jared ignored the voice in the background and said, "Can you stay there for a while?"

Knowing the urgency to get this over with, she said, "No, I'm scared, Jared. I've got the baby and I don't know where to go." She hated lying. In the past this wouldn't have bothered her, but now…Lethal was right. She was different. Even though she hated Jared for his deceit she couldn't take doing something in return to get him back.

"Stay there," he insisted. "I'll be there soon. Don't talk to anyone else." The line clicked.

She hung up the phone and sat down on the couch trying to feel better about what she was doing. Nervously, she bit her nails and decided to keep her mind off what was going on.

"Stop biting your nails," Onyx said in her ear, but her tone of voice wasn't so hard.

"How'd you know what I was doing?" Erica said.

"It's in your nature," Onyx said. "Lethal say's I have a way of seeing things without being there. Isn't that the weirdest thing to say?"

"Not if it's true."

Onyx chortled. "You did alright, lady. They're in route to your location according to Lethal, so sit tight."

*   *   *   *   *

Pacing back and forth, Whitney fretted to herself. Dakota was nothing but calm and that helped because De was becoming upset by his mother's anxiety.

"I think you should sit down," Dakota said.

"I can't sit, when my sister's out there risking her life for me. I don't think I could stand to lose someone so close to me again when I'm not around."

"Ruining a very good carpet with your pacing is not going to make things better," Dakota teased.

She stopped her pacing suddenly and looked at Dakota thoughtfully. "You should know how I feel, since you almost lost Armando a year ago. I know knowing he was lost at sea must have been hard on you. Did you think he was dead like everyone else thought?"

He corrected her. "Everyone except his aunt. She insisted on Dalton keeping up the search until a body was found."

"Do you think he would have died if they hadn't kept up the search?" Whitney asked.

"If I know Armando, he would have eventually found a way to get off that deserted island he was stranded on." Dakota set his son in the playpen and returned to the couch. "He lived. That's the important aspect of it all and so will Erica. We just have to wait."

Huffing in aggravation, she said, "I hate waiting for anything."

"If you leave to help her, you'll get her in even more trouble," he warned.

"And you actually care about that?" she asked incredulously. "I care that she means a lot to you obviously and your happiness is important to me."

Whitney instantly stopped her pacing and smiled wondrously at him. "So you have no hard feelings for Erica? I mean she was just like you, just a pawn in Eric's game. Even more so because he was her father."

Tightly, Dakota said, "Let's just say I understand her position and I forgive her, although it's taking me a while to forget. Don't press me, Whitney."

"So having her as my maid of honor won't be a problem?" she asked, sitting in his lap wrapping her arms around his neck.

There was a strained look on Dakota's face, but she tenderly kissed that away feeling his need for her grow underneath her thigh.

"As long as I have you, Whitney, I don't give a damn who you have in the wedding," he said before kissing her deeply.

                    *   *   *   *   *

"What if he wants to see the baby?" Erica said, looking at the baby car seat with the doll covered up.

"Tell him the baby's asleep," Onyx said as if it were obvious. "That thing is real enough to fool people from a distance."

Erica looked back at the doorway of the bedroom. "Maybe I'll just lay the doll down in the bed and make it look like it's sleeping."

Indifferently, Onyx said, "That sounds like a good idea. I'll check back with you in a moment."

Getting up from the couch, she walked to the doorway of the bedroom door. Slowly opening up the door as if Jared would jump out at her, she could barely see what was in the room. Finding a light switch, she turned it on and gasped at what her eyes beheld.

"What's wrong?" Onyx asked in her ear.

"H-His room. I'm in his room," she said too amazed to move.

"What do you see?" Onyx questioned with curiosity.

"I don't think I'm suppose to see this side of Jared," Erica said amazed.

Onyx chortled amused. "I take it you didn't know this side of Jared?"

Erica looked around the room dumbfounded. "I don't think I want to know this side of Jared."

"He's not as spooky as it seems," Onyx said with assurance. "When you think about, it's actually quite erotic."

Erica turned off the light and closed the door behind her. "Well, I don't plan to know him anymore than I already do. He's a back stabbing traitorous animal."

"Never judge a book by its cover," Onyx said simply. "You might be amazed at what you read."

Snorting in disbelief, Erica said, "I don't want to touch Jared's cover and judging by that room, I know for sure, I don't want to be in his presence any longer than I have to."

"Scared?" Onyx questioned.

Lying, Erica said flatly, "No, he's just a man."

"I hope you remember that when it's all over."

Erica could tell Onyx had pushed a mute button by the click in her ear. At the same time, she heard a car driving up. Going over to the window, she saw Jared getting out the car, with his father in tow.

"They're here," she said to Onyx and rushed over to the couch to gather herself.

"I know," Onyx said coming on the line. "Try not to touch your ear as often and everything should go fine, if you do your part."

Her heart was going a mile a minute as she listened to them coming up the stairs. Onyx was going to prompt her with questions, but the beating in her ears made Erica worry that she wouldn't be able to hear anything.

Facing the door, she took deep breaths to calm her nerves and get this all over with. Jared stepped in first looking very concerned at her. His father followed behind him. In Jared's hand was a large yellow envelope and Erica determined that must be the package Jared had received in California.

Jared immediately started for her, but Erica put her hands up to stop him.

"Are you okay?" he asked warily.

"I'm fine," she said stiffly.

"Where's the baby?" Nathaniel asked.

"He's in the bedroom sleep," she said, keeping eye contact with Jared. "I put him in there so we wouldn't disturb him."

Nathaniel started for the bedroom, but Jared stopped him. "He's safe for now," Jared said to his father and then looked at Erica. "You went in my room?"

Erica looked away from him unable to meet his eyes anymore knowing what she knew. "Yes, I did."

He was about to say more, but Nathaniel interjected. "This don't seem safe to be here, Jared. I've been real itchy about all this since…you know."

Jared looked pained. "Did anyone say anything to you about Whitney?"

Erica shook her head and repeated Onyx's prompting. "I got out the house just in time and ran for my life. Someone's been trying to hurt us for a while – you know that, but I never thought…" She bit her lip. "I never thought they would actually kill us."

Anxiously, Nathaniel looked out the curtains. "We better go, son." He looked at Erica. "You better come with us. You and the baby."

"I'll go get the baby," Erica said.

Jared stepped forward to follow her, but she again put her hands out to hold him away.

"Please, Jared, let me go by myself."

He didn't move as she went into the bedroom and picked up the doll as if it were a real child. Carefully she covered it up and held it in her arms as if she were really holding De. Turning around to leave, she stopped because Jared stood at the doorway.

"So you've found out my secret?" he asked, closing the door to give them privacy.

Looking around the room, she said, "If this is a secret Jared, then yes, I have, but we're not going to discuss your other nasty secrets are we?"

"It's not as bad as you think Erica-"

Cutting him off, she snapped, "I don't want to hear another word. Where are you going to take me and the baby?" she demanded to know.

Nathaniel knocked on the door. "Hey, what are the two of you doing?"

Jared's eyes turned to a deep stone. She could tell his mind was working a mile a minute and sensed he wanted to say something very important.

"Don't worry about it," he told her quietly.

She left out the room with Jared behind her.

Nathaniel went over to the back door and opened it as if to leave out.

Jared seeing that his father was a distance away, caught her shoulders and pulled her against him. In a whisper, he said, "I won't let them hurt you."

Turning around to look at him, she said guardedly, "I'm not sure I should leave. I'm scared to be found by anyone."

"And rightly so," Eric said at the doorway of the loft.

Erica gasped as she watched her father come in the loft. Nathaniel closed the door behind Eric.

Eric looked older. Stress had gotten to his features and gray hair had started to set in around the edges of his dark brown hair. He was thinner and his shoulders didn't seem so broad and strong. All her life she had tried to earn his love and respect and realized the only time she had ever earned it was when she had done his dirty work for him. Other than that, she was just in the way.

"You followed us?" Jared asked angrily.

"When Nathaniel called me and told me he was meeting you at the airport, I had to find out if Erica was still alive. I knew my daughter would deliver to me what I rightfully should have." Eric looked greedily at the bundle she carried. "Is that the baby?"

Erica held the doll close to her chest. "Yes, but it's not yours, Eric. You can't have him."

"How do you know what is suppose to be mine?" he sneered coming to her. "You've been so consumed in your parties and friends. You've been nothing but selfish and spoiled all your life Erica. You don't care about anyone but yourself and you certainly don't know what's right and wrong because you're so stupid you let others think for you."

She backed into Jared to get a distance away from her father. Her father's words had hurt her, but she couldn't let that deter her from what she was there to do. Eric was deliberately trying to hurt her. "I know this child can't be used like I was used by you," she said fearlessly.

"The Canton family owes me everything they have. They destroyed my family a long time ago. I've worked hard to get everything back from them that my father carelessly threw away to Lyle Canton. How dare you side with them?!" Eric hissed. "You're my

blood. You're a Thompson through and through, Erica. Don't you feel some loyalty to your family!"

"I am loyal to what is right. Keeping Whitney hostage like a prisoner all her life just to get her money was not fair!"

"You wouldn't have had the education and wealth without other people's sacrifices and stupidity," Eric refuted. "You wouldn't have had the luxuries in life. Don't you want that again? Don't you want it all?"

Shaking her head, she said, "Not at the cost of someone else's life, Daddy."

"Money makes the world go 'round, Erica. He who has the gold rules."

"You tore apart Lyle Canton's life for some silly past revenge that your own father was the cause of?" she asked incredulously. "You deceived Dakota out of his business and stole many more businesses just to get your hands on more money. You destroyed my mother to the point that the only way to get away from you was to kill herself."

"I would do anything to make sure I had the power, Erica. You should know. My blood flows through your veins. Even now, you can understand why I had to do all these things," he admitted.

Shaking her head even harder, she said, "No I don't see it. You used me without any thought of what it might do or the effects that would happen. You covered up the truth of who my mother was all my life and I had to watch her die without ever telling her how much I loved her and now you've taken away my sister." Tears streamed down her cheeks rapidly almost blinding her vision. "Why Eric? Why did you have to be apart in killing everyone I loved?"

"They were weak," Eric seethed, coming within arm length of her.

She couldn't back up any farther because Jared was behind her. Bravely, she said, "Whitney wasn't. She was stronger than even you were. She knew you were evil even before anyone told her. She got away from you. She took away everything you worked so long to get and would have succeeded in everything if you hadn't killed her. Whitney took away your company all over again and you ordered that guy to hurt her? You hired him to blow her office and her home, didn't you?"

Losing patience, he snapped, "I ordered him to kill her for me. I told him to do whatever it took to get her out the picture. I wasn't going to see Canton's company successful again. It had taken too much to run it in the ground without the board being notified."

"And how did you pay him? Where'd you get the money from to fund his efforts?" she demanded to know.

Eric smiled elatedly and glanced back at Nathaniel. "From Whitney, of course."

She heard Jared gasped.

"How?" Jared asked.

Nathaniel looked embarrassed. "I came here to put my past behind me, but I couldn't. I knew I had to do right by Dakota and I wanted to show you I could do something good with my life. When the opportunity came for me to help the little lady, I did, but when Eric called me up saying he was broke and needed some cash, I got him the connection he needed here in Florida to get some extra money. He didn't know about my connection to Whitney until I told him where all the money I got came from."

"So you're his Florida contact?" Jared asked his father.

"Small world, huh?" Erica sneered, remembering the words Whitney had uttered before.

"Drug money?" Jared sneered disgustedly. "You said you put that all behind you in California."

Nathaniel tried to sound desperate. "I did, but obviously the courts in California didn't feel the same way. I'm still a wanted man in California and Eric was going to turn me in. So I gave him a little of the money I borrowed from Whitney so he could buy the drugs he needed to get something going in California." Defensively, he said, "I never let the drug money I got touch the club. I didn't want Dakota to be involved in all mess."

"And that's suppose to justify what you did?!" Jared bellowed.

Erica was shocked as she stepped around Jared to see him, but without her back to her father. She had never seen Jared this emotional before and to see him enraged like this was almost frightening. She was glad she had never angered him to this point.

Jared continued with pain and hurt in his voice. "You promised! You promised to never bring what you did to California to our doorstep. Do you know what this is going to do to my mother?

Do you know what this does to me?" He grabbed his chest as if he wanted to rip his heart out his body. "She's dead! After all she did for you! After all we've done for you! You helped kill Whitney!"

"No, I didn't!" Nathaniel cried defensively.

Jared protested pointing at Eric, but still yelling at his father, "You helped him! You funded his evil intentions."

Nathaniel burst out in loud guilty sobs. "I had no choice! Don't you see? He would have turned me in."

"I could have helped you," Jared said achingly.

Erica turned to Jared accusingly. "How dare you stand there and judge him after you've betrayed Whitney and I too?!"

"None of this matters," Eric said coolly. "I still come out the winner in this whole situation, Erica. Now all you have to do is turn the baby over to me. They'll never have to know he was found in the fire and I'll get custody of the child. When the time is right, I'll make Lyle pay enough to keep us in luxury for the rest of your life."

Not believing her father could use people so casually as if they were pieces of property, she said with revulsion, "You are sick. You will never get me to turn this baby over to you. You've used people! You've killed people! You sold drugs to get money! Can't you see what you're doing is wrong?"

"AND I WOULD DO IT ALL OVER AGAIN!" Eric screamed. "Now give me the goddamn baby you stupid b-"

He didn't finish that sentence because Jared's fist connected to his mouth, sending Eric flying back over the couch and to the floor.

Erica's mouth dropped wide open at what Jared did. She looked over the couch at her father, who was passed out on the floor and then she looked at Jared who was shaking off the sting in his hand.

"I owed you a favor, remember?" he said.

"Thank you."

Nathaniel eased to the door to sneak out, but with the quickness Jared was blocking the exit. Nathaniel pulled a blue steel automatic from the back of his pants and aimed it at Jared's face.

Erica gasped. "He's got a gun," she said out loud. Jared glared over at her. "Don't you think I know that?"

She pursed her lips together feeling silly and hoping Onyx had heard her.

"You're going to shoot me?" Jared asked Nathaniel.

"If I have to," Nathaniel said bravely.

"After all I've done for you? This is what it comes down to?" Jared asked incredulously. "You're my father."

Nathaniel snorted disgustedly, "You've never loved me like a father."

"How the hell was I suppose to do that when I saw how you beat my mother when I was young until she went out and made money on the streets for you. You left us with nothing to our name and homeless. Now you come back into our lives pretending you're a changed man and now you do this? You expect me to love you?"

"I brought you in this world, you bastard," Nathaniel sneered. "And I'm going to take you out."

"You won't get away with this," Erica cried out.

"They'll eventually find you," Jared agreed.

Nathaniel smiled evilly. "Oh yes I will. One shot to the leg and then to the heart will do just fine. No one knows the girl and the baby are here, but everyone knows Eric wants her dead too. I'll put the gun in Eric's hand while he's still unconscious and kill her and the baby. By the time he awakes the police will be climbing all over this place and convinced he did the crime. I'll be long gone and with a valid alibi from your own mother."

"You bastard," Jared hissed.

"You're the bastard, Jared. Your mother only loved you because you were apart of me. How do you think it was so easy to take me back?"

"If you died, I would swear on my life, she wouldn't miss you."

Nathaniel scoffed. "You're the one who's going to be dead." He prepared to shoot the gun.

"Wait!" Erica wailed. "The w-window! I-I mean, you won't get away with this." She gave Jared a desperate look over at the window.

Jared frowned not understanding what she was trying to tell him.

"Back away, Jared," she sneered.

"Of course I'll get away with this," Nathaniel said with a degree of cockiness. He moved back to the table where Jared had set the package. "And no one will be the wiser because no one knows Eric's contacts and they'll identify Eric immediately as a drug supplier.

They'll assume you were the contact, Jared. No one knows I was here. Do you think it was a surprise I met you at the airport? I was just biding my time until I let you know I was the contact for Eric."

"You son of bitch," Jared growled angrily taking a step back towards the window.

With arrogance, Erica said, "You still won't get away with this, Nathaniel."

Irritated, Nathaniel barked coming closer to Jared with the package in hand, "Why the hell won't I?"

Erica took a deep breath and ripped open her shirt to revealed wires taped to her stomach and chest. Jared was first to take advantage of the visual distraction and kick the gun out his father hand as it went off, but at the same time a shot rang out through the room. Erica fell to her knees praying she wouldn't be killed. Everything seemed to happen in slow motion as she peeked up to see Jared fall to the ground clutching his chest and Nathaniel fall back with blood spurting from his neck.

The door burst open and it seemed as if a million DEA and FBI agents came through the door.

Her eyes went back to Jared, who was falling to his knees holding his top right shoulder as blood seeped through his fingers. She screamed in agony and rushed over to him catching him in her arms and slowing his progress to the floor cradling him close to her.

Through her tears, she saw he looked as if he were in a lot of pain and winced when she held him tight.

"Please don't die," she sobbed. "Please don't." She pressed her face against his.

"Why?" he asked weakly his eyes wide open.

Erica thought of those horrible movie scenes, when the hero died in the woman's arms. She didn't think she could stand losing Jared even though he betrayed her. She still…loved him.

"Because," she said obviously to his question. "I love you."

"You do?" he asked breathlessly wincing. "Yes!" she howled.

"Even though you think I…" he paused to catch his breath. "You think I betrayed you?"

"Did you?" she asked hopefully. "Whitney said it was probably a good excuse that you were doing what you did."

"Do you think so?" he asked faintly.

"I hope so."

"Will you love me more?"

She cried because it seemed as if he was getting weaker and weaker. "Yes!" she said fervently. "I'll love you more than anything, Jared."

He closed his eyes and she wailed burying her face in his chest. He mumbled something, but she had been crying too loud to hear her, so she lifted her head and pressed her ear to his lips thinking this would be his last words to her.

"What did you say, Jared, my love?" she begged.

"W-Would you give m-me some?"

Frowning not believing what she had heard from him. She looked into his eyes. "What did you say?"

There appeared this brilliant wicked smile on his face and his eyes were dancing in amusement as he asked again with more strength, "Would you give me some?"

Narrowing her eyes suspiciously, she asked, "You're not dying?"

"No," he said obviously.

Lethal stepped into the room and stood above them. "Why the hell are you lying on the ground, Jared? It's just a fucking flesh wound you ass."

"If you knew how to shoot," Jared growled. "I wouldn't be shot." He winced again because Erica shoved him off her lap and stood up.

"You weren't dying!" she cried.

"Of course he wasn't dying," Lethal said obviously. "He just can't take a bullet."

So upset, Erica threw the ear patch out her ear because she was tired of hearing Onyx laughing in her ear and marched right out the loft screaming in frustration.

Whitney knocked on the door for the tenth time. No one answered on the other side and she looked at Dakota helplessly.

"I don't think she will come out until she wants to," he surmised.

"But she can't stay in there forever," Whitney said irritated. "It
was just the wrong time for Jared to actually have a sense of humor."

"I thought it was quite funny after I heard it," Dakota said chuckling, but instantly stopped when he saw the evil expression on Whitney's face.

Lethal entered the penthouse suite. Whitney and Erica had occupied this space for the past three days. Lethal had been too busy to come there sooner since he was overloaded with paperwork from the government. Whitney remembered him muttering that's why he had gotten out the government business because of all the paperwork and red tape.

"When you shoot a man, you ought to be able to just write one report!" he had complained.

Even Jared was knee deep in reports and couldn't be contacted because he was being interrogated by several different agencies.

Dakota had been taking care of some of Jared's urgent businesses with Erica's help, but trying to get her to help was the most difficult because she was too angry to speak to anyone.

"Where's Erica?" Lethal asked after looking around the room. When no one answered right away, he surmised, "She's still locked in her room?"

Whitney nodded. "She's too upset. She won't tell me anything and when I try to talk to her all she mutters is that men are evil. What really happened, Lethal?"

He smirked knowingly. "I told you everything, Ms. Carlton. Jared went ridiculous over a flesh wound, Erica thought he was dying and said she loved him. I just don't think she wanted it to be like that, but if that was the only way to get her to admit she loved him, I would have pulled the same shit too."

Whitney huffed. "So Jared was deceiving us? Or can you
tell us what was really going on?"

Lethal sighed tiredly. "Like I told you before, I met Jared while he was in jail. He was the only man that could man an undercover rig for the government by himself when it usually took three men. So in returned the government hired me to help him out with his criminal problem. Jared was bothered about the fact that Eric was stalking you, so he called on some government contacts to see what they could do about it and found out they had already started an investigation on Eric. He stepped in as a contact for Eric to find out who was Eric's Florida contact, but even Jared didn't know it was Nathaniel."

Dakota said, "He had been acting real edgy lately, but I thought it was just the stress of the club becoming so big, so I never thought anything about it."

"Well, it was more than that. Eric was basically blackmailing Nathaniel. It would have been easier if Nathaniel had just turned himself in," Lethal said. "And cheaper. He gave over to Eric over five hundred thousand dollars."

Dakota whistled while Whitney looked highly perturbed.

"So Jared was never going to give us over to him?" Whitney asked.

"No," Lethal said apparently. "He was just trying to get Eric to give over information and then turn him over to authorities. No one expected it to go so well and Erica was a big help in turning her father in. When all this is over, Eric will be going to jail for a long time. I don't think you'll ever have to worry about him ever again."

"What about Jamison?" Whitney asked. "I know Erica said she heard him answer the phone which meant he was still in Eric's employ."

Lethal shrugged undeterminably. "Jamison was questioned, but according to records, he was never involved in any of what Eric was doing. He was a butler and that was it."

Whitney smiled in satisfaction. "I'm glad. I hope he'll retire and be happy." She looked worriedly over at the door. "Erica, did you hear that! Jamison is alright."

There was no answer from the door, but Whitney had a feeling Erica was listening.

"What about Nathaniel?" Dakota asked.

Lethal sighed as if tired of talking. "He'll be alright. I just nicked a collar bone." He said this as if it were nothing but a pinprick. "I served three years as a sniper in Cuba. I think I can hit the right spot a hundred miles away."

"You're bragging," Whitney said chuckling.

"And rightly so. I'm damn good."

"Will he live?" Dakota questioned Lethal.

"He'll be out the hospital in a couple of weeks, but then California wants him first and then other agencies will have a go at him. The IRS is still looking over the books he kept, but I think he was actually telling the truth about the club. I don't think they'll hurt your business." Lethal went over to Erica's door and tried to knob to discover it was locked.

"She's not going to open it," Whitney said. "She's being stubborn as a mule."

Lethal shot her a glare as if she didn't know exactly who he was. Sizing up the door, he pounded on it hard. "Erica open this damn door before I knock it down!"

Something clicked on the other side and Lethal tried the knob again. This time it opened and he stepped inside closing the door behind him.

Whitney went over to the door to see the knob was locked again so she pressed her ear against the door to hear what was being said.

"Isn't that called spying?" Dakota asked.

"Hush!" she hissed, but even when it was quiet she could only hear mumbling on the other side of the door.

After a few more minutes, the door opened up and Whitney had to back away to get out of Lethal's exit.

"What did she say?" Whitney demanded to know as Lethal closed the door again.

He shrugged indifferently this time. "Lots of woman stuff. She's scared of sex."

Dakota asked, "She told you that?"

Lethal shook his head. "She didn't have too. She just mentioned Jared's bedroom and said she didn't want to be with an animal."

"What's in Jared's room?" Whitney asked.

Lethal smiled wickedly. "I think that's a question you need to ask Jared." He checked his watch. "I got a flight to catch to Chicago." Going to the door, he paused as he stepped into the doorway turned back around to the two of them and stood akimbo pushing away his jacket and revealing a concealed weapon as if he was standing at high noon at a gunfight. The hard glare in his black eyes was directed at Dakota and the room felt like it had suddenly gone cold.

"Before I leave town, Mr. Traylor, isn't there something you need to ask Mrs. Canton which I interrupted the other day?" Dakota demanded icily.

Dakota looked a bit relieved that there really wasn't a problem. He stood up and promptly went over to Whitney taking her hand and going down on one knee. "Whitney Canton, would you marry me…again?" he asked looking up into her eyes.

Whitney smiled and leaned down kissing him gently. "Yes, Dakota Traylor. I'll gladly be your wife again."

Bringing her down to his level, Dakota tipped her back in his strong arms and coveted her lips with his own. The kiss he gave her made them both forget that Lethal had been standing at the doorway, but when they realized that they had been lip locking for quite awhile they drew away reluctantly and looked over to where Lethal had been standing.

The door was closed and Lethal was nowhere to be seen. "You think De will be sleep for a while?" Dakota asked his voice filled with passion.

She smiled wantonly licking her lips hungrily. "De will be taken care. Erica will hear him if he wakes up." She pulled on his hands to

lead him into her room excited about making love to her soon to be
husband again.

Erica huffed at the itchy chiffon/silk gown. She hated the
godawful maroon gown with gold flecks, but it was what Whitney
wanted.
"It's called Morning Glory," Whitney had protested when Erica
had bawked about the color.
"I've got other names for it, but those two words don't come
to mind," Erica had muttered.
She had basically locked herself away in her new villa
apartment only to come out and help Whitney with this ridiculous
wedding when she really needed it. Otherwise she kept out of
Whitney's hair and did her own thing. Whitney had insisted that Erica
come live with them in the house Dakota had bought, but Erica was not
going to do that. Instead, she had saved enough money to get a place
of her own over in the Town and Country area of Tampa and
had started doing some accounting for small home businesses.
Quarters were ending and she was able to drum up a lot of work. On
top of that, she worked from home so she didn't have to go out as
much. If Whitney wanted to see her, Erica's door was always open
for her sister, but anyone else was off limits unless it was a client.
"You've got to talk to him, Erica," Whitney had insisted.
"I don't have to do anything but be black and die and I'd rather
die than lay my eyes on that man again."
Whitney had questioned her about what she had seen in
Jared's bedroom, but Erica wouldn't say anything and Whitney
had said when she had asked Jared, he wasn't talking.
Erica knew exactly why Jared wasn't saying anything.
"I think I have the right to know," Whitney said. "I think I
could better help you understand what he was all about if you told me."
Erica had refused. She didn't talk about that although for the
past couple of months she had been having these weird dreams
about that room and Jared and being in his bed….
There she went again. The room she was in at St John
Baptist church had suddenly grown hot. Whitney was humming a
little tune amazingly calm while Lyle paced. Erica was very aware
how Whitney had gotten that awful habit of pacing.

Whitney looked up suddenly in the mirror she was facing and
met her sister's eyes with a wishful smile. "You look like Momma."

"I do?" Erica asked with a frown.

Whitney turned around. She was dressed in the most beautiful Vera Wang wedding gown Erica had ever seen. It had been Erica who had convinced Whitney to get the designer to make the dress for her and Whitney loved it. So did Erica and she hoped if she ever got married she could afford a Vera Wang dress.

Whitney answered her sister's frown. "Yeah, when she would be thinking about Lyle and didn't want anyone to know that she was thinking about him."

"I'm not thinking about Lyle."

"Daddy, why don't you check on the baby for me?" Whitney requested politely.

Lyle looked as if he really needed to do something other than being cooped up in the room waiting for the wedding planner to stick her head in and tell them it was time.

When he was gone, Whitney got up very carefully as not to crease her dress, and sat down next to Erica. "I know you're not thinking about Lyle."

Erica looked away from Whitney and pursed her lips together. "I wasn't thinking about Jared either."

Whitney took Erica's hand in her own. "Are you sad about your father?"

Erica shook her head changing the subject. "What does Lyle think of you marrying Dakota?"

"Just as Lyle forgave you, he also forgives Dakota, but he did insist Dakota sign a pre-nup agreement. I think Daddy insisted only to make things difficult for Dakota, but he wouldn't give his blessing on the wedding until Dakota said he would"

Erica gasped shocked Lyle would request something like that. "Did Dakota put up a big fuss?" she asked.

With a whimsical chuckle, Whitney said, "You would think, but he actually had the nerve to really agree because he said his bitch of a business wife might try to overthrow his business."

'Why would he say a cruel thing like that?"

"Because with the ten percent ownership of the club I already have and Nathaniel dividing his share of the partnership between

Dakota and Jared's mother, marrying Dakota would give me an advantage over his business in ownership." She smiled wicked. "Dakota said he wouldn't want an argument about leaving his socks on the floor to turn into a corporate take over by his own wife." Whitney caught the depressing look on Erica's face and became serious again. "You were thinking about Jared, weren't you?" When Erica didn't answer right away, Whitney said, "For once be honest with yourself, Erica. Denying what you were thinking only adds to the undue stress in your life."

Biting her lip, trying not to cry, Erica nodded and admitted, "I was thinking about Jared."

He hadn't called or even tried to come see her at her new home in the past two months. Occasionally he had asked Whitney just how Erica was doing, but nothing else. Erica was so confused about what she was feeling she didn't know what to do and she didn't know how to discuss her feelings with anyone.

When Lethal had come in and asked her what the deal was, she had been perfectly honest with him. She felt so intimidated by Whitney's newfound happiness and she didn't know how to deal with seeing Whitney and Dakota together when she felt her own deep longing to be with Jared, but was so scared to feel what felt so right in her mind, but wrong in her body. On top of that, knowing the kind of man Jared really was and how he had dealt with her up until she knew his secret was really confusing.

Lethal had told her three words, "Get Over It."

That had been in Lethal's character. He wasn't a man that could deal with a woman's emotional episodes and that was his advice on anything. He said it made him sound good.

So she was trying to deal with her own problems, which she thought she could do so in the short time, but with getting her own business together, it had taken more time. Was she to figure Jared didn't want to wait for her?

"Do you remember how sad Momma was when she died?" Whitney asked.

"I don't think remembering her is the right time, Whit."

"Yes it is, because I don't want to see you like that. I don't want you to always wonder what could have happened if you had listened to your heart. I know you're scared and I know you've been

through a lot of things, but I think, if you just listened to your heart for
once, your body will follow and the fear you have inside of you that everyone told you was wrong will go away in Jared's arms."

Erica couldn't stop the tears from falling. She could feel all the loneliness and emotional pain creeping up on her again. How much time had she wasted in pining away at her feelings when she could have been so happy just like Whitney had been. Her sister was so much stronger than she was. "How would you know, Whitney?"

"Because every time I'm in Dakota's arms, there's no where in the world I'd rather be. Fear is only as strong as you believe it to be. If you tell yourself there's no fear, then you can conquer the world. He loves you and you love him. You two could be so happy together if you just let go and don't fear what people have told you to fear." Whitney gently turned Erica's face so she could look in her sister's eyes. "Erica have I ever deceived you before?"

Erica had to be honest and say, "No, Whit. You've always been honest with me."

"Have I ever lied to you?"

Shaking her head, Erica said hoarsely, "No, Whitney."

"Then believe me when I say, Jared would never hurt you physically or emotionally and whatever this big secret is shouldn't be anything to stop you from being happy. If Lethal isn't worried about the man, then I am not worried and you shouldn't be worried."

Teasingly, Whitney added, "Plus if Jared does hurt you Lethal will jump on the first plane and beat the crap out of him."

Erica couldn't help giggling with her sister.

There was a knock at the door and the wedding planner said outside the door that they were almost ready.

"What should I do?" Erica asked desperately.

"Well your make up is a mess, but I'm sure we can fix that," Whitney said simply.

"No. About Jared?"

Whitney gleamed. "We've come this far and figured cut so much stuff together. I'm sure we can wrap that man around your finger sooner or later."

*   *   *   *   *

The wedding planner informed Whitney upon the bride's request to find out if Jared Parker had arrived while Erica fixed her makeup. The young lady returned and informed Whitney Jared Parker had just arrived and he was escorting his mother to sit on the groom's side.

"Why is he sitting on Dakota's side?" Erica questioned. Whitney rolled her eyes in exasperation. "He and Dakota have been bonding lately. Jared's been extremely grateful to Dakota for all his help while he finished up with the investigation on Eric and they've been finding a lot more to speak about. I told you he comes for dinner every once in a while. Probably to see if you will join us." Whitney had a 'hint-hint' in her eyes, but Erica wasn't falling for that.

"That man won't miss a meal to save his life, Whit. Don't pull that crap on me." Become a little agitated, she asked. "Why did he bring his mother? I bet she won't like me."

"You're crazy, girl!" Whitney said laughing. "She'll love you. He brought her because she's been especially depressed ever since…well you know."

Erica did understand what Whitney was referring to. Eliza Parker, Jared's mother missed Nathaniel and was falling into a void of depression her son wanted her to desperately get over.

Whitney continued, "He brought her to dinner last week. I think she's been so use to Nathaniel keeping her underfoot that now she's had to readjust to the world again."

Lyle entered the room again to let them know it was time. The sisters smiled at each other both excited over the moment Whitney had waited so long for.

Erica felt she was more nervous than Whitney as the double doors opened to the large packed church. Between Whitney's business contacts and Dakota's there was standing room only as Erica glided past everyone. She kept her eyes forward not daring to look in the crowd, but she knew he was there. She could just feel those smoky gray eyes visually caressing her from head to toe.

'Don't you dare trip,' she told herself. 'Eyes forward, Erica, and remain calm. Breathe, Girl! Breathe!'

Once she made it down to the end, she turned around as
practiced, but kept her eyes on Whitney as she came down the aisle
gliding with an ethereal smile that seem to light up the sanctuary.

Glancing over at Dakota, she was surprised to see him nervous even
though this was their second time getting married, but the way his
eyes beheld the mother of his child, was one Erica had never seen on
his face. She was positive that Dakota had never really loved her and
she was so glad that he had found love. At least he would have a
happy ending to all this mess.

The wedding seemed like a blur to Erica. The vows were
said and once the pastor pronounced Whitney and Dakota husband and
wife – again, which garnered chuckles throughout the congregation,
the pair was ready to receive their guest personal
congratulations. Whitney leaned over to Erica during the
handshakes and well-wishers to whisper, "Go check your makeup."

"Is it running again?" Erica asked nervously, wishing she had a
mirror.

"No, but you are so spaced out, you need a break for a
moment before we head over to the hall. It's a good thing we took
pictures yesterday. You are almost a mess up here." Whitney
touched Erica's head, while rubbing down a cowlick of hair that kept
straying.

"Why don't you all go to the reception hall without me and I'll
meet you there?" Erica suggested. "I don't think I could really deal
with all the revelry without spoiling your good time."

Whitney looked at her worriedly. "Are you sure?"

"Yeah. I can catch a ride with someone who is going
there," Erica assured her.

Nodding, Whitney said, "If you don't show up, I'll assume you
changed your mind and decided to go home and get some rest? And
don't worry about De, my father says he will enjoy spending time with
his grandson while Dakota and I are on the honeymoon."

Erica ducked behind the wedding party and went down the
back stairs to find the woman's bathroom. Opening her purse she
realized her hands were shaking as she tried to put on more make
up. She thought she heard the bathroom door open, but when no one
came in she assumed she was hearing things.

Turning to leave, she was abruptly stopped as she met Jared's
soulful cloudy undetermined looking eyes. He leaned against the

door with his arms crossed over his chest and his legs apart. Dripping in arousal, she forced her eyes to stay on his face as she clutched behind her the edge of the sink. Her legs felt like Jell-O. His cologne wafted up to her nostrils causing ethereal stimulation throughout her whole body. She had missed him physically, mentally, and visually.

"You look beautiful," he said.

The room was so quiet; she could hear her own heartbeat pounding away in her chest.

"You shouldn't be here," she pointed out. "This is the women's bathroom."

"I'm not leaving, Erica. Not until I get what I want."

Those words alone made her feel as if the room was spinning. Licking her lips, she spoke very slowly to hide her own nervousness. "What do you want Jared?"

"You," he said simply.

Turning around to collect her thoughts she tried to stop the shaking that was starting to over come her. "I-I can't stay here. I have a reception to go to."

"Don't," he said. His voice was closer and she had been so consumed with her own thoughts that she didn't hear him move closer.

To terrified to speak, she bit her lip praying she wouldn't scream out her frustration of the mess she had caused.

"Erica," he said softly. "I miss you. I'm sorry for deceiving you."

"It's okay," she responded breathlessly. "You were trying to help."

"I'm sorry my sense of humor surfaced at the wrong time."

"You had your reasons. I'm not mad at you about that."

"Then tell me what you want from me, Erica." He gently took her shoulders and tenderly forced her around to face him. "What can I say or do to make it all better so we can be together? If you want me to take it slow, I'll take it slow. I'll do whatever it takes to make you happy."

She could see the distressed in his eyes and she could certainly hear it in his voice. "It's not you, Jared. It's me."

He took her hand in his nudging her to turn around and face him. "They aren't expecting us and they won't miss us. Don't make excuses."

To take the edge off the air and give her time to collect her thoughts and emotions, she asked him, "Why did you decide to risk yourself to help Whitney and I?"

"I wanted you to be safe."

"And Whitney?"

"Of course I cared for Whitney's life, but you were my main concern. All your life Eric told you to be afraid and never want or need emotional and physical pleasure. I wanted you to see there was nothing to fear anymore Erica. I wanted to take him out of your life and open you up to me. Just because he didn't physically hurt you Erica, he still mentally abused you by not helping you to heal after what was done to you." He pulled her close to him removing the space between their bodies.

Bravely she said with pride, "I don't fear him anymore, but I don't think I've healed."

"You have. You just don't know yet." He used the tip of his nose and his cheek to caress her face. "I know you're scared Erica, but I want you to understand that you don't have to be anymore. Not as long as you're with me."

Trying to remember Whitney's words, she forced herself to relax and allow the swirling heat stirring in her loins to rise up to her chest, flow through her veins until her fingertips were tingling, yearning to touch something.

Whispering in her ear, he said, "You should understand there's nothing wrong with what you feel right now, Erica."

"H-How would you know what I feel, Jared?"

His hands moved to lightly touch the goose bumps on her arms and he entwined his strong fingers with her. "You feel like you can't breath." His nose nuzzled into the crook of her neck and his moist lips brushed the skin under her chin. "Your body wants to relax, but tighten up at the same time," he said.

She quivered in anticipation of what was to come as his mouth continued an upward path above her chin and traversed over her lips briefly before paying extra attention to her cheeks, forehead and earlobes.

In a soft accent, he said, " You're warm and cold at the same time. You want to throw your arms around me and kiss me all over as if this is the last days. Do it Erica. Do what your mind wants you to do."

Slowly her arms moved around his neck. The heels she wore were perfect for his height and her body molded against his flawlessly. "Is this all just a scheme to get me to do…those things?"

"What things, Erica?" he asked innocently.

She moved away slightly to look up into his eyes and said, "I not going to say what you're trying to make me do, Jared."

"Then you're not going to ever be able to open up to this experience, Erica." He swayed to a melody that wasn't there and she was so in tuned to his body that she swayed along with him. His arms were around her waist and he was pressing her close to him.

Erica thought again what Whitney said and how she had felt these past weeks without Jared. Just being in his arms again was pure magnificent, but to take the steps he wanted…"You want me to say those words?"

He nodded eagerly bringing those wonderful lips down to her. "I want you to tell me what you want, Erica."

"What if I don't know what I want?" she asked confused.

"Then tell me what you really fear."

Erica started to push away, but she could hear Whitney's voice in her head telling her to stay with it. She wasn't afraid that Jared would hurt her. She wasn't even afraid of allowing herself to give into the erotic pleasures he could give her. "I don't think I could please you, Jared. I know you want to make our friendship into something more, but I don't think I could live up to your expectations. Especially after seeing...well you know."

"Are you talking about my room?" he asked.

She nodded. "Don't you think I would have found out about that sooner or later?"

"True, but I think you're reading too much into." He pulled her over to a small loveseat in the waiting area of the bathroom. "After I got out of prison and was done with all my legal problems, I decided to go with Onyx to India on assignment as a vacation for myself," Jared explained casually.

"You could actually put up with Onyx for a long period of time?" she asked incredulously.

"No not really but she wasn't in my way, most of the time. She had to guard a powerful Sheik whose sister happened to be a Karma Sutra historian and artist. She took a liking to me and I got to know a lot about the art of lovemaking." He smiled to himself wickedly.

"So all those paintings and statures were from her?" she asked with a little jealousy filling her voice.

"Yes, and the books and oils were added for my own knowledge once I returned to the States. When my mother moved in, I didn't think it was appropriate to have the seven different statues poised in various sexual positions from the Karma Sutra in my home, so I moved all of it to the loft."

"So you aren't some kind of sexual deviant?" she asked.

He shook his head. "Just a connoisseur of sexual pleasure."

Those words were shocking to her system, but she was highly curious. "Is that why you're such a good kisser?"

Arrogantly, he said, "I was a good kisser before knowing all that. I just got better." He winked wickedly. "Plus it's not all about joining with a woman that creates the spiritual pleasure the Karma Sutra teaches."

She smiled mischievously. "And what other things can be done other than joining?"

Jared actually looked a little strained as he said, "I don't think I could tell you properly, Erica."

"Then show me, Jared," she encouraged.

He leaned in slowly and kissed her softly, tenderly increasing the pressure on her lips. His kisses didn't just stop there and Erica relaxed as he seared his hot mouth down her neck, while unzipping the back of her gown. His mouth further descended to the white strapless bra, which seemed to disappear revealing her hand full sized breasts and aroused tips that seem to call for his wet scorching tongue to wrap around. Hungrily he answered their cries giving each one plenty of attention and while the other was unattended, his hands kept the dark peak busy. Her heart was doing cartwheels in her chest and the fluttering sensation deep in her loins was now like molten lava shooting through her veins like a sweltering river spreading through her body.

His free hand shot under her dress and to his surprise she wore only a garter belt with knee high stockings making his access to her womanly chasm easily obtainable. Hiking her dress above her waist and moving her underwear aside, his head sunk lower.

"Jared," she breathlessly called with warning unable to figure out what he was about to do, but when his mouth attached to her soaking abyss, she screeched in surprise. Her jaw dropped open and she was positive for the first five minutes of the cataclysmic turmoil

she didn't breath. He had moved her thighs over his broad shoulders to gain further access with his tongue as he seem to draw all life out her of body and fill it with the most glorious tumultuous heaven sent pleasure the good Lord had ever created. Her back arched so tight she was sure her spine would break and she wildly scratched at the loveseat's cotton cover digging her nails in so deep she swore she would rip the fabric with her bare hands.

Jared didn't stop and she didn't want him to. The waves of desire built so high that when they came crashing down, she cried repeatedly.

Suddenly there was a quiet knock at the door and she covered her mouth as Jared abruptly stopped pleasing her.

"Is everything alright in there," an older female voice said on the other side of the door.

"Y-Yes," Erica said frantically. "I'll be out in a moment." The look of guilt was in her eyes, but Jared didn't speak until they heard the footsteps on the other side of the door walk away.

"Come to my place," he requested, planting soft kisses on her neck. The aroma of her on his lips was arousing. "Let me show you some more."

"I don't think I could walk out of here, Jared," she said.

Taking off his jacket and putting it over her shoulders, he scooped her up with the quickness and hurriedly walked out the church. She giggled in his shoulders as he went straight to his car and helped her inside the passenger's side.

Once he sat beside her in the driver's seat, she asked, "Won't they be expecting us at the reception?"

He looked incredulously at her. "Hell no. I told Whitney I wasn't leaving this church until I had you. She told me where to find you."

Erica smiled knowing her sister had purposely sent her down

to the bathroom to give her this time to reconcile with Jared. She remembered Whitney saying, "If you don't show up, I'll assume you changed your mind and decided to go home and get some rest?"

The marina was five minutes away from the church and she knew Jared would waste no time in getting there.

Snuggling up close to him, she said smiling wickedly, "Let's go to your place and get some rest."

He gave her a curious look and then leaned in to her stealing a kiss. "Erica, you know I'm going to marry you." He said this as if it were a fact that she couldn't refute.

"Good, because becoming Mrs. Jared Parker would make me the happiest woman in the world."

Jared smirked with satisfaction. "Will you let me make love to you, Erica?"

With a promising look, she said, "All night long."

Jared burned rubber heading to the marina's loft with promises of love and pleasure to come. Erica wasn't the least scared because she had Jared and she couldn't wait to tell Whitney of her upcoming nuptial.

The End

37839237R00134

Printed in Poland
by Amazon Fulfillment
Poland Sp. z o.o., Wrocław